Numerology and Your Future

Other Books by Dusty Bunker

Dream Cycles

Numerology and the Divine Triangle
(Co-authored with Faith Javane)

Numerology
and
Your Future

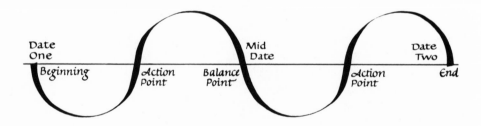

by Dusty Bunker

Para Research
Rockport, Massachusetts

Copyright © 1980 by Dusty Bunker
Illustrations © 1980 by Para Research

All rights reserved. No part of this book may be reproduced or
used in any form or by any means—graphic, electronic, or
mechanical, including photocopying, mimeographing, recording,
taping, or information storage and retrieval systems—without
written permission from publisher. A reviewer may quote brief
passages.

International Standard Book Number: 0-914918-18-4

Rider Waite Tarot Deck Copyright © 1971 U.S. Games Systems,
Inc. Used by permission.

Type set in 10 pt. Paladium on a Compugraphic Editwriter 7500

Cover Calligraphy by Margaret Shepherd

Printed by R.R. Donnelley & Sons Co.
on 55-pound Warren-Sebago paper

Published by Para Reserch, Inc.
Whistlestop Mall
Rockport, Massachusetts 01966

Manufactured in the United States of America

First Printing, September 1980, 6,000 copies
Second Printing, April 1981, 5,000 copies
Third Printing, November 1981, 4,000 copies

"God is a number endowed with motion."

It has been said that "only the truly faithful dare to question their faith." This book is dedicated to "the truly faithful."

Acknowledgments

To my husband, as always my rock and my comforter; to Faith Javane and Dottie Limont, my teachers and examples; to Faith again, Sarah & Matthew Bunker, Melanie (Bunker) McIlveen, April (Bunker) Worley, Peggy Masse, Lucile Bennis, Vikki Knowles and Tom Boyd for help with ideas and in locating certain information; to my friend, Jeanette Sawyer, who took dictation longhand and typed while my writing arm was in a sling; to Frank Molinski, Doug Hall, Hartley Ferguson, Barbara Kassabian, Steve Kravette and the wonderful people at Para Research for their encouragement and able assistance; and last but never least, to Charlie.

CONTENTS

CONTENTS

CONTENTS

I

INTRODUCTION

HAVE YOU EVER wondered about those people who
always seem to be in the right place at the right time
doing the right thing—making money, getting ahead in
business, enjoying their relationships, raising happy children,
and taking extended vacations? What is it that makes them
different from those less successful people around them? We
cannot believe that certain people are selected above all others
in some mysterious manner to be successful and happy, while
others are relegated to less fulfilling lives. If this were true,
there would be no purpose to life and we would be
automatons merely carrying out orders from a higher authority, with no will or goals of our own. However, we do have
free will and we do have choices, and it is by our free will and
right to choose that we determine the rewards we receive as
the results of our efforts. Many succeed admirably because
they have, along with determination and a will to achieve, a

keen sense of timing. They know what to do when, with whom, and why. The intent of this book is to show you how important timing is, and how you can use your number cycles to succeed in unbelievable ways.

Think of the situations that could arise when knowledge of your personal cycles is invaluable: a business meeting where acceptance of your idea could promote you to a position with better pay and more prestige. Should you be aggressive, assertive, and show your mental independence, or should you be passive, receptive, and cooperative? There is a time for each, but you need to know when each will be effective, and how each fits into your cycle for achievement. While you are experiencing a quiet introspective period, your mate may be in an outgoing social cycle. Rather than accuse him or her of being a social gadfly while you are accused of being a stick-in-the-mud, some understanding of your separate states of mind could help you cooperate with each other more lovingly to avoid unnecessary unhappiness. Your child may be going through a cycle in which the need for freedom and learning are uppermost. It would be wonderful if you knew what that cycle was. You could then help by giving your child more room to move in, or perhaps by a trip to the museum or the zoo. Our lives are intricately interwoven, and with a little effort we can learn to help each other through the sensitive periods by an awareness of our own cycles and the cycles of those around us.

This book contains some of the most valuable information you may ever encounter. Spend just a few moments learning to follow the simple steps necessary in determining your personal numbers and cycles and you will see what will happen to you on any given day, in any given month, and in any given year of your life.

Numerology, one of the oldest metaphysical practices in the world, is a method of reducing names (using a number-letter code) and dates to special numbers that reveal the character, quality, and cycle of the person or thing being examined. (Businesses and countries have names and birthdates as well, and therefore have qualities and go through cycles just as we do.) Note that numbers and figures are not the same. Figures are used to measure how much, how far, how heavy; whereas numbers represent qualities and character traits. For example, when you say, "You are one person," you are expressing an entirely different meaning from, "You are number one." The first sentence indicates a quantity, the second a quality.

Numerology does run into double numbers. However, this book will deal with the meanings of the digits 1 through 9 and the Master Numbers, to which all double numbers eventually reduce. These basic meanings are correlated with your Personal Year Cycles, the Period Numbers within those year cycles, your Personal Months, and your Personal Days.

I want to introduce here two new concepts that, to my knowledge, have never been explored in any other numerological system. I call them the *Peak Point*, or the *Balance Point*, and the *Action Points*, and they occur in any cycle, great or small. Since I began working with these points I have found them to be correct and meaningful, thus adding to my mounting amazement at the crisp accuracy and simple beauty of the numbers.

The Peak Point is simply that point halfway through any cycle in your life when the energies represented by that cycle come to their fullest expression. They peak, or come to a head. The Action Points are the quarter and three-quarter points through any cycle when you are urged to the action determined by the cycle you are examining. In other words, the Peak Point and the Action Points divide any cycle into quarters, marking those dates within the cycle when events occur.

The Moon in its four phases is a good analogy. The new Moon is the beginning of its cycle, and the first quarter corresponds to an Action Point, the second quarter (or full Moon) to the Peak Point or Balance Point , and the third quarter to another Action Point. Each cycle will have one Peak Point and two Action Points. Perhaps it is indeed the Moon, along with the other planets and stars in our universe, that influences our cycles—not only on a daily, seasonally, and yearly basis, but also on a personal level determined by our unique birth pattern.

Marilyn Ferguson in *The Brain Revolution* (Bantam Books, 1973) states that the human being is "astonishingly vulnerable to light, to magnetic fields, free electricity, and extraterrestrial forces," and that the human brain "responds to a sea of radiation, and by its responses controls [his] every function." We are indeed subject to the energies around us, just as a flower responds to the warmth of the sun and the cool of the evening. However, rather than accepting this theory as a denial of free will, I choose to believe that time is not linear but elliptical, and if we survive after death then we must have lived before birth. If this is the case, we chose our moment to be born knowing full well the pattern we selected for ourselves. Once we are born we have to live within a certain framework of our own choosing, which is controlled loosely by the energies of the moment of our birth and the ensuing cycles. We cannot change our cycles but we can choose how we will handle them. Therefore, for me, we have always had free will and we always will. When we ate of the apple (which, by the way, reduces numerically to wisdom), of the tree in the Garden of Eden, we took on knowledge of ourselves as godlike beings able to choose our destiny. We were expelled from Eden because we had lost our innocence and taken on self-consciousness, free will, and the wheel of karma. The wheel turns rhythmically, moving us through the necessary stages in our evolutionary spiral of growth. Numerology is one method of examining that wheel.

Numerology is a vast field and much has been and could yet be written on it. If your interest is fired by this book, you will want to read more on the subject. My previous book co-authored with Faith Javane and titled *Numerology and the Divine Triangle* (Para Research, 1979), explores character more deeply through the Soul, Outer Personality, Path of Destiny, and Life Lesson Numbers, and shows you how to lay them on the Pythagorean right triangle, a blueprint of your life. It correlates the seventy-eight keys of the Tarot and the planets, signs, and decans in astrology with the numbers. It also examines the numbers in the Bible, and places the name and birthdate of the sleeping prophet, Edgar Cayce, on the Divine Triangle.

The present work stresses the predictive side of numerology.

Chapter 2 shows you how to find your personal numbers and what is happening to you now and what is likely to happen in your future. Chapter 3 explains additional techniques and introduces new ideas and possibilities. The astrological signatures of the numbers 1 through 9 and the Master Numbers are discussed in Chapter 4 along with corresponding mythological relationships. Chapter 5 explores numerology's influence on each decade of the 1900s in America, offering predictions for the 1980s and beyond. In Chapter 6, the significance of the numerological order of the Presidents is examined along with corresponding Tarot keys. Included here is a discussion of the death cycle haunting every President elected in twenty year periods since 1840, and the possibilities for the fall election of 1980. Chapter 7 goes into the calendar, a brief history, and how the numbers of the calendar months affect us. Chapter 8 deals with the nine Gifts of the Spirit spoken of in I Corinthians 12:7-10, and how these gifts relate to the special numbers derived from our birthdays. Chapter 9, Thoughts From My Notebook, is very special. It was written in one day; however the ideas had been gathering for a long time and just happened to coalesce at that particular time. For me, this chapter is the very essence of what numerology is all about—the wonder and joy of discovery that God's language reveals about ourselves and the world around us. I hope you enjoy reading it as much as I did writing it. And may it stimulate your mind towards greater dimensions of understanding about yourself and your place in the universe.

In the last two chapters you will find Personal Number Delineations and Temporary Number Delineations. Because this book is basically a predictive tool, the Personal Number delineations which describe your character are brief. Famous personalities are listed after each number so that you can more accurately get a feel for the type of individual that the number rules.

Under the Temporary Number Delineations, the numbers are more fully explored as current energies operating in your life. They describe what is happening now—the events you can expect and the areas you need to focus on.

Numerology is one method of examining the cycles in your life. This study can be fascinating and enlightening, and can unlock the secrets to your future.

1

THE NUMBERS AND YOUR

NUMEROLOGICAL CHART

NUMEROLOGY IS AS OLD as time itself. In the beginning there was the One, from which all else evolved.
Thus numbers were born and have been as close to us as our
hands and feet. The most logical place to learn to count is on
our ten fingers, where nine of the fingers represent the digits 1
through 9, and the tenth finger solidifies the system by beginning again at 1, thus exemplifying the continuance of the
cycles.

Most every counting system in the world is based upon
the 9 digits, and each of the digits has its own peculiar
unchanging vibration because of its unique placement in the
numerical order. A brief description of the numbers follows:

1. The beginning, a restlessness, the start of something new,
2. Seeking companionship, peace, compromise,

3. Expansion, growth and creativity as a result of two entities coming together,
4. Form built as a result of merger and expansion,
5. Experience needed to deal with the new world of form,
6. Love, balance and harmony resulting from the experience of 5,
7. Physical completion, rest and a turning inward to listen,
8. Responsibility and karma, the result of past efforts,
9. Final completion, reward, ending and transition.

The numbers 1 through 9, 11, 22, 33 and 44 are delineated briefly as Personal Number vibrations in Chapter 10 of this book. (See page 207.)

Delineating your chart may seem awkward at first, as does any new technique—for example, learning to walk or to ride a bicycle—but with patience and a little practice it will become easier.

To begin delineating a numerological chart, it is best to use the keywords for each of the numbers. You will notice that in Chapter 11 Temporary Number Delineations, the keywords are listed in heavier type beside each of the numbers. Use these keywords as a beginning tool in reading your numbers and the numbers of those whose charts you decide to work on. Do not try to remember every word that falls under each of the numbers as that can be confusing at first. Give yourself time. After you have read and reread the delineations (and thus have gained experience and insight through working with and understanding your own cycles and the cycles of others), you will be able to add more meanings to the numbers than you find here. You will also learn to synthesize the number vibrations in the chart for a more meaningful and cohesive analysis. Time, patience, and observation are the keywords here.

This book deals with the numbers 1 through 9 and the four Master Numbers, 11, 22, 33, 44 to which all numbers eventually reduce. When you reduce a number, you merely add the digits together. For example:

$41 = 4+1 = 5$, written as $41/5$
$36 = 3+6 = 9$, written as $36/9$
$48 = 4+8 = 12$, (a double number, so add again.)
$12 = 1+2 = 3$, written as $48/3$

To reduce a four-digit number, add the four digits together in the same manner:

$2014 = 2+0+1+4 = 7$, written as $2014/7$

7

Before we examine the predictive dimension of numerology, we will talk about your Personal Number Vibrations. This information will be used later in determining your future cycles.

Your Four Personal Numbers

You were born with four special numbers that are uniquely your own. They were determined by the day you were born and the full name you were given at birth. These four personal numbers describe your character and qualities and your purpose in life, and set the cyclical rhythm of your life's pattern. In my previous book, *Numerology and the Divine Triangle*, co-authored with Faith Javane (Para Research, 1979), we used these four personal numbers for character analysis. As this book emphasizes the predictive side of numerology, we will figure your four personal numbers so that you can use them to work out your cycles in the next chapters.

The most important number you have is your *Life Lesson Number*, which is arrived at through your birthdate. The Life Lesson Number reveals your reason for being here, your purpose in life, and what you have chosen to learn in this incarnation. We shall use the following example of:

Sarah Melanie Houlton, born July 7, 1952

To find Sarah's Life Lesson Number, we start with her birthday, July 7, 1952. First, reduce the full year of birth by adding it through once. (Do not use the abbreviated form, '52, or your result will be incorrect.)

$$1952 = 1+9+5+2 = 17$$

Add the month (July = 7) and day of birth (7) to the reduced year total 17.

$$7+7+17 = 31$$

Reduce the 31 by adding it through once.

$$31 = 3+1 = 4, \text{ written as } 31/4$$

Always keep your double number over the digit in your final result because you will be using some of these double numbers later on. For now, read the meaning of the single number of your Life Lesson Number in Chapter 10 of this book, under Personal Number Delineations, which begins on page 207.

Here is another example of a Life Lesson Number: Birth-date November 8, 1937.

Reduce the year by adding it through once.

$$1937 = 1+9+3+7 = 20$$

Add the month (November = 11) and day of birth (8) to the reduced year total 20:

$$11+8+20 = 39$$

Reduce the 39 by adding it through once.

$$39 = 3+9 = 12$$

You still have a double number, so add it through once again.

$$12 = 1+2 = 3$$

This Life Lesson Number will be written as a 39/3 because 39 was the original total which then reduced to a 3.

This is the first of your four personal numbers. The three other personal numbers result from reducing your full name at birth numerically. You will need to work with the following number-letter code which numbers the letters of the alphabet from 1 to 26; e.g.: A=1, B=2, C=3,...Y=25, which reduces to 7, and Z=26 which reduces to 8.

$$1 = A \ J \ S$$
$$2 = B \ K \ T$$
$$3 = C \ L \ U$$
$$4 = D \ M \ V$$
$$5 = E \ N \ W$$
$$6 = F \ O \ X$$
$$7 = G \ P \ Y$$
$$8 = H \ Q \ Z$$
$$9 = I \ R$$

By adding the value of the vowels in your full name given at birth, you arrive at your *Soul Number*, or what you really are inside and what you may have been in past lifetimes. Others do not always recognize this aspect of your self. To find Sarah's Soul Number, place the value of the vowels in her

9

full name above the vowels (Vowels are A, E, I, O, U, Y*.):

$$1 \quad 1 \qquad 5 \quad 1 \quad 95 \qquad 63 \qquad 6 \quad =37$$
SARAH MELANIE HOULTON

Reduce the 37 by adding it through once:

$$37=3+7=10$$

Reduce the 10 by adding it through once:

$$10=1+0=1$$

Sarah's Soul Number is a 37/1. Always keep your double number for use later on. For now, turn to Chapter 10 of this book under Personal Number Delineations (page 207), and read the single number of your Soul Number.

The total value of the consonants in your name equals your *Outer Personality Number*, or how others see you. This is not necessarily the way you really are. This number also reveals what others will expect from you because of how you appear to them. Place the value of the consonants below the name and add:

SARAH MELANIE HOULTON
$$1 \quad 9 \quad 8 \quad 4 \quad 3 \quad 5 \qquad 8 \qquad 32 \quad 5 \quad =48$$

Reduce the 48 by adding it through once.

$$48=4+8=12$$

Reduce the 12 by adding it through once.

$$12=1+2=3$$

Sarah's Outer Personality Number is a 48/3. Figure out your Outer Personality Number, and then turn to Personal Number Delineations to determine what this number means for you.

The total of the full name at birth, or the total of the Soul and Outer Personality Numbers, is called the *Path of Destiny Number*. This number reveals the path you will walk this lifetime in order to learn the lessons indicated by your Life

*If you have a "Y" in your birthname, please read the section on "The Mysterious Letter Y' page 13, before going on.

Lesson Number (your birthday). Two people may walk the same path, for instance medicine, but one may be developing compassion and understanding while the other is developing discipline.

To find Sarah's Path of Destiny Number, add the double numbers of the Soul and Outer Personality Numbers. (This is the same as adding the entire name.) Then turn to the second part of this book to read the meaning of your Path of Destiny Number.

> 37 *Soul Number (vowels)*
> 48 *Outer Personality Number (consonants)*
> —
> 85

Reduce the 85 by adding it through once.

$$85 = 8 + 5 = 13$$

Reduce the 13 by adding it through once.

$$13 = 1 + 3 = 4$$

Sarah's Path of Destiny Number is an 85/4. Her numerological chart now looks like this:

Sarah Melanie Houlton, born July 7, 1952.

Life Lesson Number: 31/4
$$1952 = 1 + 9 + 5 + 2 = 17$$
$$7 + 7 + 17 = 31$$
$$31 = 3 + 1 = 4$$

Soul Number: 37/1	1 1 5 1 9 5 6 3 6 =37
Outer Personality Number: 48/3	SARAH MELANIE HOULTON
Path of Destiny Number: 85/4	1 9 8 4 3 5 8 3 2 5 = 48

Master Numbers

All rules seem to have exceptions. Numerology has its deviations as well. There is a point where you do not reduce a double number, and that is when you arrive at what is called a Master Number. There are four Master Numbers: 11, 22, 33, and 44. When, upon reducing, you discover you have a Master Number, you do not reduce it further. Example: If your birthday were November 8, 1945, you would determine your Life Lesson Number in the following manner:

Reduce the year 1945.

$$1945=1+9+4+5=19$$

Add the month (November = 11) and day of birth (8) to the reduced year total 19.

$$11+8+19=38$$

Reduce the 38 by adding it through once.

$$38=3+8=11$$

You have arrived at one of the Master Numbers, the 11; therefore hold that number and record it as a Life Lesson Number 38/11.

If your Soul Number adds to a 47, for example, reduce it by adding it through once.

$$47=4+7=11$$

11 is a Master Number; therefore do not reduce further but write it as a Soul Number 47/11.

This same procedure applies to any of the Master Numbers 11, 22, 33, and 44. Keep in mind that the Master Numbers do reduce to a single digit; e.g.: 11/2, 22/4, 33/6, and 44/8. Therefore, while you are under the influence of a Master Number, you will feel the effects of both the Master Number and its base digit. The effects of the Master Number however, give you an opportunity to achieve something more unique, on a higher level of consciousness. Since these Master Number vibrations can be intense, you will fluctuate between the Master Number and its base digit so that a rest period will be afforded. The Master Number energy is neither negative nor positive, it just is, and it demands more from you than the other numbers do. You should be in control of how you will handle it.

Exercise: Work out the following example to determine the four personal numbers: Life Lesson Number, Soul Number, Outer Personality Number, Path of Destiny Number. The answers are found on page 235.

Birthname: APRIL JANE BUNKER
Birthdate: April 20, 1959

The Mysterious Letter Y

Pythagoras, the father of mathematics and numerology, a mystic and a philosopher, felt there was a mystery contained within the letter Y. To experience the vibration of this letter personally, he used a name containing the Y sound for some years. He felt that the Y was a letter that indicated a dual path and perhaps choices because of this duality.

Many numerology books have explicit rules on the use of the letter Y, which in the English language is sometimes used as a vowel and sometimes as a consonant. The duality of the letter's usage may indicate that its double role is taking the place of a letter or sound yet to be discovered. (Perhaps the English language will soon adopt a 27th letter and relieve the Y of its double duty.) At the present time, however, its presence indicates a multifaceted vibration.

Through my own research I have found that the Y seems to work as both a vowel and a consonant within the same name, thus offering the individual more variety of expression and experience at those periods in his or her life when the Y is activated. (See "Table of Events" on page 51 for further explanation.) Using Y as both a vowel and a consonant results in two vowel totals, or Soul Numbers, and two consonant totals, or Outer Personality Numbers.

Consider the following name containing a Y:

Sandra Louise Coby, born April 6, 1945

Place the value of the vowels above the vowels and, using Y as a consonant, the value of the consonants below the consonants.

```
  1      1  639 5   6    =31,3+1=4, or 31/4 Soul Number
SANDRA LOUISE COBY
1  549  3    1  3   27 =35, 3+5=8, or 35/8 Outer Personality
                                               Number
```

Now reverse the position of the Y and use it as a vowel.

$$1 \qquad 1\ 639\ 5 \quad 6\ \ 7 = 38,\ 3+8=11,\ or\ 38/11\ (Master\ Number)$$

SANDRA LOUISE COBY   *Soul Number*

$$1\ \ 549 \quad 3 \quad \ 1 \quad 3 \quad 2 \quad = 28,\ 2+8=10,\ 1+0=1,\ or\ 28/1\ Outer$$

Personality Number

Therefore, Sandra has two Soul Numbers, 31/4 and 38/11, and two Outer Personality Numbers, 35/8 and 28/1. You will notice that there is a difference of 7 between each of the Soul Numbers and each of the Outer Personality Numbers which is the value of the letter Y. Also notice that the Path of Destiny Number, or the total value of the entire name, will always remain the same regardless of whether the Y is used as a vowel or a consonant. If you have more than one Y in your name, use all the Y's first as vowels and then as consonants.

The double vibration in both the Soul and the Outer Personality Numbers of Sandra's chart indicates that she has a multifaceted personality. She may have many talents, and may have lived a double life in a past lifetime. She may have two careers, perhaps one public and the other private. The double Outer Personality Number vibration may indicate that she is seen differently by different groups of people. She may appear one way at one time and another way at another time. She may be something of an enigma to many people.

Double vibrations may also come into play if you are currently using another name—for instance a married name, a professional name, or a nickname. Use this name along with your birthname to give you another set of special numbers, which will operate along with your birthname (which is with you for your lifetime). Your other name will be in effect as long as you use it.

It has been said that women are more adaptable than men in many ways, mentally, emotionally and physically. Since it is usually the custom for the woman and not the man to change her name upon marriage, she is the one who has an additional set of numbers to work with. Therefore the woman learns to be more adaptable, juggling two sets of number vibrations. The man continues throughout life with the same name, seldom changing it for any reason. Could this be one outward manifestation of a universal truth as expressed in the Yin and the Yang? It is something to think about.

Your Personal Cycles

In the following chapter you will learn how to arrive at your Personal Year Cycles, your Period Number Cycles, your Personal Month Cycles, and your Personal Day Cycles. It is important to remember that whenever you are in a cycle number that corresponds to one of your four personal numbers, then the effects of that cycle are emphasized and the cycle has greater importance for you in relation to the personal number it matches. For example, if your Life Lesson Number is a 5, and you are in a Personal Year Cycle 5, then this personal year contains some lesson you need to learn. If your Period Number Cycle is a 7, and your Outer Personality Number is a 7, events oriented towards your public image and how people see you as a person can occur in that cycle. Use the information revealed by your cycles to understand where and how you can grow and evolve as a creative individual.

2

YOUR CYCLES OF LIFE

WE BEGIN THE GREATEST JOURNEY of our life at the moment of our birth. We embark upon our journey with detailed maps that depict the major highways, detours, and rest stops along the way; yet most of us never stop to consult these maps. We drive straight on, unmindful of the directory signs along the way, until we hit a pothole or drive off a bridge and suddenly find ourselves lost and our vehicles badly in need of repair.

One of these maps is our numerological chart, which is determined at our moment of birth by our birthdate and the particular name we are given at that time. Our vibrational patterns are then set in motion, and turn and continue to turn incessantly until that moment when we choose to leave our vehicle behind at death and take on a new vibrational pattern within an overall wheel.

By examining your cycles of life and what they mean for you, you can move into the driver's seat and take control. You can learn to work and flow with your cycles rather than fight them. When you are aware of your seasons, aware that winter follows autumn and spring winter, you can then be prepared to deal with the changes as you choose. You cannot change your cycles, which are determined at birth, just as you cannot change the seasons, but you can learn to recognize your cycles and learn how to use them to your fullest advantage.

Your Personal Year Cycle

We live our lives in nine-year cycles that are repeated throughout our lifetime. Each person is born under a different cycle, represented by the numbers 1 through 9. You may have been born under a 3, or a 7, or an 8. Your beginning cycle is determined by your birthdate in the same manner as is your Life Lesson Number. If you were born under an 8, for example, 8 would be your Life Lesson Number as well as your first cycle. On your next birthday you would begin a 9 cycle, the following birthday a 1 cycle, then a 2 and so on.

The yearly cycles are called Personal Year Cycles, and the reason for the repetition of cycles is personal growth. Just as we learned our multiplication tables in grade school by repeating them over and over, so do we learn our life's lessons by repeating our cycles over and over during our lifetime. We grow through each series of nine cycles, so that each successive series finds us in a happier, healthier, and more evolved state of consciousness.

The yearly cycle, which begins on your birthday and runs from your birthday of one year to your birthday of the following year, is called the Personal Year Cycle. It has nothing to do with the calendar year. Your day of birth is the first day of your life and you do not complete a full one year cycle until your next birthday. If you were born July 9th, it would take one full year to complete the cycle, or until the following July 9th. Of if you were born January 4th, it would take one full year to complete your cycle, or until the following January 4th.

Your Personal Year Cycles begin with the year you were born. (Remember, your first Personal Year Cycle is also your Life Lesson Number.) By determining the Personal Year Cycle you are in now, you can determine the vibrational pattern you are now experiencing and the reason for it. Similarly, by determining your Personal Year Cycle for next year and the year after that, you will know what kinds of events to expect during those yearly cycles.

To work out your *present* Personal Year Cycle, we will use the example of Sarah Melanie Houlton, born July 7, 1952. To determine her present year cycle, take the year of her *last* birthday. As of this writing, February 1980, the year of her *last* birthday is 1979. Reduce the 1979 by adding it through once.

$$1979=1+9+7+9=26$$

Add the month (July = 7) and day of birth (7) to the reduced year of the last birthday, or 26.

$$7+7+26=40$$

Reduce the 40 by adding it through once.

$$40=4+0=4, \text{ written as } 40/4$$

Sarah will be in a Personal Year Cycle 40/4 from July 7, 1979 to July 7, 1980. Upon July 7, 1980, her Personal Year Cycle will change to a 5; on July 7, 1981, her cycle will change to a 6 and so forth.

Another example: Birthdate January 24th.
Reduce the year of the last birthday. (1980 was the year of the last birthday as of this writing, February 1980.)

$$1980=1+9+8+0=18$$

Add the month (January = 1) and day of birth (24) to the reduced year 18.

$$1+24+18=43$$

Reduce the total 43 by adding it through once.

$$43=4+3=7, \text{ or } 43/7$$

This birthdate of January 24th yields a Personal Year Cycle of 43/7 from January 24, 1980 to January 24, 1981, when the Personal Year Cycle 8 begins. Although the Personal Year Cycle will increase by one digit each year, it should still be figured, because you may arrive at a Master Number Cycle during one of your even numbered cycles.

Example of a Master Number Cycle: Birthdate September 3rd. Reduce the year of the last birthday, or 1979 (as of this writing, February 1980).

$$1979 = 1+9+7+9 = 26$$

Add the month (September = 9) and day of birth (3) to the reduced year 26.

$$9+3+26 = 38$$

Reduce the 38 by adding it through once.

$$38 = 3+8 = 11 \text{ or } 38/11$$

This Personal Year Cycle is written as 38/11. You have a Master Number; therefore do not reduce further.

Exercise: Determine the Personal Year for the following example. Check your answer with the correct answer which will be found on page 235 in the back of the book.
Birthdate: September 10, 1948.
Find the Personal Year Cycle beginning in the fall of 1981.

Now that you have your Personal Year Cycle Number, turn to the delineations of the temporary cycles 1 through 9, 11, 22, 33, and 44. Use the Temporary Number Delineations because the Personal Year Cycle is an energy you are experiencing temporarily, not for a lifetime as you do with your four personal numbers. Remember, if you are operating under a Master Number cycle, read both the Master Number and its base digit because you will fluctuate between the two vibrations. The Master Numbers reduce in the following manner: 11/2, 22/4, 33/6, and 44/8. The delineations of these number cycles will validate the accuracy of this system. You will begin to see a pattern forming when you examine your nine-year cycles. Whatever is happening in your life now was happening nine years ago and nine years before that, and will happen again nine years from now, and so forth into the future. The events will not be identical, but the trends and the areas of focus will be the same.

Purchase a notebook and make a list of your nine-year cycles since birth. Fill in the events you can remember under the appropriate years. You will not remember all of your past experiences at once, so plan to enter them as they come to mind. Soon an amazing synthesis will unfold before your eyes and the pattern will become quite clear. You may discover facets of these numbers that are not mentioned here. It would be impossible to make note of every eventuality that could occur under each number, but you will understand how the events you experience are exclusive to your particular cycle and qualify under that number and no other.

19

Peak or Balance Point in Your Personal Year Cycle: During any cycle, there is always a beginning, a growing, a culmination, a decaying, and a transition point. This is a vital sequence which deserves our attention in relation to numerology, because it can designate with great exactness particular dates when certain events will occur. This process is exemplified by the phases of the Moon, a perfect model of the workings of the universal waxing and waning process present in all cycles.

Your birthday each year is like the new Moon. It is a beginning. A seed has been planted, the seed of your new Personal Year Cycle. Ideas are stirring, and the universal life process comes alive. As the Moon waxes, energies increase and the seed begins to push its way up through the ground. Your ideas, gaining momentum, produce events which demand your attention.

Then, upon the full Moon, the seed bursts through the ground into the sunlight, alive with the fullness of life's energy. This is the Peak Point in your cycle when the energies of that cycle come to a head, events occur, and the process becomes visible.

The waning of the Moon returns the energies inward, and the seed that became a plant now returns to the earth, nourishing and fertilizing the soil so that the new growth that follows will benefit from its sacrifice. As your cycle wanes, it sends its message deep into your subconscious, its experience nourishing you subliminally so that your next cycle will be richer and fuller because of what you have learned from the previous one.

Each cycle, whether year, month, or day, will fulfill this universal process. In your Personal Year Cycle, the full Moon of your Personal Year is halfway through your cycle, or exactly six months from your birthday, just as the full Moon is halfway through its cycle two weeks from its beginning. This is your Peak Point, or full Moon aspect when your energies of that particular cycle peak. (Notice how many major events happen in people's lives on their birthdays or six months later.)

If your birthday is February 13th, the Peak Point in your Personal Year will always be August 13th, six months later. If your birthday is September 9th your Peak Point will always be March 9th. The energies that peak on that date, the Peak Point, reflect the Personal Year Cycle number you are under at that time.

Lay out the experiences of your past few years numerologically in the manner of the accompanying graph. Give yourself time to think about what happened during those

years. So often I have talked with people who at first could
not remember anything happening in a given year on a given
date, but then discovered that after a few minutes thought
they suddenly recalled an automobile accident in which they
almost died, or a residential move that changed their life. Not
every year brings such drastic events, but if you allow yourself
or the person whose numbers you are working on time to
think, you will discover that the numbers are uncannily correct.

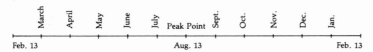

If, after adding your month and day of birth to the reduced year of your last birthday, you discover for example
that you are in a Personal Year Cycle 8, your energies are then
focussed on your work and on money situations in which you
feel more pressure and have more responsibility. These
energies began when your cycle began, on your birthday, and
they will peak six months later. At that Peak Point, if you
have worked well, you may receive a raise or a promotion. Or
perhaps you received the promotion at the beginning of your
Personal Year Cycle; at your Peak Point, if you have not
worked well, you could lose that position. You will see how
the energies of that 8 cycle have built to the Peak Point. The
remainder of the Personal Year, the last six months, should
bring either continued rewards and an inward growth, or
despair over the failure. However, this despair can be used as
a point of growth if you examine it and decide to utilize what
you have learned in the process. It is true that we learn
through our mistakes, but too often we overlook the fact that
we learn from our successes as well. I tend to like the latter
process.

On occasion, the Peak Point may not bring an obvious
outward event, especially during an introspective cycle.
However, events and ideas do begin on your birthday, continue to grow, and then reach a peak in six months. That Peak
Point could be a profound attitude change, a deep realization
that may not be obvious to those around you but to you is
very tangible. However, since our thoughts are potent and do
create our reality, more times than not the events are visible
outside ourselves.

Another way of looking at the Personal Year Cycle and
its Peak Point is to visualize it as energy or light waves traveling in an undulating motion. Energy conforms to this pattern.
A life cycle with a birthday of May 4th could be laid out on
this frequency:

In the waxing period the energy of your particular Personal Year Cycle builds to a Peak Point, where it bursts forth. As the energies are given off, they gradually soak into the earth or subconscious as experience. The waning process fertilizes the earth and gives nourishment to the subconscious. At the same time it clears the way for the new growth that begins as the result of the entire cycle.

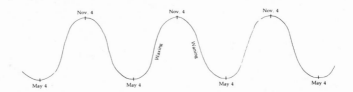

One notorious case that immediately comes to mind is the Reverend Jim Jones of the People's Temple. He was born May 13, 1931. On November 19, 1978. Almost exactly six months past his birthday, at his Peak Point, he was responsible for and died himself in a horrible massacre-suicide in Guyana where 911 of his followers met their deaths. Of course, positive events occur at this Peak Point as well which will be shown shortly; however, it is interesting to keep track of world events in this manner.

The following examples came from my files (the names are fictitious):

Case 1: Mrs. Brown always had difficulty relating to her mother and she could never understand the tension between them. When she was 34 years old, she discovered quite by accident that as an infant she had been abandoned by her mother. Authorities, finding her on a doorstep, took her to the local welfare agency where she remained for some months until miraculously a family member recognized her photograph from a newspaper story. The family claimed the child and some weeks later, the mother, after experiencing great mental suffering over the act, returned to her family and her child.

During her abandonment, Mrs. Brown was in a Personal Year Cycle 1, a new beginning, a time of isolation when she felt alone even when there were many people around. It was a time of learning to stand alone. It was also a time for decisions; and, although an eighteen-month-old child cannot consciously make decisions, it was obvious that subconsciously she had made certain assessments about trusting others because of her experiences. This cycle peaked at the time her mother returned and she was reunited with her. However, a lesson in independence had been learned at an early age.

When Mrs. Brown realized the cycle she was in at that time and the purpose for it, she then found more acceptance in her heart for her mother's actions.

Case 2: Mr. White had a serious cigarette habit. He had tried everything to rid himself of the problem, to no avail. In desperation, he finally took a friend's advice and enrolled in a well-known mind control course, even though he had no faith in it. The intensive forty hour course was soon over and Mr. White set about practicing what he had learned.

He began his course six weeks after his Personal Year Cycle 7 had begun, and, three days before the Peak Point in this cycle, he discarded a full "just-in-case" pack of cigarettes, which had been lying on top of his refrigerator since the day he finished the course.

A Personal Year Cycle 7 is a time of withdrawal, a going within to think and analyze, a time to perfect skills, a time of completion. It is also a health number. Upon examining his numerological chart, Mr. White realized how well his cycle had fit his needs.

Action Points in Your Personal Year Cycle

I have also been experimenting with the following technique and to date it has proved accurate.

Just as any cycle has a Peak Point that occurs midway, and in astrology relates to the opposition (σ^{o}), so there appear to be two other very strong points in a cycle when events also occur. I call these the Action Points. They relate to a square ($\square$) aspect in astrology. The square in astrology is a dynamic factor in a chart urging the individual to do something to relieve the pressure caused by the square's influence. Therefore I propose that the Action Point in numerology causes the same type of reaction.

The junctures where Action Points fall are the times in your life when events take place that energize you. These are times when you are urged to do something that brings about a major event in your life. Conversely, these points would draw those same major events to you through others, at which point you are forced to react.

To find the Action Points in your cycle, divide your Personal Year Cycle of twelve months into quarters of three months each, beginning with your month and day of birth, as in the accompanying example of a birthdate, November 5. Mark your month and day of birth at each end of the line. Six

23

months into the cycle, mark your Peak Point. Then, mark three months and nine months or one-quarter and three-quarters, into the cycle as Action Points.

	Action Point	Peak Point	Action Point	
Nov. 5	Feb. 5	May 5	Aug. 5	Nov. 5

Another example:

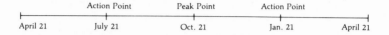

	Action Point	Peak Point	Action Point	
April 21	July 21	Oct. 21	Jan. 21	April 21

Upon these Action Point dates you can expect the energy of the cycle that you are experiencing to become strongly activated, so that you are moved to action or are caused to react.

Thomas Jefferson, born April 2 under the old calendar (the Gregorian calendar added 11 days in 1752), had an action point of July 2. Two of the most important events in his life occurred on July 4 (in different years): The Declaration of Independence and his death.

The conception, fetal growth, and birth of a child further exemplifies this universal cycle. The cycle begins at conception. At about three months, the first Action Point in the cycle, life is felt within the womb. If abortion is considered, it is usually suggested by this time. At six months, the Peak Point of the cycle, the fetus is about twelve and a half inches long, with fully developed hands and feet. It exercises actively by stretching and bending, and forcefully moving its arms and legs. Then at nine months, the last Action Point in the cycle, the child is born.

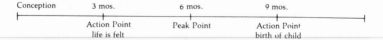

Conception	3 mos.	6 mos.	9 mos.	
	Action Point	Peak Point	Action Point	
	life is felt		birth of child	

The ancient axiom, as it is above, so it is below, continues to hold true. If we examine any cycle in heaven or on earth, we find this Universal Law applies. One must stand in awe of the Cosmic Mind that so knowingly planned lifes' cycles.

An event that just occurred in my life fits well here. Last August 3rd, my previous book (co-authored with Faith Javane, entitled *Numerology and the Divine Triangle*) was finally delivered to the publisher after much work and a long wait. My birthday is November 5th; therefore, my Action

Points in a Personal Year Cycle are February 5th and August 5th. The books were delivered on August 3rd. However, August 5th of last year, 1979, fell on a Sunday, and since there are no deliveries on the weekend, the closest dates to my Action point of August 5th when the books could have been delivered were August 3rd and August 6th, and they arrived on Friday August 3rd! On the same day, our publisher offered us a contract for the computer rights to the book, and this was agreed upon the following Monday, August 6th! That series of events graphically pointed out the accuracy of the Action Point of August 5th in my Personal Year Cycle.

February 5th is also an Action Point in my cycle. This month of February, I am working on the present manuscript. I met with my publisher and his associate on February 4th, and they expressed interest in the ideas for this book and gave me the go-ahead. I have been working four to five hours a day since February 5th, the following day. Again, the Action Point of my Personal Year cycle has definitely urged me to action. The following is another example from my files:

Case 1: Mr. Black was in a Personal Year Cycle 5. This was also his Life Lesson Number, so it was obvious that this particular Personal Year Cycle would be an important one in his life. He had never married because he had never found anyone he could relate to. His birthday is August 15th. At the end of this particular August, when he had turned 29 years old, he began dating a beautiful young woman. By the middle of November this young lady had won his heart. He asked her to marry him on a day that coincided with his first Action Point. They were married the middle of February, the Peak Point of his Personal Year Cycle, and in May, his second Action Point, he left his job of some years to operate a small business they had bought.

I was amazed at how perfectly the events of this Personal Year Cycle fit the Action Points and Peak Point. Perhaps this will not always work so precisely. No rule is ironclad. However, I have seen this happen so often that it seems to me there is truth in it. The four distinct seasons bring new life to the earth. Perhaps we also have our four seasons which revitalize our earth, our bodies and our minds.

Your Period Number Cycle

Your Personal Year Cycle can be divided into three four-month blocks of time called Period Number Cycles. Through

these Period Number Cycles you can discover the more specific events that will be occurring within a shorter span of time. The Period Number Cycles have a narrowing down effect within your Personal Year Cycle . You may be in a Personal Year Cycle 7, for example, and may want to know not only what is going to happen within the rest of that year, but also, more specifically, when. The Period Number Cycles can help you focus on certain months within your Personal Year Cycle when particular energies will be operating; energies that are working towards a manifestation of the potential of the larger Personal Year Cycle. All lesser cycles always work towards accomplishing the goals of the greater cycle.

To arrive at a Period Number Cycle within your present cycle, begin with your month and day of birth and count four months ahead. Continue until you have divided the year into thirds. Using October 18, we would divide the Personal Year Cycle as follows: October 18 to February 18, February 18 to June 18, June 18 to October 18. We shall use our previous example: Sarah Melanie Houlton, born July 7, 1952. In the following chart we have labeled each block according to this division:

Personal Year Cycle	July 7-Nov. 7	Nov. 7-March 7	March 7-Nov. 7

Now write the year you are working with in each block under the four-month Period Numbers. Since we are working with July 7th, the year of her last birthday (as of this writing, February 1980) is 1979, so we place 1979 in each block under the 4-month Period Numbers.

To the first Period Number, add the age in the year you are working with. In 1979 Sarah is 27 years old.

$$1979 + 27 = 2006$$

Reduce the total by adding it through once.

$$2006 = 2 + 0 + 0 + 6 = 8$$

From July 7th to November 7th Sarah will be operating under an 8 Period Number Cycle which is geared towards the larger realization of the Personal Year Cycle.

To discover what Sarah can expect to experience and deal with under this Period Number Cycle 8, turn to the Tem-

Personal Year Cycle	July 7-Nov. 7	Nov. 7-March 7	March 7-July 7
	1979 27 ‾‾‾‾‾ 2006 = 8 add age	1979	1979

Under the second Period Number Cycle, from November 7th to March 7th, add the Life Lesson Number to the year. The Life Lesson Number is arrived at by adding the full birthdate. With her birthdate July 7, 1952, we know that Sarah's Life Lesson Number is 31/4. This is the point when the double numbers are used. Add the double number of Sarah's Life Lesson Number to the 1979 in the second Period Number Cycle.

$$1979+31=2010$$

Reduce the 2010 by adding it through once.

$$2010=2+0+1+0=3$$

Personal Year Cycle	July 7-Nov. 7	Nov. 7-March 7	March 7-July 7
	1979 27 ‾‾‾‾‾ 2006 = 8 add age	1979 31 ‾‾‾‾‾ 2010 = 3 add double no. of Life Lesson no.	

From November 7, 1979 to March 7, 1980, Sarah will be operating under a Period Number Cycle 3, and she can expect the events of that period to reflect the 3 vibration.

Under the last Period Number Cycle, from March 7th to July 7th, add the double number of the Soul Number, or the total of the vowels in the full name at birth, to the year 1979. Sarah's vowel total, or Soul Number is 37/1.

$$1979+37=2016$$

Reduce the total 2016 by adding it through once.

$$2016=2+0+1+6=9$$

27

In the third Period Number Cycle, from March 7th to July 7th, Sarah will be working with a 9 vibration.

Personal Year Cycle	July 7-Nov. 7	Nov. 7-March 7	March 7-July 7
	1979 27 ――― 2006 = 8	1979 31 ――― 2010 = 8	1979 37 ――― 2016 = 9
	add age	add double no. of Life Lesson no.	add double no. of Soul no.

In every delineation, when you divide the Personal Year Cycle down into Period Number Cycles, you will follow this procedure:

1. Divide the Personal Year Cycle into three four-month blocks of time beginning with the day of birth.
2 . To the first Period Number Cycle, add the age during that year you are working with.
3 . To the second Period Number Cycle, add the double digit from the Life Lesson Number (from the birthdate).
4 . To the third Period Number Cycle, add the double number of the Soul Number (from the total of the vowels in the birthname).

Using our previous example, Sandra Louise Coby born April 6, 1945, in the same manner, we remember that Sandra has a Y in her birthname and therefore has two Soul Numbers. Therefore, you would add both Soul Numbers in the third Period Period Cycle yielding a double experience at that time.

Personal Year Cycle	Period Number Cycles		
April 6	April 6-August 6	August 6-December 6	December 6-April 6
4 + 6 + 1979 (26) 4 + 6 + 26 = 36 36 = 3 + 6 = 9	1979 34 ――― 2013 = 6	1979 29 ――― 2008 = 10 = 1	1979 31 ――― 2010 = 3 1979 38 ――― 2017 = 10 = 1

From December 6th to April 6th, Sandra will be working with two vibrations, a 1 and a 3. These two vibrational patterns will join to produce a more complex series of events, thereby adding another dimension to the quality of the experience, as well as working towards achieving the goals of the Personal Year Cycle 9.

Exercise: Work out the following example to determine the Period Number cycles for April 1982 to April 1983 and check your answers on page 235 in the back of the book.

Birthname: APRIL JANE BUNKER
Birthdate: April 20, 1959

My son is in a Period Number Cycle 11. A preliminary comment here—we feel we have instilled a good sense of values and judgment in our children. During their teenage years, we discuss their desires carefully and nine times out of ten let them follow through on their own decisions. The reason for this attitude is twofold: we believe in giving the children a certain amount of latitude because we feel they have a strong foundation from which to work, and, secondly, there is something to be said for experiencing the results of your own decisions.

Last month, our 17 year old son came to us with a request for a motorcycle which he intended to finance. This was one of the few times I had to say no.

His birthday is December 9th. He is in a 47/11 Personal Year Cycle (as of this writing April 1980). With a Life Lesson Number of 39/3, his second Period Number Cycle from April 9 to August 9 is an 11. Double 11's! Now, I know that 11's can bring great recognition and rewards, however they can also bring sudden unexpected and sometimes upsetting incidents.

The son of a woman I know had a similar period in his life recently. Although entirely innocent, he happened to be with a "friend" who shoplifted at a department store. This boy met his friend on the way out of the store and was arrested along with the guilty boy. His mother had quite a time exonerating him.

I always expect the positive side of the numbers to operate but I also believe "an ounce of prevention is worth a pound of cure." When we are aware of our cycles, we must act wisely. My instincts told me that my son, in double 11's from April 9 to August 9, should not be riding a motorcycle. We have told him he will have to wait until next year when he graduates from high school. The double 11's will still operate—no one can change that now—but free will helps direct the positive or negative direction of the number vibration. "Forewarned is forearmed." My son has seen the accuracy of these cycles and has accepted this decision well.

Peak Point Within Your Period Number Cycles: Just as your Personal Year Cycle has its Peak Point, your Period Number Cycle does also, and it operates under the same basic principle. The Peak Point within your Period Number Cycle is halfway through the four-month block of time. In our example of Sandra Louise Coby, born April 6, 1945, the first Period Number Cycle is from April 6th to August 6th. The Peak Point within this Period Number Cycle is June 6th.

29

Since Sandra is operating under a 6 Period Number Cycle during those four months, she can expect that the energies of that 6, which represent domestic changes and considerations, to peak around June 6th. Since this Period Number Cycle occurs within a Personal Year Cycle 9, a time of endings, this activity in her home, which peaks around June 6th, could bring an end to a current domestic situation.

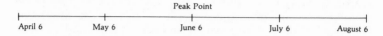

		Peak Point		
April 6	May 6	June 6	July 6	August 6

Similarly, the Peak Point within the second Period Number Cycle from August 6th to December 6th, occurs on October 6th. Sandra will be experiencing a Period Number Cycle 1 at that time, indicating new beginnings when she must make major decisions by herself. These new beginnings will peak around October 6th.

The last Period Number Cycle from December 6th to April 6th will peak on February 6th, halfway through the Period Number Cycle. Under the 1 and 3 vibrations, she is now experiencing a time when not only must she stand alone and make decisions, but also, because of the 3, she is more noticeable in a social way; her life is beginning to expand and grow through others' acceptance of her ideas.

These three Period Number Cycles have all been building to bring about the necessary changes indicated by the Personal Year Cycle 9.

Notice the emphasis on the Peak Point October 6th. It is the Peak Point of Sandra's Personal Year Cycle and her second Period Number Cycle. This reinforces the importance of this date on her chart. The Peak Point of the Personal Year and the Peak Point of the second Period Number Cycle will always coincide. Perhaps that is why major events seem to occur either at the beginning of your year or half way through. You may want to make note of these Peak Points on your numerological chart.

A synopsis of the above chart would go something like this: Sandra is in a transitional year (Personal Year Cycle 9), when necessary changes must occur in order to free her for the future, so she will be prepared for the brand new cycle that will begin with her next birthday (Personal Year Cycle 1). These changes may occur in her home or a domestic area where the current situation will not be in effect for long (Period Number 6), and may happen around June 6th (Peak Point). In August, she will need to take matters into her own hands and make some decisions that may be unpopular with those around her; however, she must stand her ground (Period Number 1). Some key decisions may have to be made the first week of October (Peak Point). As December begins, her stand will bring her the admiration and respect of those who had earlier opposed her, and she will begin to respond to that positive feedback, enjoying her newly found attention so much that she decides to accept the social invitations that are being proffered (Period Number 3). The first week of February should be especially active (Peak Point). However, the overall trend for this personal year is a transitional one. Sandra must be ready to let go of the things that are no longer necessary in her life. She must be ready to move in the new directions that will open up for her on her next birthday.

Action Points in Your Period Number Cycles Your Period Number Cycles also have two Action Points. Divide the four-month Period Number Cycle into quarters of one month each beginning with the first month of each cycle. Halfway through the Period Number Cycle, or two months, mark the Peak Point. One month and three months into the Period Number Cycle, mark the Action Points. Use this method for each of the three Period Number Cycles in each Personal Year Cycle.

Example: Birthdate November 5th.

	Action Point	Peak Point	Action Point	
Nov. 5	Dec. 5	Jan. 5	Feb. 5	March 5

Example 2: Birthdate April 21st.

	Action Point	Peak Point	Action Point	
April 21	May 21	June 21	July 21	August 21

The Action Points will energize the number vibration of the Period Number Cycle in which it is found. For example, this month of February in which I am writing this book falls within a Period Number Cycle 5, which signifies communication of all kinds, and writing is a form of communication. February 5th happens to be one of my Action Points, and this Action Point would instigate events that coincide or work towards the accomplishment of this Period Number Cycle 5. As you recall, February 5th was the date that, because my publisher expressed interest in this book, I began writing. The Action Point urged into action the energies of the Period Number Cycle 5 of communication.

Case 1: Miss Violet was in a Period Number Cycle 6 in a Personal Year Cycle 5. 6 is a love vibration and 5 is communication and change. I could tell her with some confidence that she was about to enter a yearly cycle in which she would be socially active and have many opportunities to date. There was a good chance that during her Period Number Cycle 6 she would meet one special man, and because her Action Point fell on March 18th, I suggested that on or around that date, she accept invitations to parties and community activities. She called some months later to thank me for the advice. I told her that she should thank herself for being wise enough to listen to her own cycles and flow with them.

If you lay out the Period Number Cycles under the Personal Year Cycle, you will find that certain dates are emphasized. This will hold true for each year of your life. In other words, once you find your points of emphasis, those same dates will be accentuated each year of your life.

Example: Birthdate November 5th.

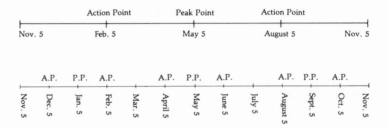

Notice that February 5th is accentuated as an Action Point in both the Personal Year Cycle and the first Period Number Cycle. This date has added emphasis and should bring about an event that will fall under the synthesis of the first Period Number Cycle and the Personal Year Cycle numbers.

May 5th is accented as the Peak Point in both the Personal Year Cycle and the second Period Number cycle, and is an outstanding date in the year's activities. The energies of the second Period Number Cycle will dovetail into the larger Personal Year cycle, and May 5th should be the approximate date when this activity becomes observable.

The Action Point of August 5th is also accented through the Personal Year cycle and the Period Number Cycle; here again the lesser Period Number Cycle number vibration will work toward the goal of the greater Personal Year Cycle: August 5th should be a telling date as to when and how these events will manifest. Do not overlook the other Action Points and Peak Points, however. They blend in with the more obvious points in your cycle in a constructive symphony of harmony in your life.

Your Personal Month Cycle

Your circle of experience expands once again with the introduction of the Personal Month. Just as we divided your Personal Year Cycle into segments of Period Numbers, we now divide the Personal Year Cycle and the Period Numbers into smaller units by the addition of your Personal Month.

To arrive at a Personal Month, we divide the Personal Year Cycle into twelve-month segments beginning with your day of birth, and moving ahead each month to the same day of the month.

Example: Birthdate April 6th.

| April 6 | May 6 | June 6 | July 6 | August 6 | Sept. 6 | Oct. 6 | Nov. 6 | Dec. 6 | Jan. 6 | Feb. 6 | March 6 | April 6 |

Through the use of the Personal Month you can narrow down the specific energies or events that will occur within a given Period Number and Personal Year Cycle. The value of this technique is obvious. If you are anticipating a big business venture and need to know when you should make your plans, when you should seek financing, and when you should begin the project, these Personal Months can be a guiding force.

Imagine that Mrs. Peacock is in a Personal Year Cycle 8, a big business cycle, and she needs financial backing. Looking at her chart, you may find that she is under a Period Number 4 from May to September. You can then suggest that the best time for her to make her plans is between May and September. If May were a Personal Month 7, June a Personal Month 8, July a Personal Month 9, and August a Personal Month 1 (they will run in sequence), you could tell her that during May she should spend her time thinking, analyzing, and planning mentally, but this would not be the month to push ahead because she would be opposed or might become ill. In June, when she is in her Personal Month 8, previously closed areas will open for her and influential help may become available. July sees her tying up loose ends, and by August she should be on her way to instigating her new plans.

The Personal Months, being a minor vibration, may not necessarily bring major events into your life because by themselves they are a lesser force. However, when they are in a larger cycle that is reinforced by their presence, the events designated by that Personal Month will be emphasized. A Personal Month 8 within a Period Number 8 would emphasize the 8 energies just as a Period Number 6 within a Personal Year Cycle 6 would emphasize the 6 vibration. Wherever you find the numbers duplicated, there will be an added emphasis on that number's energies.

Again, your Personal Month runs from your day of birth in the beginning month of Your Personal Year Cycle to your day of the birth in the following month, and so on to the end of Your Personal Year Cycle. So again, if your birthday is May 9, for example, your Personal Months run from May 9 to June 9, from June 9 to July 9, from July 9 to August 9, etc.. Or if your birthday is November 21, your Personal Months run from November 21 to December 21, from December 21 to January 21, from January 21 to February 21, and so forth.

To arrive at your Personal Month Cycle, add the number of the calendar month to your double Personal Year Cycle Number.

Example: Birthdate April 7th. As of this writing, February 1980, you will find the Personal Year Cycle number by adding April 7 to the year of the last birthday, or 1979.
Reduce the year by adding it through once.

$$1979 = 1+9+7+9 = 26$$

Add the month (April = 4) and day of birth (7) to the reduced year 26.

$$4+7+26 = 37$$

Reduce the 37 by adding it through once.

$$37 = 3+7 = 10$$

Reduce the 10 by adding it through once.

$$10 = 1+0 = 1$$

This is a Personal Year Cycle 37/1, from April 7, 1979 to April 7, 1980. If you wanted to know what March of 1980 would bring, add 3 (March is the third month of the calendar year) to the double number of the Personal Year Cycle 37/1.

$$3+37 = 40$$

Reduce the 40 by adding it through once:

$$40=4+0=4$$

March 7th to April 7th would be a Personal Month 4.

If you wanted to know what November of 1979 was, you would add 11 (November is the 11th month of the calendar year) to the double number of the Personal Year Cycle 37/1:

$$11+37=48$$

Reduce the total 48 by adding it through once.

$$48=4+8=12$$

Reduce the 12 by adding it through once.

$$12=1+2=3$$

November 7th to December 7th would be a Personal Month 3.

Example: Birthdate January 26th.
Find the Personal Year Cycle by adding the month and day of birth to the reduced total of the last year. 1980 was the last year, as of this writing Feburary 1980. Reduce the year 1980:

$$1980=1+9+8+0=18$$

Add the month (January = 1) and day of birth (26) to the reduced year 18.

$$1+26+18=45$$

Reduce the total 45 by adding it through once.

$$45=4+5=9$$

The Personal Year Cycle of this birthdate is 45/9 from January 26th, 1980 to January 26, 1981. To the double number of the Personal Year Cycle 45/9 add the number of the calendar month you are investigating; for instance October, which is a 10 month:

$$10+45=55$$

Reduce the 55 by adding it through once.

$$55 = 5 + 5 = 10$$

Reduce the 10 by adding it through once.

$$10 = 1 + 0 = 1$$

October 26th to November 26th will be a Personal Month 1 in this chart.

In this process, add the month to the double digit of the Personal Year Cycle because in this manner you may arrive at a Master Number, whereas if you only used the single digit of the Personal Year Cycle you would not necessarily do so.

Exercise: Work out the following example to determine the Personal Month cycles and then check your answer on page 235 in the back of the book.

Find the Personal Month Cycles for the cycle from April 20, 1982 to April 20, 1983.

As before, use the number delineations in the second portion of this book, remembering that Personal Month Cycles are minor, helping to key in on the larger Personal Year Cycle and Period Number Cycles. However, they are still accurate.

Often I have looked ahead in my own chart to the following month and thought at the time, "There is no indication whatsoever that these things will happen." But each time they do. The most recent example is the writing of this book now in February, 1980.

I am presently in a Period Number 5 from this past November 5 until this coming March 5th. 5 indicates writing amongst other activities. However, last November I had no plans to write this book. Early in January, last month, I noticed I would be in a Personal Month 8 from February 5th to March 5th. My calendar for that month was empty except for a course I had planned to take on Monday evenings. I mentioned to my husband how strange it was that I would shortly be in an 8 month and I had absolutely nothing planned. And to make matters even more odd, the course was cancelled two weeks later, leaving my Personal Month 8 absolutely blank! I have learned to trust the Higher Forces, and I have found the numbers, being an expression of these Higher Forces, to be unfailing. So I knew my calendar had been cleared for the month of February for a reason.

I am always playing with numbers and keeping notes, and new ideas had been moving inside my head since late fall of 1979. But I had made no plans for them, other than enjoying them and recording them in my notebook.

On January 5th as I entered my Personal Month 7 the serious thinking began. I woke up each morning and jotted down numerous ideas which had come to me through my dreams. During the day I kept my notebook close by for those thoughts that suddenly appeared out of nowhere. I spent some time alone because I felt the need for it, even though, under the Period Number 5, I still had many outside activities to attend to. Then, on February 1st, a Friday, I was impelled to call my publisher and set up an appointment for the following Monday to discuss these ideas as a possible book. Over the weekend, I put together an outline and an introduction.

On Monday morning, February 4th, I met with the publisher, Frank Molinski, and the marketing manager, Douglas Hall, for an hour discussing this proposal. They liked the idea and asked when I could have a rough manuscript to them. I told them in about a month. It was not until I was driving home that afternoon that I realized that the next day, February 5th, when I would begin the discipline of writing four to five hours each morning, was the exact day my Personal Month 8 began! My calendar would be very full for the entire month, and the discipline, pressure, responsibility, and business vibration of the 8 had indeed been fulfilled. Not only that, but since this Personal Month began, I have already received two lecture requests and a pleasant check in the mail for a business arrangement. I continue to stand in awe of those spiritual messengers, the numbers.

Peak Point in Your Personal Month Cycle: As in the Personal Year Cycle and the Period Number Cycle, every cycle has a Peak Point that occurs halfway through that cycle. Your Personal Month also has a Peak Point, approximately two weeks beyond the beginning of your Personal Month, or halfway through the month of four weeks. At that time, the events designated by the number of the Personal Month will culminate.

Because the number of days varies with each month, an approximate date can be chosen, or you could work out the exact date for each month.

Example: Birthdate November 5th.

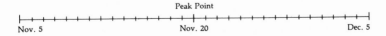

Peak Point
Nov. 5   Nov. 20   Dec. 5

This person's Personal Month, from November 5th to December 5th, contains 30 days. Half of 30 is 15; therefore, the halfway point, or Peak Point, of this Personal Month is 15 days from November 5th, or November 20th.

From December 5th to January 5th, this person's Personal Month Cycle contains 31 days. The halfway point, or Peak Point, is 15½ days from December 5th, or December 20-21st.

Since each month (except February) contains 30 or 31 days, you can add 15 to 15½ days to the beginning date of each Personal Month Cycle. This will give you a two-day period as a Peak Point in that Personal Month. When you are working with the Personal Month of February, which has 28 days (except for leap year when it has 29), add 14 days to the beginning of the Personal Month Cycle in order to find the Peak Point.

Example: Birthdate March 27.

The Peak Point in each month for this person born on March 27th is 15 to 15½ days from the day of birth, or the 27th.

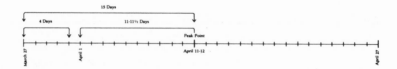

Counting 15 to 15½ days from March 27, you arrive at April 11 to 12th, the Peak Point of that Personal Month.

The Peak Point for the Personal Month of April 27 to May 27th is 15 to 15½ days from April 27th or May 12th to 13th.

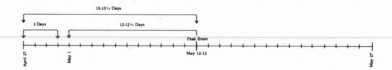

I use the following chart in my delineations. Notice that the Personal Months are located at the base of the Period Numbers.

In the the example you will notice that the Peak Points in the Personal Months vary between the 11 and 12th and the 12th and 13th, depending on whether there are 30 or 31 days in the individual month. The very last block to the far right in the Personal Months is the February block; therefore add only

14 days to the 27th and arrive at the Peak Point of the Personal Month.

Personal Year Cycle	Period Number Cycles			
March 27, 1955	March 27-July 27	July 27-Nov. 27	Nov. 27-March 27	
3+27+1979 (26) 3+27+26=56 56=5+6=11 Master Number Year 9/27	1979 24 ─── 2003 =5 add age	1979 50 ─── 2029 =13=4 add double no. of life lesson no.	1979 31 ─── 2010 =3 add double no. of soul no.'s.	1979 38 ─── 2017 =10=1

Personal Months	5	6	7	8	9	1	2	3	4	5	3	4
Peak Points	4/11-12	5/12-13	6/11-12	7/12-13	8/11-12	9/11-12	10/12-13	11/11-12	12/12-13	1/11-12	2/11-12	3/11

Case 2: Mr. Green knows numerology, trusts it, and uses it well. In his early days with numerology he needed some cash to boost both a sagging business and his morale. He had just begun his Personal Year Cycle 5, a time of change, communication, and exchanging of ideas. Encouraged by the new energy and the many ideas he was coming up with, he began planning for a business seminar under a Period Number 4. After much work, organization, and the proper advertising, along with a small investment on his part, the seminar was held during a Personal Month 8, a business and money vibration. His seminar, which was well attended and very successful, was held on a Saturday, the 9th. On the following Monday, the 11th, the Peak Point in his Personal Month Cycle, he made a substantial deposit to his bank account.

He used the information he gathered from his numerological chart as a guide in turning the unhappy state of affairs he was enduring into a profitable and mentally rewarding experience, not only for himself but for all those who attended his seminar. He gave well and received much in return.

Action Points In Your Personal Month Cycle: You can determine the Action Points in your Personal Month by dividing the month of approximately thirty days into quarters of 7½ days each, beginning with the month and day of birth. Halfway through the Personal Month cycle, or 15 days past the day of birth, mark the Peak Point. Then mark 7½ days past the day of birth, or ¼ of the month, and 22½ days past the day of birth, or ¾ of the month, as the Action Points.

Example: Birthdate September 7th.

	Action Point		Peak Point		Action Point	
Sept. 7	Sept. 14-15		Sept. 22		Sept. 29-30	Oct. 7

DATE	PERSONAL YEAR CYCLE	PERIOD NUMBER CYCLE	PERSONAL MONTH CYCLE
November 12-13			A.P.
November 20			P.P.
November 27-28			A.P.
December 5		A.P.	
December 12-13			A.P.
December 20-21			P.P.
December 28-29			A.P.
January 5		P.P.	
January 12-13			A.P.
January 20-21			P.P.
January 28-29			A.P.
February 5	A.P.	A.P.	
February 12			A.P.
February 19			P.P.
February 26			A.P.
March 12-13			A.P.
March 20-21			P.P.
March 28-29			A.P.
April 5		A.P.	
April 12-13			A.P.
April 20			P.P.
April 27-28			A.P.
May 5	P.P.	P.P.	
May 12-13			A.P.
May 20-21			P.P.
May 28-29			A.P.
June 5		A.P.	
June 12-13			A.P.
June 20			P.P.
June 27-28			A.P.
July 12-13			A.P.
July 20-21			P.P.
July 28-29			A.P.
August 5	A.P.	A.P.	
August 12-13			A.P.
August 20-21			P.P.
August 28-29			A.P.
September 5		P.P.	
September 12-13			A.P.
September 20			P.P.
September 27-28			A.P.
October 5		A.P.	
October 12-13			A.P.
October 20-21			P.P.
October 28-29			A.P.

Example: Birthdate April 25th.

	Action Point	Peak Point	Action Point	
April 25	May 1-2	May 9-10	May 16-17	May 25

The days of the months vary from 28 in February (29 in leap year) to 31. Each month can be figured separately by counting the number of days from the day of birth in one month to the day of birth in the following month, dividing the total into quarters and marking the Action Points and Peak Point in each Personal Month cycle. Or you can approximate the date in each month by adding 7½ and 22½ days for the Action Points and 15 days for the Peak Points to the day of birth, which will be off by 1-1½ days at the most in any given month. However, once you have taken the time to determine these Peak and Action Points in your Personal Month cycles, the dates will remain the same year after year, as they do in all the cycles. Therefore, you may want to make a chart like the one on page 40 marking the points and their corresponding dates.

Example: Birthdate November 5th. (See page 40.)

Your Personal Day Cycle

If you have an important appointment on a particular day, it may be vital that you know how you are going to feel on that day. Knowing what your mood will be on any given day can enable you to plan your calendar more in keeping with your personal ups and downs.

You can determine the trend of any day by using your Personal Day Cycle. It can help you understand why on one day you feel tired and need to be alone and on the next you are ready to tackle the world. By using your Personal Day Cycle wisely, you will know what day is best for your more aggressive activities, what day is best for that special party, when you can expect an important contract to be signed, when family gatherings will be more harmonious, what days are ruled by love, why you spend more money on one day and less on another, and so on.

To find your Personal Day Cycle, add the month and day in question to the double number of your Personal Year Cycle.

Example: Birthdate October 7th.
Find the Personal Year Cycle by reducing the year of the last birthday, or 1979 (as of this writing February 1980).

$$1979 = 1+9+7+9 = 26$$

Add the month and day of birth to the reduced year total 26.

$$10+7+26=43$$

Reduce the total 43 by adding it through once.

$$43=4+3=7$$

This is a Personal Year Cycle 43/7. Add the month and day you are examining to the double number of the Personal Year Cycle 43/7. If you want to discover the Personal Day Cycle for March 5th for example, add 3+5 (March 5) to the double number of the Personal Year Cycle 43/7 for a total of 51.

$$3+5+43=51$$

Reduce the 51 by adding it through once.

$$51=5+1=6$$

March 5th to March 6th would be a Personal Day 6 for this birthdate of October 7th.

Example: Birthdate January 20th.
Find the Personal Year by reducing the year of the last birthday, or 1980 (as of this writing, February 1980).

$$1980=1+9+8+0=18$$

Add the month and day of birth to the reduced year 18.

$$1+20+18=39$$

Reduce the 39 by adding it through once.

$$39=3+9=12$$

Reduce the 12 by adding it through once.

$$12=1+2=3$$

The Personal Year Cycle is a 39/3. Add the month and day in question, for example, May 3rd, to the double numbers of the Personal Year Cycle 39/3.

$$5+3+39=47$$

Reduce the 47 by adding it through once.

$$47=4+7=11$$

The Personal Day Cycle for May 3rd for a birthdate of January 20th is a Master Number.

If you want to find the Personal Day Cycle for September 14th for this same birthdate, add the month and day to the same double number of the Personal Year Cycle 39/3.

$$9+14+39=62$$

Reduce the 62 by adding it through once.

$$62=6+2=8$$

September 14th would be a Personal Day Cycle 8 for this birthdate of January 20th.

Exercise: Work out the following example to determine the Personal Day Cycles and check your answers in the back of the book on page 235.

Birthdate: August 7th.

Find the Personal Day Cycles for May 7, 1980 to June 7, 1980.

Your Personal Day Cycle runs from your time of birth on one day to that same time on the following day, or exactly twenty-four hours later. For instance, if you were born at 10:30 AM, your Personal Day Cycle would begin at 10:30 in the morning and continue until 10:30 the next morning, at which time you would enter your next Personal Day Cycle. Similarly, if you were born at 11:28 PM, your Personal Day Cycle would begin at 11:28 in the evening and continue until 11:28 the following evening. If you do not know your exact time of birth, there is a section on page 45 that may help you determine what your time is.

For a delineation of your Personal Day Cycle, turn to Chapter 11, page 216, under Temporary Number Delineations. Remember that the shorter the cycle, the less emphasis it has; however, it will still work. And when used in conjunction with the larger cycles, the Personal Day Cycle can pinpoint a specific day when you can expect the events of the larger personal Month Cycle to come to a head.

Peak Point in the Personal Day Cycle: The Peak Point in your

Personal Day Cycle, or that point at which the energies of this cycle will culminate, is determined by dividing the day of twenty-four hours in half, or twelve hours, and adding this twelve hours to your exact time of birth. For instance, a birth-time of 10:38 AM would yield a Peak Point of 10:38 PM, and the energies of that Personal Day Cycle will begin at 10:38 AM, wax during the intervening twelve hours and reach their maximum at 10:38 PM.

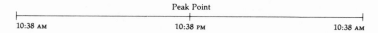

Peak Point

10:38 AM	10:38 PM	10:38 AM

Similarly, a birthtime of 7:04 PM will yield a Peak Point of 7:04 AM, twelve hours, or halfway through the cycle, from the start of the Personal Day Cycle. This Personal Day Cycle will begin at 7:04 PM, increase during the intervening night hours and reach a peak at 7:04 AM.

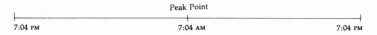

Peak Point

7:04 PM	7:04 AM	7:04 PM

This Peak Point in a Personal Day Cycle could easily account for day people and night people. There are some people who are wide awake early in the morning, bouncy and ready to go. These same people are often extremely fatigued in the afternoon and into the evening. Conversely, there are others who can barely drag themselves from bed each morning, unable to communicate with more than a few grunts, but watch them sparkle as evening approaches. These are the night owls among us, the late night talk show fans.

I am a morning person. I was born at 10:38 PM and have since childhood gone to bed early. Even today, at age forty-two, I am still in bed between 10:00 and 10:30 PM. You might wonder how a person's cycle can increase during the night. Mine does through my dreams. I have always had vivid and plentiful dreams, many of them prophetic. I have recorded my dreams for periods of years, four to six a night, and wrote a dream column for five years for a large daily newspaper. I still lecture on this subject. Much of my work then, is done during the dark quiet hours of night. When I awake each morning I lie still for a few minutes waiting for any information my subconscious has to give me. I depend upon it for much in my life. When it speaks, I jot down ideas, suggestions, warnings, or changes in a manuscript I may be working on. 8:00 AM to noon are my best hours when much of my writing and other work is accomplished.

On the other hand, my son, who is now seventeen, was born at 4:38 PM. He is definitely a night person. As I write this, at 10:45 on a Sunday morning, he is still asleep in his room. He loves to read, often into the early hours of the morning, because he cannot fall asleep before midnight. Even as a child he had difficulty going to bed early. Getting him up in the morning for school takes nothing less than block and tackle. His hours of increasing vitality are between 4:38 in the afternoon and 4:38 in the morning. After that his vitality goes downhill and by 7:00 AM, he is hard to shake awake. He is very creative, and it seems that this is because his cycle peaks during his sleeping and dreaming hours.

To Determine Your Time of Birth: If you do not know your exact time of birth, try the following methods:

1 . Determine whether you are a night person or a day person. This is not failproof but it can be an indicator. Keep a daily record for a few months noting the time of day when you feel the most energetic and that part of the day when you are the weariest.
2 . Determine your Personal Day Cycle, and mark each cycle number in the appropriate block on a monthly calendar. (see diagram.)
3 . Select two days for examination; for instance, Personal Day Cycles 7 and 8. You will notice the Personal Day Cycles 7 and 8 fall on, in our example, May 12 to 13, 21 to 22, and 30 to 31st.
4 . Determine the pattern you find in these daily cycles. There is a great difference between a Personal Day Cycle 7 and a Personal Day Cycle 8, which you will discover by reading the number delineations at the back of this book.
5 . Keep a record of the type of events and the exact time at which they occur during the day on these Personal Day Cycles 7 and 8. This should enable you to determine a point at which one cycle begins and the other ends.

Example: Birthdate April 5th.
To find the Personal Year Cycle, reduce the year of the last birthday, or 1979 (as of this writing, February 1980).

$$1979 = 1+9+7+9 = 26$$

Add the month and day of birth to the reduced year total 26.

$$4+5+26 = 35$$

Reduce the total 35 by adding it through once.

$$35=3+5=8$$

The Personal Year Cycle is a 35/8. To find the Personal Day Cycle, add the month and day you are examining to the Personal Year Cycle 35/8; for instance, May 5th.

$$5+5+35=45$$

Reduce the total 45 by adding it through once:

$$45=4+5=9$$

May 5th is a Personal Day Cycle 9. The Personal Day Cycles will run in sequence on consecutive days within the cycle; therefore, May 6th is a Personal Day Cycle 1, May 7th, an 11/2, and so on. Fill in the Personal Day Cycle numbers in the appropriate blocks on your monthly calendar. The calendar shown here is for a birthdate of April 5th.

			May			
SUN	MON	TUES	WED	THURS	FRI	SAT
		1	2	3	4	9 5
1 6	11/2 7	3 8	4 9	5 10	6 11	7 12
8 13	9 14	1 15	11/2 16	3 17	4 18	5 19
6 20	7 21	8 22	9 23	1 24	11/2 25	3 26
4 27	5 28	6 29	7 30	8 31		

Let's say that our birthdate of April 5th belongs to Miss Scarlett. On Wednesday, May 30th (see calendar) Miss Scarlet goes to bed around 10:00 PM, feeling more quiet and withdrawn than she did during the day. She wakes up at 6:30 and goes to work with the same feelings. She is not as communicative with other employees as she usually is. She refuses a luncheon date under pretense of a headache when she really just wants to be alone. That evening she is happy to curl up with a good book by the fireplace, planning to go to bed a little early. But then, on a sudden impulse, around 10:00 PM she decides to balance her checkbook for the month and pay a few bills. She eventually goes to bed at 11:30 PM.

The next morning she is up bright and early, eager to go to work. At work she organizes her desk and digs into the pile of papers left from the day before. Around 10:00 AM the phones start to ring, the typewriter breaks down, and the boss wants her for dictation. The pressure peaks. By noontime, however, she has taken care of the phone calls, repaired the typewriter and transcribed the dictation. She gets through the rest of the day with a lot less pressure. That evening she feels good about how she handled herself and what she accomplished that day at work.

There is a pattern here that seems to begin late evening and peak middle morning. The quiet introspective Personal Day Cycle 7 may have begun May 30th when Miss Scarlett went to bed feeling more subdued. It could have peaked on May 31st when she refused the luncheon date. That evening when she suddenly decided to work on her checkbook, she could have just entered her Personal Day Cycle 8, a pressured business and money vibration. This seems to have peaked the next morning around 10:00 with the ringing phones, broken typewriter and dictation. If she also confirmed our suspicion by stating that she is a morning person, then we would proceed on the assumption that Miss Scarlett's Personal Day Cycles begin about 10:00 in the evening and reach their Peak Point around 10:00 in the morning. Using this example as a pattern to follow, you could then proceed by testing each Personal Day Cycle by noting the high and low peaks, the time of day that certain events occur and how they qualify under the number of the Personal Day Cycle in which they are happening.

Action Points in Your Personal Day: To find the Action Points in your Personal Cycle Day, divide the day of twenty-four hours into quarters of six hours each starting with the exact birthtime of the day. Halfway through the day, or twelve hours past the birthtime, mark the Peak Point. Then, mark six hours and eighteen hours past the time of birth as the Action Points.

Example: Birthdate November 5th, 10:38 PM.

	Action Point	Peak Point	Action Point	
10:38 PM	4:38 AM	10:38 AM	4:38 AM	10:38 PM
Nov. 5	Nov. 6	Nov. 6	Nov. 6	Nov. 6

Example: Birthdate September 9th, 6:30 AM.

	Action Point	Peak Point	Action Point	
6:30 AM	12:30 PM	6:30 PM	12:30 PM	6:30 AM
Sept. 9	Sept. 9	Sept. 9	Sept. 10	Sept. 9

These Action Points mark the time of day when you will be challenged or urged to action by some circumstances in your environment or within yourself. You may wonder how Action Points can work in the middle of the night. My birthtime is 10:38 PM; therefore my Action Points each day occur at

4:38 in the morning and 4:38 in the afternoon. Through observation I have found that when I awake in the middle of the
night from a dream or some unknown restless prompting, it is
usually around 4:30 in the morning. Often, I make notes
about some idea or dream that seems significant. Challenges
seem to arise around 4:30 in the afternoon as well. For instance, if I am dieting, I have to fight my way past late afternoon, then I have won the battle for the day. These are small
examples but they add to the mountain of proof.

3

ADDITIONAL TECHNIQUES:

PROBABILITIES AND

POSSIBILITIES

NUMEROLOGY IS BY NO MEANS a closed field. There is always room for questioning, searching and discovery, as there is in any field. The techniques offered in this book are not ironclad rules. They have worked, and worked well, in the past, but that does not mean they cannot be improved on in the future. Just as the discovery of the outer planets, Uranus, Neptune, and Pluto, brought a consciousness change to the world during the periods when they were dicovered, so this Aquarian Age demands questioning and searching minds to explore the possibilities of new discoveries that will change the consciousness of the future. I am constant-ly thinking of different ways of working with the numbers, and I would like to share some of these ideas with you. Not all of the techniques presented here are new, but they contain interesting possibilities so they are included along with other new material. Some of the ideas are not worked out fully, but perhaps there will be enough information to trigger in your mind a thought that will lead you towards discovery.

"Select Three Numbers"

I watched a numerologist on a television program perform the following trick. He asked a member of the audience to give him three numbers quickly without thinking. The woman did so, and he proceeded to explain what thoughts were paramount in her life at that time. He did this with several people with great accuracy.

I thought: He could be psychic and is using the numbers as a point of focus; or the numbers themselves are giving him all the information he needs; or it's a combination of both. So I decided to experiment on my own. I found that the numbers tell the story, at least as far as I can tell in discerning between my psychic abilities and working with just the facts (the numbers). Everyone is psychic to a degree so to try to separate our psychism from any act we perform would be virtually impossible. However, I believe that if you obtain a thorough knowledge of the digits 1 through 9, you could do the same things this numerologist did with the television audience.

We all have an innate understanding of the meaning of each number, and even without a deep study of the numbers, you will be amazed at how well you will do with this technique. Great knowledge is stored in the subconscious, and this storehouse of information surfaces through our daily language without our awareness. A recent experience brought this to me quite graphically. I was asked to appear on a Boston television show with a number of other people to explain the meaning of the number 8 for the coming 1980s decade. A gentleman who appeared before me, from the telephone company, was asked why the WATS line (the telephone service that businesses pay for so that customers can call in free) is an 800 code number. Was there a special reason 8 was chosen? Why not 600 or 200? The man explained that the number was chosen arbitrarily and that any other number could just as easily have been used. When it was my turn to speak, I explained that, with all due respect to this gentleman from the phone company, no other number but an 8 could have been used because 8 represents the world of big business. The phone company officials had chosen the only number that fit the enterprise they were introducing to the public. Some might say the chances were one in nine that the 8 would have been selected. That is true, although how many times could you pick the correct number from a series of nine. If this were the only instance of this kind of an occurrence with the numbers, I would agree with the skeptics, but the proof mounts day after day when you begin to observe.

Why don't you try it now? Ask someone for three numbers, then tell them exactly what comes into your mind regardless of how foolish it may sound. For example:

Sally: Give me three numbers quickly, the first three that pop into your head.
Richard: 7–4–3.
Sally: You need a vacation but before you can take one, there are matters to be straightened out, perhaps financial ones. Once these are settled, you will have much more freedom and perhaps the money to take a long trip during which you will meet new and interesting people and have a good time socializing.

The 7 indicates rest. Matters will come to a head and be solved. The 4 represents organization, work, and the handling of money matters. The number 3 brings travel, greater social contact and expansion. By synthesizing the three selected numbers, 7–4–3, you can see that the 7 and 3 both indicate that Richard needs to get away but the 4 stands as an obstacle, a problem that must be solved before the number can work in harmony to bring about the results desired by Richard.

As you experiment with this technique, you will become more efficient at it, and you will soon realize that we all know at subconscious levels what we need and what is about to happen in our lives. How else could the selection of three random numbers tell so much about our innermost thoughts and needs?

Table of Events

There is a technique called the Table of Events, which can reveal the general trends under which you will be operating for periods of years in your life. The Personal Year Cycles tell what any given year will bring, but the Table of Events will group a number of these cycles together under one vibration that will operate during that time. Again, using this technique requires synthesis with the other cycles in your life.

Use your full name at birth. You may also work with a name you are currently using if you use it often. Place the value of *all* the letters above your name.

```
1 6 8 5        1 6 1 5 7 8         1 6 8 5 1 6 5
J O H N        J O S E P H         J O H N S O N
```

The numbers that you will place *below* the letters in your name will be your progressive ages. Each name of your full name is worked independently. Start with your first name, in our example: John. The value of the J is 1, therefore we place a 1 (for his age) under the first letter J. The first age we write is always the value of the first letter of the name; it is not always a 1. To the 1, we add the value of the second letter O, or 6. 1+6=7. Under the letter O, place the age 7. To the 7, add the value of the third letter H, or 8. 7+8=15. Place the age 15 under the third letter H. To the 15 add the value of the final letter N, or 5. 15+5=20. Place the age 20 under the letter N.

```
1  6   8  5
J  O   H  N
1  7  15 20
```

Now start a second row of figures. Taking the 20, the last age total in the first row, add to it the value of the first letter J, or 1. 20+1=21. Place the age 21 under the letter J and 1. To the 21, add the value of the second letter O, or 6. 21+6=27. Place the age 27 under the letter O and 7. To the 27, add the value of the third letter H, or 8. 27+8=35. Place the age 35 under the third letter H and 15. To the 35, add the value of the last letter N, or 5. 35+5=40. Place the age 40 under the letter N and 20.

```
 1  6   8  5
 J  O   H  N
 1  7  15 20
21 27  35 40
41 47  55 60
```

To start the third row of figures, take the age total from the end of the second row, or 40, and add to it the value of the first letter J, or 1. 40+1=41. Place the age 41 under the J, 1, and 21. To the 41, add the value of the second letter 0, or 6. 41+6=47. Place the age 47 under the O, 7, and 27. To the 47, add the value of the third letter H, or 8. 47+8=55. Place the age 55 under the H, 15, and 35. To the 55, add the value of the last letter N, or 5. 55+5=60. Place the age 60 under the letter N, 20, and 40.

You may continue this for another row, and follow the same procedure with the remaining names in your full name, remembering to work with each name individually. These numbers under the name represent your ages. For instance, from birth to age one, the age under the letter J, John was working with a 1 vibration, the value *above* the letter J. From age 1 to 7, the age under the letter O, he was working with a 6 vibration, the value over the letter O. From age 7 to 15, the age under the letter H, he was influenced by an 8 vibration, the value over the letter H, and from age 15 to 20, the age under the letter N, he was working with a 5 vibration, the value over the letter N. From age 20 to 21, moving from the age at the end of the first row to the age at the beginning of the second row, he was working with a 1 vibration, once again, the value above the letter J.

You can see by the repetition of the number vibrations throughout your life caused by the particular letters within your name, why your name is so important, and why all literature abounds with references to names. For example: A rose by any other name would never smell as sweet; the emphasis in the Bible on Adam "naming" every creature so they would be "known;" and the emphasis placed on selecting the right name for a new born baby. Think how many times your name is spoken *towards* you by others, and how this particular sound vibration travels through the air and impresses the cells in your body with its unique pattern. You are molded into that vibration through repetition. You become it. That is why authors select the names of their characters so carefully—the name reflects the personality, the traits of the character. We all know the characters of Barnaby Rudge, Long John Silver, and Madame DeFarge. There is indeed something in a name that makes each one of us different from another.

By individually working out each name in John's full name we have a Table of Events that looks like this:

1 6 8 5	1 6 1 5 7 8	1 6 8 5 1 6 5
J O H N	J O S E P H	J O H N S O N
1 17 15 20	1 7 8 13 20 28	1 7 15 20 21 27 32
21 27 35 40	29 35 36 41 48 56	33 39 47 52 53 59 64
41 47 55 60	57 63 64 69 76 84	65 71 79 84 85 91 96

If you wanted to know what types of events are going to happen to John at age 31, for instance, locate that age under each name.

In the first name, John, age 31 is located in the second row between ages 27 and 35. Because age 31 is beyond age 27, the vibration of age 27 has been passed. Age 31 will be influenced by the age towards which it is approaching, or age 35. The letter over the 35 is an H with a value of 8. Therefore, at age 31, John will be working with an 8. John will be influenced by this 8 from ages 27 to 35. At age 35, he moves to the next age block of 35 to 40, or the vibration of the N, a 5 energy. Therefore, the first name in our example yields an 8 cycle for age 31.

Working with the second name, you find age 31 located in the second row between ages 29 and 35, under the J and the O. This indicates that from age 29 to 35, he is influenced by a 6 cycle, or the value of the O. Remember, you work towards the next closest age.

In the last name, age 31 is located in the first row between ages 27 and 32, under the 0 and N; therefore, at age 31, John will be working with a 5 cycle under the letter N, the letter towards which he is working.

John has three cycles working at all times because he has three names. At age 31, he will be influenced by cycles of 8, 6, and 5. You can find the meaning of these cycles in the back of the book under Temporary Number Delineations. These three cycles will not all change at the same time. For instance, the 8 cycle from the first name will change at age 35 in our example, the 6 cycle from the second name also happens to change at age 35, and the 5 cycle from the last name changes at age 32. Therefore, new elements are constantly being introduced into John's life at differing ages, thus providing a gradual synthesis of change as he evolves.

Although it is not true for all of us, more often than not the full birthname has three names. Perhaps we might look upon this three-in-one, three separate names within one whole name, as a manifestation of the Trinity: the conscious, the subconscious and the superconscious, which synchronizes the three parts of ourselves into one cohesive working unit. Perhaps the first name is the conscious mind because it is the one we are most commonly called by. It is the one we hear the most often and it is the one most people recognize us by because of its visibility.

The middle name could be the subconscious, or the present motivating force behind our every thought and action; that part that is not often consciously heard and is very seldom known to others. Yet it binds our first and last names, a sort of mediary or consultant between the two.

And the last name is perhaps the superconscious, which stretches from our distant past, the family name, and is the true foundation of our personal present vibrations. It is the umbrella vibration under which like souls, entities with

similar frequencies, unite in order to preserve their continuance.

By using this analogy in reading the three cycles from the
three names at any given age, we can say that, at the age of 31,
John's cycles of 8 and 5 indicate that he will feel more pressure
and responsibility in his life (the 8 will manifest outwardly as a
conscious event), but this test will only strengthen his ability
to see the justice in any situation and perhaps enable him to
love others more easily (the 6 working on a subconscious
level). The entire experience will help him adapt and communicate more easily with others, thus improving his
character (the 5 absorbed into the superconscious). The three-
in-one, the Trinity, is at work even in our names.

The Power Behind You

There is a number called your Power Number which indicates
the motivating force behind your entire being in this lifetime.
It is your source of energy, your battery so to speak. It usually
does not come into play until your middle thirties, after you
have gained your soul, as Plato said of the age twenty-nine.
Astrologically, this seems to hold true as well because at age
twenty-nine, Saturn has completed one entire transit of your
horoscope, crystallizing all your character traits. It is at this
time in your life, at the age of twenty-nine, that you become a
whole person with the capabilities of exercising your potential
to its fullest. So the thirties are the real testing ground
astrologically, and perhaps numerologically as well when the
Power Number begins to become more apparent in your life.
Talents, abilities, and acts you would never have thought
yourself capable of often surface at this time in your life. Your
wholeness shines through.

My Power Number is a 3. I was a timid child throughout
school, never raising my hand to participate in class. Through
my twenties I never spoke out at public meetings. My Power
Number 3 came into effect in my thirties. Now I lecture and
appear on radio and television, and I am completely calm and
relaxed. If anyone had told me this would happen I would
never have believed it. So be aware that, when you are talking
to a person under the age of thirty, they have not yet reached
their fullest potential and may not necessarily recognize all
they are capable of.

To find your Power Number, add the total value of your
full name at birth, or your Path of Destiny Number, to the
total of your birthday, or your Life Lesson Number. You
might also try adding the name you are presently using to
your birthdate for an additional vibration. Always add the

55

double numbers and then reduce because you may arrive at a Master Number.

$$1\ \ 6\ \ \ 8\ \ 5 \qquad 1\ \ 6\ \ 1\ \ 5\ \ 7\ \ 8 \qquad 1\ \ 6\ \ 8\ \ 5\ \ 1\ \ 6\ \ 5 = 80$$

J O H N   J O S E P H   J O H N S O N

$$October\ 16,\ 1953\ (1+9+5+3)$$
$$10+16+18=44$$

Add the double number to the full name, or Path of Destiny Number, 80, to the double number of the birthdate, or Life Lesson Number, 44.

$$80+44=124$$

Reduce the 124 by adding it through once.

$$124=1+2+4=7$$

John has a Power Number 7. Turn to the second portion of this book under Personal Number Delineations for an understanding of this number as a Power Number, remembering that it will come into effect in the thirties.

If John had a birthday of February 19, 1953, his Life Lesson Number would be:

$$2+19+18\ (1+9+5+3)=39$$

Add the 39 to the full name total of 80.

$$39+80=119$$

Reduce the 119 by adding it through once.

$$119=1+1+9=11$$

Do not reduce further because John now has a Power Number that is also a Master Number. You could say he has a Master Power Number 11. Find the delineations for these numbers in the chapter on Personal Number Delineations. Remember, the number always has the same meaning but you must place it in the proper context. If the 7 is your Soul Number, then this is what you already are; if it is your Life Lesson Number, then it is what you must learn; and if it is your Power Number, it is what you will begin expressing in your thirties as a power source.

Ages in the Calendar Year

Some numerologists feel that because we work universally with a January to December year that the ages you are in a given calendar year are significant and will affect you during that calendar year. For instance, if during the calendar year you turned from age 27 to 28, you would add these two ages.

$$27+28=55$$

Reduce the 55 by adding it through once.

$$55=5+5=10$$

Reduce the 10 by adding it through once.

$$10=1+0=1$$

During this calendar year from January to December, during which you turned from age 27 to age 28, you would be influenced by a 1 vibration.

If you turned from age 32 to age 33 in a given calendar year, you would add these two ages.

$$32+33=65$$

Reduce the 65 by adding it through once.

$$65=6+5=11$$

Do not reduce further because 11 is a Master Number. You would then be operating under a Master Number 11 in this particular January to December calendar year during which you turned from age 32 to age 33.

These numbers would have the same meaning as the number delineations in the second portion of this book under Temporary Number delineations.

More Master Numbers?

I was taught that there are three Master Numbers, 11, 22, and 33. At night, when the house was quiet and I was snuggled in bed with a notebook and pencil, I would lay these numbers out in the following manner:

```
11   22   33   ?
1 2 3 4 5 6 7 8 9
```

11 reduces to a 2, 22 to a 4, 33 to a 6. It was obvious to me that something was missing—all the even numbers had a Master Number vibration except the 8. Even symmetrically, the layout was imbalanced. It seemed there should be a fourth Master Number, a 44, to correspond to the 8, and thus fill in the missing space. My teacher and I worked on this concept, which resulted in our first small book, self-published and no longer in print, entitled *13—Birth or Death?* In it we introduced the possibility of a fourth Master Number, the 44, and we called it Atlas for superior strength. 8 represents strength, and 44 is a higher vibration of 8. Curiously enough, *Atlas* reduces to an 8. In mythology Atlas supported the heavens on his shoulders while standing on earth. The Atlas bone at the base of the neck supports the head (the mind or heaven) while resting on the body (earth).

And then the question arose, if the even numbers have Master Numbers, why shouldn't the odd numbers have Master Numbers also? The layout would then look like this:

$$55 \quad 66 \quad 77 \quad 88 \quad 99$$
$$11 \quad 22 \quad 33 \quad 44$$
$$1 \quad 2 \quad 3 \quad 4 \quad 5 \quad 6 \quad 7 \quad 8 \quad 9$$

This completes the 1 through 9 cycle, supplying each of the digits with a Master Number vibration. See how beautifully the pattern interlocks. Perhaps all similar double numbers are Master Numbers, from the 11 through the 99. It may be that the repetition of the numbers so emphasizes the quality of that number as to raise its vibration to a higher level of intensity or consciousness, therefore it becomes a Master Number vibration.

Playing with some possibilities, imagine the Master Numbers as Masters who physically walk the earth or, at least, hover above the earth influencing the proper persons in the appropriate places when things get so out of hand that the entire earth is in danger of destruction. We can pretend that each of the nine Master Numbers rules a department in the government complex of life that is overseen by nine separate groups of Master Agents, thus ensuring that all phases of life here on earth are adequately protected. We have already delineated the Master Numbers 11, 22, 33, and 44 in the back portion of this book, so we shall now concentrate on the Master Numbers 55, 66, 77, 88, and 99.

55 WE MIGHT SUGGEST that Master Agents 55 are assigned to the department of communication and investigation. They must separate the true from the false, and make sure that this truth is made public when the need becomes pressing. Researchers, investigators, detectives, writers, salespersons, and so forth might fall under their influence.

The Ace of Swords in the Tarot would be a good card to reflect upon for more truth about this department.

66 MASTER AGENTS 66 are in charge of truth and beauty. They must assure that harmony, symmetry, and balance are maintained in the necessary places on earth to serve as oasis of inspiration in a parched world for the right persons. They supply the compassion and protection of the necessary balance needed for those young souls who are placed in the care of parents for a certain period of years. Judges, doctors, artists, domestics, homemakers, interior decorators, and those who beautify the environment in any way come under the care of the Master Agents 66.

The Queen of Pentacles in the Tarot may shed further light upon this vibration.

77 UNDER THE MASTER AGENTS 77, silence reigns. They see to it that the material world slows down at certain times so that the great minds of the world have the time and support they need in order to think. Thinking is a powerful energy that can create or destroy, and Agents 77 must watchfully observe the direction of the world's thinking processes. Inventors, religious leaders, mystics, and scientists would fall into this category.

The Nine of Pentacles in the Tarot relates to this Master Number vibration.

88 MASTER AGENTS 88 must see to it that the super builders and champion athletes continue to inspire the proper new souls in each generation. They must be sure the appropriate philanthropic acts are carried out so that foundations are available to support necessary projects. Institutions that supply the material world with goods must be maintained in the right areas of the globe. Master Agents 88 rule the world of business, high finance, and physical strength. Corporate executives, bankers, philanthropists, and famous athletes are in their domain. Here the God-power is emphasized in the four zeros: 88.

The Tarot keys end with the 78. Again the 8 and 9 stand alone as unique number vibrations in the family of digits 1 through 9.

99 GREAT BURDENS LIE on the shoulders of the Master Agents 99. They must ensure the continuance of Grand Masters, Holy Avatars and Supreme Teachers. They must help guide those who will be teachers of teachers, those who have climbed the mountain and overcome, and must now turn to teach those who have newly achieved the peak. The 99 in its lines pictures the teacher behind the teacher, and perhaps these Grand Masters and Holy Avatars eventually go on to join with and help the Master Agents in the loving task of running the heavenly government.

These Master Numbers would work through their base digits.

Thinking again about the doubleness of the numbers, we look upon the birth of twins as something different and more curious than the birth of a single child, and it seems ever more curious when the twins are identical because then most people cannot tell them apart. Perhaps our Master Number, being identical twins, takes on this same unique personality. You may want to play with this possibility by determining through your own experience how these numbers work in your own life and in the lives of those people you encounter.

In the following chapter we see that each number has a planetary assignment. The Master Numbers are assigned to the outer planets; i.e.: 11–Uranus, 22–Pluto, 33–Neptune, and 44–an occult point at this time. Undoubtedly more planets will be discovered in our solar system, thus supplying planetary assignments to the "new" Master Numbers, 55 through 99.

Our Coat of Many Colors and the Numbers

Everything is surrounded by an electromagnetic energy field called the aura by the mystics. Artists, who are traditionally known for their sensitivity to the subtle emanations in their environment, have always pictured the saints and holy persons with a glowing nimbus, a halo, or an aura around their heads. However, we all have auras, albeit not as powerful as the saints, and they change color, size and intensity according to our moods, feelings, attitudes and spiritual progress. A sensitive can tell your temperament and your mood on any given day by the colors in your aura.

In *Color Psychology and Color Therapy*, (Citadel Press, 1950) Faber Birren states: "The aura of the superman is filled with iridescent hues . . . there is a yellow nimbus about his head which shines like the rays of the sun." The American Heritage Dictionary defines the word "iridescent" as lustrous, rainbow-like colors. So, what Mr. Birren is saying is the truly good and perfect person, the super-person, is filled with and perhaps surrounded by a rainbow. His or her aura is rainbow-like, a perfectly balanced, harmonious array of colors.

While reading this I suddenly realized that when we are perfectly balanced in all ways, we are wrapped in a rainbow, and our energy field or our aura is all colors in perfect balance, radiating outward to all those we encounter, spreading the light, sharing the harmony of life's treasures, sharing our "pot of gold" at the end of the rainbow. And could this pot of gold at the end of our rainbow be our head: a pot that contains the truest treasure of all, pure and loving thoughts?

Do not these pure and loving thoughts, sent out, bring back equal treasure? To give from the pot of gold is to have the treasure replenished; the universal boomerang law is in effect. As ye think, so shall it be; for every action, there is an equal and opposite reaction; whatever you send out comes back to you in equal measure.

We may be able to find a correspondence between the nine digits and the rainbow. It is known that each color gives off different frequencies of vibratory rates which differentiate one from another. At one end of the spectrum is red, and at the other end, violet. Let us assign numbers to the colors in the following manner:

1-red
2-orange
3-yellow
4-green
5-blue
6-indigo
7-violet

There are only seven colors in the rainbow. 7 rules the material world in the sense that all the archetypes of all form are in existence by the cycle 7.

God created the world in six days and rested on the seventh. With the 7, we are given all the tools; all the vibrations we need in order to work. These tools exist in the first seven numbers and the seven colors of the rainbow. Now we must take this palette of seven colors and paint a beautiful self-portrait. Could the number 8 be the free will to consciously select and blend these hues, and thereby weave a coat of many colors with which to wrap ourselves, a coat that becomes our aura, the quality and appeal of which is determined by the strength of our color combinations and the wisdom of the threads we have chosen? Did Joseph's coat of many colors in the Bible signify his perfected aura, his spiritual superiority over his brothers?

Under the 8, a picture has been painted, and we have woven our aura and wrapped ourselves in a raiment of color. Again we see the meaning in the axiom, as it is above (in our head or in our minds), so it is below (in our body and in our life's affairs). If we mix the seven colors of our rainbow improperly, our pot will be empty or filled with sludge, and therefore our bodies will be sick and our lives unhappy. However, if we have chosen and painted well, under the 9 we find the peace that passeth all understanding in our minds, our heads—the pot containing the gold at the end of the rainbow.

The Bible says that God created the world in six days, or six
stages, and rested on the seventh. The number 7 is a real cycle in
our lives on a physical level, much like an animal's cycle. A common saying is that one year in an animal's life is equal to seven
years in a human's life. Number 7 is rest from physical activity,
and completion on a physical plane, a time to let the higher forces
take over for you.

However, it is not the cessation of all activity. Much mental
work is done under a 7. And it is here that we branch higher than
our beloved animal friends. It is here that we go beyond the seven
days of creation and take on our God-given power. Our free will
and higher consciousness manifest in the 8 and 9 cycles. Under the
8, we find that karma rules. It is said that animals do not have karma because they are ruled by a group soul, and react purely on instinct, free from revenge, hate, jealousy, and passion; therefore
they respond to a numerological cycle of 7. Because we live with a
higher level of consciousness, our cycles expand to include the 8
and the 9. Under the 8, the efforts of the past seven cycles come
back to us in equal measure—exemplified by the drawing of the
figure 8 as a perfectly balanced form, one circle above the
other—as it is above, so it is below; as ye sow, so shall ye reap.
Here the responsibility is squarely upon our shoulders and we
either rise or fall according to our past intentions and works.

Under the 9, the wisdom or the folly prevails. Either we have
gained knowledge from our past cycle and attained our pot of gold
(and then realized the necessity of sharing this wisdom with others,
emptying our coffers so there will be room for more coin of the
realm in our next cycle), or we enter our 9 cycle with an empty
pot, poor as paupers, unable to give because of the sorrow and
failure we have encountered from erroneous past actions. But this
can also be a turning point for those with eyes to see their past
mistakes, and the intention of using the wisdom gained from those
past mistakes to change the future cycle. But woe to those who
have gained much and refuse to share it with others under a 9 cycle. Their coffers are only temporarily full and if they make no
room for more by sharing in their 9 cycle they will not grow but
will stagnate at their present level. The ripe fruit will rot on the
branches.

Even a cursory look at the kundalini divulges the same story.
The kundalini is the sleeping serpent, the fiery life energy, the liquid fire, the force that lies coiled at the base of the spine in unevolv-
ed persons. The goal of life is to raise the kundalini up the spine
through the 1 through 9 cycles by positive actions and thoughts to
the higher centers in the head, number 9, where the kundalini or
life force is then spiritualized, transformed, regenerated into liquid
gold, the pot of gold. Often the kundalini becomes trapped in the
lower centers of the body where desire, lust, passion, hate, and
love on a personal selfish level overcome and imprison the in-

dividual. The struggle with the emotions is most difficult, and it is only when, through great effort, the individual can meet these emotions impersonally yet lovingly that the battle is won.

The Shapes of the Numbers

The shapes of the numbers themselves relate still another similar version of this story. Imagine that the number 1 represents the soul entering life with no possessions, totally stripped of any tools but the body. We can almost visualize this state of affairs by looking at the stark nature of the shape of the 1, a clean straight line. Through the 2 and 3 shapes, the 1 begins to bend, meld, and conform to the material world it encounters, but still is urged on by its own needs. By the time the 1 reaches 4, it feels the need to own some of these things it finds in its environment, and realizes it must construct something in which to contain these things, so it begins to collect and build. The shape of the 4 as we usually handwrite it, 4 , could bring to mind a basket into which items are placed, or the beginning of a square, a foundation upon which a home is built.

The 5 opens in both directions—backward ◄ 5 ► forward. Here the 1 is offered choices. Has the experience of the past four numbers brought a comfortable feeling so that progress on the same path is acceptable, or is the present situation uncomfortable enough to demand change? The 5 is a point of decision. At the 6, some decisions have been made, perhaps the selection of a mate, and now the need for love becomes pressing. This is the beginning of a reaching forward, 6→   although still on a personal level. The shape of the 6 might remind us of the 1 with a circle at its base. Could this be the developing kundalini life force in the lower body centers where the personal desire is located? Some persons, instead of using the personal love indicated by the 6 as a learning experience towards understanding universal love, become trapped in the lower centers where personal satisfaction, lust, physical gratification, and power are paramount in their lives. The number of the beast in Revelation is 666. This refers to the unregenerated person who is locked into the illusion that gratification on the physical level is the most important goal in life. This illusory state of mind is exemplified on three levels by the three 6's: mentally, physically, and emotionally. The number 666 means the person is locked in on all three levels at the lower centers. This number is explored further in Chapter 9.

At the 7, the curves and angles seem to become momentarily suspended, almost waiting. An ancient symbol for matter or the material world was the horizontal line, ——— , and since this line is elevated above the vertical line of the 1 in the number 7, we can almost visualize the 1 stopping to think about the material world (the horizontal line raised to the head level) and its relation to

63

where the 1 has been, ⬅7 , and where the 1 is going, 7➡ , (it is leaning forward.) Physical activity has slowed but mental activity has increased.

When the 1 reaches the 8, much has been sorted out mentally, and again the material world takes over to show the 1 what the effects of its past energies will be. Number 8 is the only number (other than zero) that can be written over and over without lifting the pen from the paper. It contains two zeros, the God figure. It represents the ancient axiom: as it is above, so it is below—8. Karma rules under the 8, justice is king, the scales are balanced and the 1 reaps what has been sown.

In the 9, the kundalini has been raised to the higher centers in the head, exemplified by the zero at the top of the vertical line, 9, and now it turns to hold its light of wisdom, the pot of gold, the circle, for those who follow. 9 is also a burden, like a pack on the back. Spiritual wisdom is a heavy responsibility and the one who carries it knows the truth; therefore, this person must act in accordance with the Law. The breaking of the Law here is a great sin because it is broken with knowledge, whereas those who break the Law in ignorance have not sinned in the same sense. Number 9 is great responsibility. The outline of the 9 can be seen in the figure of Key 9 in the Tarot, the Hermit, who holds his lantern high so that others may find their way up the mountain of attainment.

Certainly we can find more analogies in every phase of life, in our bodies, in our relationships, and in our environment. The Cosmic Mind has placed life's wisdom and cycles at our disposal so that we who have eyes to see and ears to hear will learn the law of cyclicity through the repetitive nature of life around us.

4

ASTROLOGICAL

ASSIGNMENTS TO THE

NUMBERS

T HE STATISTICS OF Dade County, Florida, for a
fifteen-year period reveal a "scientifically sound" relationship between the murder rate and the phases of the Moon.
Arnold Lieber of the University of Miami concluded from this
survey that "eventually we're going to show that any
organism, human or animal, is an integral part of the
universe, and responds to changes like variations in the solar
cycle and the lunar cycle."[1]

Metaphysicians expand this linkage to all phases of life.
They believe there is a Cosmic Web, constructed of im-

---

[1] *The Brain Revolution*, Marilyn Ferguson, Bantam Books, 1973

measurable invisible threads, that connects all life in a network of subliminal communication. They feel that, from the tiniest bit of energy to the greatest mass, these threads of energy bind us one to another. You cannot pick a flower but you disturb a star, an environmentalist once said. The Hawaiian kahunas call these interlocking lines *aka threads*, and they are said to connect us to every thought we have ever entertained, every act we have ever committed, and every person we have ever contacted. The more frequent the contact, the stronger the aka thread, binding us more tightly than ever to whatever or whoever we hold strongest in our minds. Just as the spider knows when a fly lands on its web by the vibration of a single thread, so do we often know subliminally, sometimes consciously, when one of our connecting threads is activated, that something is about to happen to us or to the people we love.

In his book, *The Tao of Physics* (Shambhala Publications, 1975), fast becoming a classic in its field, Fritjof Capra finds startling comparisons between mysticism and quantum physics. Capra, a physicist, studied Eastern mysticism, and had a mystical experience while sitting on a beach one day. He and other physicists are discovering that the oneness of life and the descriptions of that oneness that the mystics have claimed for thousands of years is close to being proven as truth in the laboratories of modern physics. Even though this unity is only just now being discovered by the modern world, it nevertheless has always been true. Modern science may not have discovered yet all the threads connecting science and metaphysics, but that does not mean they do not exist nor does it mean that mystical experiences are illusory.

The perfectly constructed Cosmic Web continues to cover us all; and any science, such as astrology, that has persisted for so many thousands of years surely has woven very strong aka threads. History abounds in famous and respected personalities who strongly believed in and used astrology daily. Hippocrates, the father of medicine, claimed that no man should call himself a doctor who does not have a thorough understanding of astrology and how it relates to the physical and mental bodies. Sir Isaac Newton, when chided by Edmund Halley, the astronomer, for his belief in astrology, replied, "Sir, I have studied it, you have not." And statistics prove that some 70 to 80 percent of the people in the United States today know at least their sun sign of the zodiac. Certainly astrology has constructed a healthy durable thread in the Cosmic Web.

Astrology and numerology interlock; and although there is some debate over the assignments of particular planets to the numbers, there is a definite correspondence between the energies represented by the numbers and the energies emanating from the planets in our solar system the Sun, the Moon, Mercury, Venus, Earth, Mars, Jupiter, Saturn, Uranus, Neptune and Pluto. The Sun and Moon are also called planets for simplicity's sake. Vulcan is also used here. Vulcan, the planet located between Mercury and the Sun, is accepted by some astrologers as the ruler of Virgo. This is a more fitting application than Mercury to Virgo because Vulcan, blacksmith to the gods, was also the god of artisans. Virgo is the artisan. Atlas, an occult point, is suggested in our first book *13-Birth or Death?* (AID, Hampton, New Hampshire, 1976) as an assignment, awaiting the discovery of another planet in our solar system.

If you can mentally connect the special qualities of each planet to its corresponding number, you will find the numerological chart easier to read. For example, the energies of a 1 are typically Martian, the qualities of the 3, Jupiterian, and the 5, Mercurial. As always, examination of our manner of speaking, our cliches and expressions, reveals the truth behind the words: for example, "the martial strains of a musical piece," someone with a "mercurial nature," or a "jovial nature." By relating the specific planets to particular numbers, you will have a more thorough understanding of the numbers and therefore will be better able to read your charts.

The following assignments are the ones I have come to use because they make sense to me; however, try them for yourself. Work with them; experiment. No rule is infallible.

1. Mars, ruler of Aries
2. Vulcan, ruler of Virgo
   11 Uranus, ruler of Aquarius
3. Jupiter, ruler of Sagittarius
4. Earth, ruler of Taurus
   22 Pluto, ruler of Scorpio
5. Mercury, ruler of Gemini
6. Venus, ruler of Libra
   33 Neptune, ruler of Pisces
7. Moon, ruler of Cancer
8. Saturn, ruler of Capricorn
   44 Atlas, an occult point (waiting for a planetary assignment)
9. Sun, ruler of Leo

Because the even numbers can be evenly divided, e.g.: 8 into 4 and 4, 6 into 3 and 3, 4 into 2 and 2, 2 into 1 and 1, they are dual vibrations that require double assignments, thus the Master Numbers are included. Therefore, each of the even numbers has two planetary assignments.

1 MARS, RULER OF ARIES. 1 is that point where things emerge from a state of "being" into a state of "becoming." In the beginning there was the word, and the word was God. The word, a spoken sound, is a vibration that moves out of is-ness into the void, seeking and desirous of expressing its own creativity. Nothing stands in its way; it is the pioneer of the numbers, just as Mars, ruler of Aries, is the aggressive, assertive god of war, actively seeking mastery and power over all. Aries is also called number 1, and Arians need to be first and best at everything they do. Wherever you find a number 1 activated, you will find the individual feels this kind of energy. The personal needs will come first, and the person will stand apart, separated from the crowd in some way, either visibly, by being recognized as number 1, or mentally, by feeling the need to make decisions without help from others.

Just as spirit leaves the godhead, the father, to journey into the world of form, so may the number 1 be likened to the sperm which, after leaving the father travels through the canal seeking its creative destiny in the world of form.

Mars is assigned to number 1. Notice how like the Mars symbol the sperm's shape is: Mars (♂); sperm (⚬⌇).

Some numerologists feel that the Sun should be assigned to the number 1. However, I feel that the beginning of a cycle implies a searching, a reaching out towards a goal which is only achieved by going through the entire cycle 1 through 9. If the Sun were number 1, then the goal would be reached before the journey began.

2/11 TWO: VULCAN, RULER OF VIRGO; 11: Uranus, ruler of Aquarius. 2 implies division and separateness. We might picture this as two lines at odds with each other: (+). Awareness of this division creates in us a longing for wholeness, a need for a coming together, a desire for harmony. To bring about this desired harmony, we need cooperation, mediation, understanding of the work required, and a keen eye for the rough corners that can rip the fabric of the wholeness. Vulcan, as ruler of Virgo, answers this need.

Vulcan, an elusive planet located between Mercury and the Sun, was first seen on March 26, 1859 by M. Lescarbault, a village doctor and amateur astronomer who subsequently contacted the famous astronomer Leverrier about his discovery of a black spot, visible for 1 hour, 17 minutes and 9 seconds, crossing the rim of the Sun. Leverrier investigated and was so convinced that he asked the Emperor Napoleon to grant the Legion of Honor to the village doctor.

The occasional sightings made up to 1949 were erratic because the planet did not reappear on schedule. The two men were ridiculed and the planet all but dismissed by astronomers (but not astrologers) until June 26, 1949, when Dr. Walter Baade on Mt. Palomar, with a new 48-inch telescope, discovered and photographed the trail of a tiny, new celestial body which he called Icarus (Lescarbault's Vulcan) for the youth who flew too close to the Sun and fell to his death on Earth because the Sun melted the wax in his feathered wings.

Vulcan/Icarus is not like the other planets—its orbit, taking 411.8 days, traces a path from the edge of the Sun through the orbits of Mercury, Venus and Earth and loops around the path of Mars (see diagram).

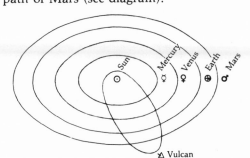

The original discovery in 1859 was thought erroneous because astronomers had assumed the planet would follow the usual elliptical orbit that the other planets follow, and had calculated the time for this regular orbit inside Mercury's path where Vulcan was first discovered.

Vulcan is 21 million miles from the Sun at perihelion (its nearest point) and 177 million miles from the Sun at aphelion (its farthest point). It comes closest to the earth, 4.6 million miles, every 19 years, a cycle which corresponds to weather cycles as recorded by the Smithsonian Institute.

Both the legends of Icarus and Vulcan place the planet very close to the Sun: Icarus flew so close to the Sun that the wax in his feathers melted, and Vulcan needed the heat from the celestial fire to forge his creations. Vulcan's expulsion from the home of the gods (the Sun) and Icarus falling so far from the Sun suggests Vulcan's orbit could be much farther from the Sun than the orbit of the other planets.

Vulcan is said to have caught Mars and made sport of him before Olympus, home of the gods. Vulcan "caught" Mars inside its orbit, i.e.: Vulcan loops around Mars in its orbit (see diagram), and Olympus, home of the gods, could be none other than the Sun, the "planet" all cultures have assigned to or worshipped as the supreme deity. We are told that astrologers in Pythagoras' time, about 600 BC, taught their students that there were "ten fiery circles," although the exoteric doctrine given out publicly counted only seven. Excluding the Sun which does not orbit, there are only nine "fiery circles": Mercury, Venus, Earth, Mars, Jupiter, Saturn, Uranus, Neptune and Pluto (the last three of which were unknown to the general public during Pythagoras' time). Vulcan would complete the number as the tenth "fiery circle." It seems that many hidden truths can be revealed through closer examination of myths and legends.

Health is a sixth house, Virgoan issue. Weather cycles, seemingly related to Vulcan through its approach to the earth every nineteen years, affect our health through atmospheric conditions and crop production. Weather determines the quality and quantity of crops that are produced each year as well as the kind of houses we must construct to protect ourselves from the elements. The feeding and housing of the public are sixth house, Virgoan matters.

Vulcan is hard to see because it is so small and because it comes so close to the Sun's overpowering brightness. Its obscurity also fits in with Virgoan characteristics of shyness, modesty and unobtrusiveness.

Even today, the history and qualities of Mr. Spock of "Star Trek" further exemplify Vulcan and Virgo as celestial partners. Mr. Spock was banished, or thrown from his home, Vulcan, by his parents (as the God Vulcan was thrown from heaven by his parents) because he couldn't achieve total indifference and objectivity. He was extremely psychic, able to read everyone's thoughts. It is said that in ancient times Virgo and Scorpio were the same sign. Virgo picks up psychic qualities from this association as well as from its opposite polarity, Pisces. All Spock's senses were heightened—notice his large pointed ears. By touching someone, he could take their pain into his body to observe and analyze it. He was very logical, almost computerized. His sensitive touch relates to Vulcan's ability as an artisan to mould beautiful things. The logic is also Virgo's.

11, ruled by Uranus, is the higher frequency of the number 2. Eleven represents sudden bursts of energy, like lightning flashes that rip through the heavens, or sudden moments of illumination. Situations that demand instant action and decision can arise without warning.

With the number 2, Vulcan quietly took the fire (Mars, number 1) and formed new life with precision, care, and an eye for perfection. With the number 11, Uranus, god of the heavens (the mind), struck with intuitive flashes and sudden demands. The fire of Mars is almost too hot to handle. I am reminded of Dr. Frankenstein who drew upon the lightning from a midnight storm to infuse his soulless monster with life.

Perhaps it was an improper use of the Uranian energy on Dr. Frankenstein's part, but the analogy nevertheless holds true. Uranian energy, number 11, if controlled and used wisely, brings great inspiration and creation. Number 11 bestows freedom and inspiration (Uranus–Aquarius–Number 11) upon the disciplined, skilled, willing worker and servant (Vulcan–Virgo– Number 2).

Under the number 2, the sperm that left its father's home (↓) seeking experience is now fulfilled by being accepted into the waiting egg (↓). The cross (+) that results represents the burden of the physical body that weighs down the free spirit upon its entry into matter.

There is some disagreement over the assignment of Vulcan to number 2. Some claim the Moon rules number 2; others, that Uranus rules here. I feel that Vulcan's role as blacksmith of the gods assigns him the task of taking the life spirit (Mars) from the gods (heaven) and fashioning form (earth). His role as mediator between the gods and humanity also reinforces his rulership of this number. No previous assignment has been given to Master Number 11.

3 JUPITER, RULER OF SAGITTARIUS. There is expansion, expresssion, and growth with number 3. The two entities seeking unity join each other at this point and the third stage is born, the three-in-one, the trinity. This may be the largest visible point of growth in the 1 through 9 cycle.

In mythology, it is said that Vulcan captured Mars and made sport of him before Jupiter (Zeus). To make sport of is to play with, perhaps to fashion. In other words, Vulcan, number 2, played with (or fashioned), with a bit of humor perhaps, the fiery life energy of Mars before Jupiter, the forces of expansion and growth. Vulcan was showing off his creation for the approval of the gods, in a sense.

3 is the first perfect number, or the first perfect form that can be constructed with straight lines; e.g.: (△). 3 is the energy that precedes physical manifestation.

Jupiter in astrology rules Sagittarius and the ninth house of the higher mind, philosophy, and long distance travel. Jupiter's assignment to number 3 lends the positive, happy, social vibration that this number implies.

Under the 3, the sperm, united with the egg, enters a period of tremendous growth and expansion, the cells multiplying with astonishing speed.

There is agreement on Jupiter's assignment to number 3.

4/22 FOUR:EARTH, RULER OF TAURUS; 22: Pluto, Ruler of Scorpio. Under the number

4, all earthly, practical, work-a-day projects are emphasized. Building, form, foundation, and security are keywords as a result of the 4's relationship to the square, the second perfect shape that can be formed with straight lines (☐). The logical planetary assignment for this number is Earth itself, a planet that somehow has been left out of the astrological scene, and yet it is the most obvious because we live upon it. Earth must have the strongest effect upon us because it is the closest to us, literally a Siamese twin.

In astrology the first point of awareness is Aries, "I am." A child is born and knows only that "it is." The second point of awareness is Taurus, "I have." The child now becomes aware of its body and that body's needs—all earthly considerations. The current ruler of Taurus, Venus, whose role is the balancer, aware of others' needs, seems out of place in this evolutionary stage of growth. This "other" awareness comes later. Earth seems to be the only fitting ruler of Taurus and the number 4.

Number 22, as the Master Number and higher vibration of the number 4, is ruled by Pluto. Pluto, as god of the underworld, was the richest of all the gods because the wealth of the Earth belonged to him. When crossing the River Styx, travelers had to pay a fee (which was their bodies, since crossing the River Styx meant dying), and all payment went to Pluto. Even today the very wealthy are called "plutocrats." If number 4 rules the material world, then 22 as a Master Number is an intensified version of the same energy, promising material resources in abundance. Pluto rules Scorpio, and Scorpio is the house of joint resources, great sums of money. One can see why the Master Number 22 should rule the wealth of the material world.

The joining of the sperm and the egg and its subsequent expansion has now produced form under the number 4. Some old assignments have given Neptune to number 4. Neptune rules Pisces, and indicates sensitivity, compassion, fantasy, and creativity of an illusory nature. These qualities do not seem to fit the nature of the number 4. 22 had no assignment.

5 MERCURY, RULER OF GEMINI. 5 is motion in order to gain experience. The number 5 is communication, travel and knowledge. The wing-footed Mercury was the messenger of the gods, transmitting information through the heavens (the mind) and sometimes to the earth (the body). In astrology, we find Mercury ruling Gemini, the first air, or intellectual, sign. Geminis are charming, adaptable, and curious. They need to know a little about everything, and with the 5 energies at work, the same attitude comes through.

The fifth step in the journey from conception to death could be the child's expulsion through the birth canal into a new world of experience.

There seems to be agreement on Mercury's assignment to number 5.

6/33

SIX: VENUS, RULER OF LIBRA; 33: Neptune Ruler of Pisces. Under the 6, love and domestic and community responsibility preside. The need for beauty, peace, and harmony are very obvious.

Venus, the goddess of beauty, arose from the ocean. When brought before the gods, they were so smitten by her beauty that each "wished in his heart to take her as a wife and lead her to his abode." She was the essence of femininity—"pure charm and harmony." She had perfect features and a perfect form and always wore a smile. Clearly Venus could rule no other sign than Libra and no other number than 6.

33 is ruled by Neptune and Pisces. Venus rose from the ocean (Neptune's domain) and Venus is exalted in Pisces. Certainly number 6, love, could find no better assignment in its higher Master Number form than to the compassionate Neptune and Pisces.

The child is born and now must learn to deal with the relationships around him or her. Hopefully, love, compassion and true understanding are the first qualities encountered.

Venus is usually assigned to number 6. 33 had no assignment.

7

THE MOON, RULER OF CANCER. God created the world in six stages and rested on the seventh; therefore, 7 is rest, completion on the physical level, contemplation, perfection. 7 rules time, a physical earth concept. There are seven days in the week, seven colors in the rainbow, seven notes in the musical scale, seven major centers, or chakras, in the body, seven original planets, and our body is completely renewed every seven years by the replacement of all our cells. 7 is the heavenly messenger bearing time into our physical world.

The lunar calendar has thirteen months governed by the thirteen Moon cycles each year. The four phases of the Moon consist of seven days each, thus again relating the Moon to time. The Moon also controls the menstrual cycle of females and a similar cycle in males, as well as all ebbs and flows, such as the ocean. Even the Earth's surface moves many inches under the gravitational pull of the full Moon. This seems to bind the Moon to number 7 through the joint connections with time and the physical flux of the cycles.

In astrology, the Moon rules the absorptive processes and the subconscious mind, which absorbs all that it contacts through physical means whether in this lifetime or past lifetimes. The zodiacal sign Cancer, ruled by the Moon, bestowing a protective nurturing nature, still active but more obliquely so than direct confrontation. As with Cancer and the Moon, the number 7 indicates activity, but activity that is more subtly directed than under a 1, a more secretive, thoughtful, meditative, perfected type of activity.

This stage of development from the sperm entry into life to the culminating point of death covers that phase of childhood when the subconscious is developed, and when the child's sense of self-worth (from the feedback of others in the environment) is established.

It seems that the Moon is a more fitting ruler of number 7 than Neptune, which is sometimes assigned here. Perhaps the outer planets should be assigned to the Master Numbers since the outer planets and the Master Numbers both imply a higher level of consciousness.

8/44

EIGHT: SATURN, RULER OF CAPRICORN 44: Atlas, an occult point. 8 is pressure, responsibility, strength and karma. The 4 as a square represents matter; 8 as a cube represents the solidification of matter. The cube reduces to an 8: a cube has eight points, twelve lines and six planes. $8 + 12 + 6 = 26$. Reduce the 26: $2+6 = 8$. Salt crystallizes in cubes, and the Bible says: *ye are the salt of the earth.* 8 is solidification. Is it not also the eighth tone of the scale that solidifies musical composition?

Saturn is the undisputed ruler of number 8. Saturn (or Cronus), one of the twelve Titan children of Uranus and Gaea, took (at his mother's bequest because Uranus had imprisoned the monsters born of his Cyclops' children), the sickle his mother had fashioned and cut off his father's genitals and cast them into the sea. Uranus, or heaven (mind), and Gaea, or earth (body), produced twelve children (the twelve signs of the zodiac), one of whom was Saturn (Satan-the Reaper). The uniting of heaven and earth produced time and form. The three Cyclops children with single eyes in their foreheads indicate the three parts of the mind that now have the ability to reason for themselves, that have godlike knowledge of wisdom and truth. Through this ability they can now choose to produce monsters (the results of evil actions), which Uranus (the mind) imprisoned in the bowels of the earth (the body). Saturn cut off his father's genitals (cut off the mind's creative heavenly power) and cast them into the ocean (the great deep of the subconscious where the mind's creative power is now lost). Thus the meeting of the mind and the body when the soul enters the body creates a knowledge of time, an awareness of separateness from others through outer form and ultimate division from the unity of the heavenly oneness. Free will is established, and ultimately karma, as the results of one's actions. Saturn is generally accepted as ruler of number 8.

Atlas, as number 44, is the bone at the base of the neck that connects heaven and earth, or the mind and the body. Atlas was a mythical figure, half man and half god. This implies that through number 44, or Atlas, we can unite those two halves of our selves, the body and the mind, through application of strength and discipline. In our previous book we suggested the use of number 44 as a Master Number and assigned Atlas, an occult point at the present, to the number. We expect that the discovery of a new planet will eventually take the place of the occult point.

Eight may be the stage of development where adulthood and its ensuing responsibility is placed upon us.

9 THE SUN, RULER OF LEO. 9 is knowing, wisdom, charity, completeness, victory, the transitional point in any cycle. Greek mythology relates that Helios (the Sun god) was one of the children of the Titans, or a product of the divisions of time (the zodiac). Helios was drowned in the ocean by his Titan uncles, then raised to the sky where he became the Sun. As the god of light, Helios, or the Sun, saw and knew everything. He shone on everyone and everything without discrimination. Pindar said: "He is the god who plumbs all hearts, the infallible, whom neither mortals nor immortals can deceive either by action or in their most secret thoughts." The number 9 has this same ability to know and perceive.

Astrologically, the Sun is ruler of Leo, the king of the zodiac, the disseminator of gifts and wisdom. It seems logical that the Sun be assigned to number 9 because true wisdom can only be attained through experience, or through the completion of a cycle. When we incarnate, or when we enter a new cycle of experience, we do so with the knowledge gained from our past lifetimes or our past cycles, but with no knowledge of the coming cycle. The fact that we have entered a new cycle implies that we have something more to learn. Therefore, in a sense, we enter that cycle "unlearned" in whatever experiences that cycle seeks to give us. At the end of the cycle, or at number 9, we hopefully have gained the knowledge meant for us through the cycle we have just completed. The omniscience of the 9 is then and only then, ours.

This is the point in our evolution where we have gained our

true realization, our sunhood, our selfhood, our true selves.

Capricorn, the tenth sign of the zodiac, solidifies the 1 through 9 cycle. As ruler of the tenth house, it covers that phase of our lives which is most obvious publicly (the world of form): profession, career, public recognition and standing.

Some place Mars with number 9, and the Sun with number 1; however, this seems backward, in the sense that these placements imply that we start our cycle with complete knowledge of ourselves and an attitude of equitable sharing of our talents and abilities through the Sun, and end our cycle with the ego-centered energies of Mars and the little self.

Thus I arrived at the planetary assignments I gave at the beginning of this chapter. Some are traditional and have not been questioned. Of the rest, however, there is some debate. Because I felt uncomfortable with particular assignments, I began research-ing the symbolism behind the name of each planet, and observed how the information found correlated to the particular numbers. Then I applied it to my experience with the number vibrations in my own life and in the lives of those I know, as well as of the strangers who came to me for counsel. Your own inner voice is the best judge of what is true for you. Just as reading a sentence aloud gives you a clearer feeling of whether or not the sentence "rings true," listening to your own feelings allows you to discover whether the information rings true to you. If it does, all well and good. If it does not, then question and seek; eventually you will find what your truth is.

5

NUMEROLOGY'S INFLUENCE

ON THE DECADES

THE GREAT PSYCHOLOGIST William James said: "Any act or thought repeated consecutively for 45 times without failure becomes a habit." A habit is something done without reasoning or thinking; it is automatic, or second nature.

I have lectured on numerology to many thousands of people over the years. My expectations of the audience's response to information about their numerological cycles have become a habit, because that response has been repeated consecutively for so many years. Audiences continue to be amazed at the accuracy of their number cycles; therefore I know the numbers work. It has become second nature for me to think in numerological terms in relation to everything around me.

The true significance of the numbers is so ingrained in our consciousness that we, as a world mind, are even influenced by the numbers of the centuries, decades, and single years dur-

Numerology's
Influence
on the
Decades
ing which we live. We have our personal cycles determined by our unique birth information, which affects us on a personal level. However, the entire world population as a unit responds to universal cycles determined by the calendar. We invented the calendar; therefore, the calendar reflects our innate knowledge of the meaning of the numbers. And now that the calendar is used more or less universally, the consciousness of the world is influenced by it.

The consciousness of a people, culture or nation is embedded in the mind of its people from the moment of birth. It is reflected in the art, language, dress and customs—all thought processes of the particular people. The measurement of time, being very arbitrary, is no exception. If a people use a particular calendar they will respond to that means of measurement—in other words—they will respond to the number vibrations they have selected. In cultures where a different system of counting is used, that culture will react accordingly. However, the majority of the world uses the present Gregorian calendar adopted in 1582; therefore, that is the system we will examine.

Each one hundred years has its own peculiar vibration determined by the meaning of the first two digits in the century, e.g.: the 1700s, the 1800s, the 1900s. In any century, the first two digits of the year are repeated one hundred times from, say, 1900 to 1999; more than twice that required by James to become a habit. How many times have you written, spoken, or heard the digits 19 in the years of this century? Far too many to count, I am sure. If your name repeated over and over throughout your lifetime impresses a particular vibration upon your cells, think how strongly the vibration of the 19 in the 1900s must be impressed upon the world consciousness when written and spoken by millions of people for a hundred years. The repetition of the numbers of any century, decade, or single year set up a certain frequency, a vibration which moves around the world and influences the thinking and therefore the events of the entire earth. This repetition forms a habit for that time.

In the following look at the decades of this century, notice how the verbs, adjectives, and phrases used to describe the events and the mood of the decade are the same words (that is, they could be interchanged as keywords) used in describing the numbers that rule the decade.

I have chosen to focus on American history rather than scattered events from the history of many countries around the world to prove the influence of the decade's numbers. It would be a simple matter to select two or three events in a ten-year period from a variety of different countries that would fit under each decade number. However, I felt that by focusing on one country and a larger number of major events occurring within one decade in that one country, the proof would be more convincing. Ten major events in one country within one decade that describe the decade's number perfectly are more convincing than two or three events within one decade from seven or eight different countries. The following examination would, however, be applicable to any country using the Gregorian calendar.

The 1900s are influenced by the first two digits, the 1 and the 9, because these two digits remain unchanged, while the last two digits change either every ten years or every one year. The 1 and the 9 of the 1900s seem to tell us that this is a transitional one hundred years in our history, a time of birth and death, a time of testing, struggling, and cleansing through regeneration. The 1 is the beginning, the 9 is the ending—birth and death. This century, of all the years of history, will stand out as the most extreme in terms of the invention, discovery, and advancement that ushered it in and nurtured it through its first seven decades. This century may also be known for the final and total desecration wrought by these achievements during the century's waning years. The digits 1 and 9 are at opposite ends of the spectrum, yet they are side by side; e.g.: 8, 9, 1, 2, 3, 4, 5, 6, 7, 8, 9, 1, 2, 3, or:

Life appears to flow in one direction: just as the planets revolve around the Sun in a set pattern; the Earth moves from west to east, and the hands of the clock move clockwise. To move from 1 to 9, we must traverse seven digits, but to move from 9 to 1 is merely a step. This may indicate that we have ample time to fashion the habits and cast the character that will form our destiny. But once the mold is cast, there is only one false move to destruction. The transition always comes quickly, tearing down the outworn structures, and using that refuse to kindle the resurrecting fires of tomorrow.

As the 1900s began, we had latitude, time to act, and room to move, ability to reason, and ideas with which to plan the future. We were given the positive, ardent, aggressive, flamboyant energy of Mars through the number 1, and the promise of the pot of gold at the end of the rainbow through the Sun, or number 9. As the 1900s bloomed, we were optimistic and full of energy. We enjoyed a pioneering zest for new lands to conquer, new worlds to see, and new pleasures to enjoy. We idolized those who lived these dreams for us.

1900-1909

The first decade combined the 19 with the 0 and the digits

1 through 9; e.g.: 1901, 1902, 1903. . .1908, 1909. The 0 ruled the first ten years: each year of the decade was ruled by blending the 0 with the digit that followed it. For example, in 1901 the 1 worked with the 0, in 1902 the 2 melded with the 0, in 1903 the 3 united with the 0, and so on in the natural sequential expenditure of energy towards the realization of the number series, the 9, which worked with the 0 in 1909. The goal had been reached, transition was imminent. This pattern applies in each decade; e.g.: in the 1920s the last digit of the calendar year worked with the 2, in the 1930s the last digit of the calendar year blended with the 3, and so on.

Each single year can be reduced in the manner described previously in this book, e.g.: 1921 would reduce: $1+9+2+1$ $= 13/4$. 1921 was a 13/4 single year. The last digit, the 1, worked with the third digit, the 2, and with the 1 and 9 to produce a 13/4 single year. This year however, as with each single year through the 1920s, was overshadowed by the 2 of the 1920s decade because the 2 is repeated through each of the ten years of the decade, a cycle within a cycle, just as we live our Personal Day Cycle within our Personal Month Cycle within our Period Number Cycle within our Personal Year Cycle. The single years are smaller cycles within the larger decade cycle within the larger century cycle within the still larger millenium cycle, ad infinitum.

In the ten-year period from 1900 to 1909, the 0 ruled. 0 is the God symbol, the cosmic egg, the is-ness, the "I am" before the creation. In the 0, the archetypes for all creation already exist. It contains all we need to create and build the world of form. The 0 decade from 1900-1909 showed us what we had to work with in this century. The circle, loving, complete, whole, and happy, bestowed a sort of "I am" pattern, a holding pattern over the first decade, as if the golden jonquils of spring had been suspended in a timeless moment, and youth and joy would last forever.

The symbology of the "I am" and the circle is deeply embedded in our consciousness. A baby lives in the "I am" every moment of the waking day. Its first awareness is "I am," and its first contact with the circle is the parent's face smiling down. He or she does not differentiate features but does see outlines, the round outline of a face radiating love. Mother's nurturing breast, or the bottle, is round as well. Round balls, rattles, and other round toys without sharp edges are the first contacts with soft, loving, sustaining, safe shapes. The circle symbology persists in the complete faith and pure joy with which a small child views the world. Watch a toddler jump down into the arms of a parent without fear that the parent would let him or her fall. Notice the ecstatic concentration of a child playing with a warm puppy. When the child first learns to write, he or she usually reveals that same loving attitude in the full loops and circles of handwriting.

We carry these associations into adulthood when we arrange our chairs in a circle at a meeting, because somehow we feel more comfortable that way. We sit around a campfire to enjoy the camaraderie. Many cultures have circle dances; and all religious teachings contain circles. From 1900-1909, the encompassing symbology of the circle seemed to hold time in abeyance. We felt that God was with us and all things were possible. *This Fabulous Century*, by Time-Life Books, captured the flavor of the first ten years: "The man of the decade, President Theodore Roosevelt, was the living embodiment of the optimism and energy of this country's mood. During his seven and one-half years of vigorous, personal leadership, from 1901 to 1909, he wielded the powers of the Presidency as no man had done before. Roosevelt called his crusade the Square Deal, and the people loved it. They loved him for himself, too. 'I have never known another person so vital,' wrote author and editor William Allen White, speaking for the nation, 'nor another man so dear.'"

Called the Cocksure Era, this was a splendid time, a wonderful country." Most Americans felt that way about the new century and they said so with exaggerated "references to Peace, Prosperity and Progress."

1910-1919

In the years 1910 to 1919, the 1 overshadowed the decade. 1 represents independence, decisiveness, aggressiveness, impulsiveness, fervor, originality, the pioneering instinct, leadership, and the need to be first and best. Henry Ford summed up this decade best when he said he wanted "to be known as a thinker of an original kind," and these years produced much that was original. It was a decade of firsts and the end of innocence; a time when the 0 bubble of optimism, faith, and an almost Pollyanna attitude towards life finally burst. Historians reflecting upon this time spoke the real essence of the number 1 in phrases like: a period of "almost tremulous unrest," of a "reviewing of all our social conceptions," a time when "we are profoundly disenchanted."

Rebellion against the past and all its traditions emerged in the attitudes, habits, customs, dress, literary tastes, films, and dances of the decade. The new woman was born. In May, 1910, the first public demonstration of women's suffrage took place. Women demanded the right to vote, which at that time was denied only to them, the mentally retarded, and

criminals. The struggle ended in 1919 when women won their
right to vote with the 19th Amendment to the Constitution.
Ironically, the 19 of the 19th Amendment was doubly reflected
in the year 1919, the beginning and the end.

Women became more aggressive and assertive. One
young woman dared to smoke in public. Others invaded the
male business world and raised the female working force by
one million in that ten-year period. The Milwaukee women's
swimming team appeared in public in a "collection of men's
swim suits," baring their arms and legs for the first time to the
shock and dismay of clergy. One could almost hear a collective sigh of relief as tight corsets were thrown away and
millions of pinched waistlines expanded. A straighter
silhouette, more like the shape of the number 1, was born in
styles that allowed more freedom.

The headlong and often confused rush into the future was
captured by the mad movie world of Charlie Chaplin, the
Keystone Kops, and the Perils of Pauline. A group of intellec-
tuals, Anderson, Lippmann, Eastman, Dreiser, Sandburg,
Lowell, and Frost, some of whom protested the lowbrow
reading tastes of the public, brought on a literary revolution
through a stream of purely American works and critiques. The
mass production of Henry Ford's Tin Lizzie freed millions of
people from isolated farms and remote country homes. The
horse and buggy gave way to instant transportation, suddenly
changing the face of America. Her cheeks now blushed with
the excitement and fervor of new places to go and new sights
to see.

Then, on April 2, 1917, war came upon the world, and
America leaped to the defense of world peace. Young red-
blooded American men marched off to fight, singing valiant
songs of victory, and the Martian quality of the number 1
reached its peak. Those who did not want to go to war were
publicly scorned and ridiculed. It was a time to stand up and
be counted.

The 1920s

The 1920s were under the thumb of the number 2, which
represents a gestation period in which to collect, analyze, and
assimilate. Secret elements, which would surface at a later
time, were working beneath the surface; therefore a quiet,
nonassertive, passive, cooperative, unsure attitude prevailed.
Choices are difficult under a 2, so often decisions are deferred
to a later day. Affairs fluctuate, situations change rapidly, and
emotions run high, causing erratic actions at times. Poise,
equilibrium, and balance are the saving factors: this is why

peacemakers and mediators are in demand. Under a 2, the seeds of creativity are planted, and artists produce deeply moving works of art.

Two principles are active: the secretive, waiting, creative energy and the suddenly erratic, impulsive, explosive energy—two sides of the same coin. The number 2 is either balanced (||) or at odds with itself (+). This decade had a little of both.

America was tired as she entered the 1920s. The need for normalcy, peace and quiet was reflected in the defeat of Woodrow Wilson, who had led the country through World War I and then demanded reform at home and American leadership and responsibility worldwide, all number 1 qualities. But the time of the 1 was finished. America was disillusioned over the death and destruction of the war and its failure to bring peace and democracy to the world, so she rejected Wilson's aggressive demands and elected gentle, lovable Warren G. Harding, who proclaimed, "America's present need is not heroics but healing; not nostrums but normalcy; not revolution but restoration; not surgery but serenity."

America's mood had changed from the militancy of the number 1 in the teens to the passive mood of the number 2 in the 1920s. "America suspended between the innocence and security of childhood and the wisdom and poise of maturity."

The creative side of the 2 blossomed. Joe Oliver, Johnny and Baby Dodds, and Louis Armstrong of the Creole Jazz Band, some of the best musicians north of New Orleans, drove the public wild by their performances. They created "that great blue New Orleans sound." Demand for the blues increased nationwide, culminating in the most celebrated musical event of the decade, George Gershwin's premier performance of "Rhapsody in Blue" at Manhattan's Aeolian Hall in 1924. Society's elite filled the hall to hear Gershwin's "symphonic jazz."

A quote from "How To Play and Sing the Blues Like Phonograph and Stage Artists" reads: "blues are more naturally blue when the melodic movements are treated with minor chords." It is perhaps coincidence that the number 2 relates to Key 2 of the Tarot, which is the subconscious, the roots of creativity; and the color of the subconscious is blue. The subconscious urgings could be described as minor chords, number 2, which are often drowned out by the conscious mind's major chords, number 1, until the right moment, the right cycle, when the "outer" is stilled and the "inner" is heard.

The twenties also ushered in Prohibition, which drove the drinking public into hiding and created the underground saloon and speakeasy. Alcohol was smuggled in from ships anchored three miles off the coast, and moonshine was brought in from country hills. Gentlemen carried flasks in their back pockets and ladies tucked theirs under garters.

Al Capone, with a 700-man army at his disposal, controlled 10,000 speakeasies in Chicago and ran bootlegging operations from Canada to Florida. Out of the dark of night a secret element emerged and racketeering was born. Emotions ran high, not only because of the furtive attempts of the public to purchase booze and avoid the law, but also because of the rackets' internal struggles to maintain supremacy over a million-dollar market.

The finale of all the underground rumblings occurred in the ninth (a time of endings) year of the decade, on Black Tuesday, October 29, 1929, when the stock market collapsed. Strangely enough, a 1921 political cartoon, warning investors of shady operators angling for victims in the stock exchange, depicted fat well-dressed male figures on top of the stock exchange building with fishing poles, at the end of which hung those poor souls who had been caught on the financial hook. This was the supreme example of one side of the number 2 coin, hidden energies suddenly emerging and creating chaos.

The 1930s

The 1930s were under the auspices of the number 3. As with all the numbers, they can be used on a lower physical plane or on a higher illumined level of consciousness. The former brings disintegration, the latter transmutation. 3 is the principle of life, which activates the physical plane, and as such its harmonious use can bestow social harmony, generosity, affability, honesty, recognition, orderly growth and expansion, and freedom from want. 3 allows planning on a grand scale, listening to dreams, and expressing talents. The inharmonious effects of the 3 power wreak destruction and chaos through exaggeration, overconfidence, wastefulness and bankruptcy.

The first two decades raised a lean cow. The early depression years of the 1930s that followed the stock market crash caused untold hardship on many Americans who had plodded through the 1920s unaware of the loss of energy caused by insidious forces. Nature lashed the lean cow with dust storms, which buried farms and suffocated the citizens of New Mexico, Texas, Kansas, and Oklahoma. On March 4, 1933, the last bank in the country closed its doors, and financial and economic starvation loomed on the horizon. America was more frightened than she had ever been before. However, on that same day in March, Franklin D. Roosevelt became president, moved into the Oval Office, and began issuing orders. He called special sessions of Congress, and his emergency banking bill passed through the House within thirty-eight minutes unchanged. Four days later the banks reopened and the panic was over. People began redepositing their money and confidence was restored. By June 16, fifteen new laws had been enacted to stabilize the economy. The New Deal, Roosevelt's alphabet soup—the NRA (National Recovery Act), the CCC (Civilian Conservation Corps), the PWA (Public Works Administration), the WPA (Works Progress Administration), and so on—nourished and slowly strengthened the weakened cow. His government programs created jobs for unemployed artists—composers, painters, writers, actors. One recipient was John Steinbeck, who produced a major work of the decade *The Grapes of Wrath*.

FDR radiated the confidence the country needed. An associate, awed by the president, commented, "He must have been psychoanalyzed by God." Roosevelt's attitude and his social programs were exemplary of the qualities of the number 3 and its Jupiterian flavor.

In this decade John L. Lewis held the limelight; his eloquent voice spoke for the downtrodden working class. After knowing terror, beatings, and death, labor finally secured for itself better wages, safer working conditions, and security on the job. Union membership swelled over the seven million mark, and the once ignored and battered worker became a first class citizen. (The recognition, relaxed conditions and affluency of the 3 began to manifest in these events.)

The need for freedom became obvious in 1933 when Prohibition was repealed. The nation celebrated wildly. The inner need for self-expression was reflected further in the expansive events and entertainment of this decade. Music carried the tone of the Big Band sound with Benny Goodman, the Dorsey Brothers, Glen Miller, Harry James, Count Basie, Duke Ellington, Artie Shaw and their female vocalists, Helen O'Connel, Billie Holiday, and Ella Fitzgerald. Stage musicals flourished, and the celluloid industry produced the greatest extravaganza of the decade: the film version of Margaret Mitchell's novel, *Gone With the Wind*. This film is still spectacular today.

Hope, faith, and optimism sprang forth in the roles played by the adorable Shirley Temple and in the characters of Little Orphan Annie, Buck Rogers, and Flash Gordon, who prevailed despite obstacles. The country's exaggerated and gullible state of mind was perhaps best summed up in its reaction to Orson Welles' radio program, "Invasion From Mars," enacted as a series of news broadcasts. Many in the listening audience actually believe the Martians had landed and were wreaking death and destruction over the countryside with their death rays.

In 1939 America put on the biggest, gaudiest, and most expensive exposition in the world. The New York World's Fair cost more than 150 million dollars, covered 1,216 acres, and boasted 10,000 trees and 1,000,000 tulips. It featured everything from transportation and Polish vodka to scientific marvels and the world of tomorrow.

The decade ended on an optimistic, rejuvenated and well-satisfied note. Some semblance of sanity and safety had returned to the world, and life seemed more comfortable. The cow was healthy and well fed.

The 1940s

The square and its four sides and all that it implies had precedence in the 1940s. The 4 represents solidity, security, caution, patience, thrift, industry, hard work, money and material possessions. It upholds the traditions of the past because it is a building block, a foundation, upon which law, order and society rest. Organization is a keyword, and debts are paid on all levels. Physical relationships are emphasized. The square is a doorway to new experience, a window through which to view the world, a boundary that defines limits and ensures safety, or a wall that imprisons. Notice that we say "boxed in," rather than "circled in," "tubed in," or "triangled in." On the negative side, 4 can be limited, restrained, fearful, stubborn and overworked.

Although parents usually feel their teenagers are nonconformists, the 1940s produced no rebels. During this decade teenagers "lived and dressed by rigid codes" that were quite conservative—loafers, rolled-up dungarees, and dad's shirt for the girls; army boots, dungarees, and school jackets for the boys. Television, just introduced to the public, came to be known as "the box." In the sense that it kept families home more often, it had a solidifying effect. Organization emerged in the clubwoman, "a ubiquitous and powerful figure on the American scene" in the 1940s. And personal relationships were explored in Dr. Alfred Kinsey's best-selling book, *Sexual Behaviour in the Human Male*, which analyzed the findings of intimate interviews with 5,300 American men.

The major event of the decade, however, was World War II, which, paradoxically, was anticipated and prepared for and yet caught everyone by surprise. The last issue of *Time* magazine before Pearl Harbor read: "From Rangoon to Honolulu every man was at battle stations." The day after the attack, December 8, 1941, House Republican leader Joe Martin exclaimed, "I don't know how the hell we were caught so unprepared." Trouble had been brewing for a decade, however. The Japanese wanted dominion over the Pacific, and the United States fleet stationed in Pearl Harbor blocked their efforts. The attack obviously was planned. Every graduating class at the naval academy in Japan from 1931 on was asked the following question on their final exam: "How would you carry out a surprise attack on Pearl Harbor?"

By the middle of 1941, events had become like a powder keg waiting for a match. Japan's actions proved she wanted to kick the "white devils" out of Asia. In retaliation the United States embargoed the American oil and scrap metal that Japan needed to prepare for war. In July Roosevelt froze all Japanese assets in the United States. Negotiations over the next few months produced no results, and at 7:55 on a Sunday morning, December 7th, the match was struck and Pearl Harbor went up in flames, catching the base and the entire world unaware. In 110 minutes, 188 planes, eight battleships, and three cruisers were destroyed, and 2,400 men were dead. The attack paralyzed American dominance in the Pacific for a year and "laid bare America's inexcusable unreadiness" for war. The optimism of the 1930s ended abruptly, and America suddenly knew she must muster her forces, organize, and solidify. The 1940s had arrived.

It was a decade of work and production. By 1942 the amount of goods made by Americans had quadrupled, and the volume of production continued until the enemy was defeated by the very mass of weaponry produced. Everyone worked. In the five months after Pearl Harbor 750,000 women donned slacks and went to work in armament plants. The thriftiness of number 4 showed in various ways: women collected and saved silk stockings and bacon grease, children saved empty toothpaste tubes and bought war stamps in school, men saved worn tires, old radiators, and scrap metal—all to be recycled for the war effort. Rationing was put into effect and stamps were issued for food and gas.

Victory gardens sprang up in the most unlikely places. Anyone who had even a small square plot of earth grew a few vegetables. Although farmers were producing enough food to feed half the world, the victory gardens made Americans feel they were contributing. War bonds raised the necessary money to fund the war. Money is a vital issue under 4, and the economy boomed. People were working, and some were making "a killing" on the war. One bombardier, home on furlough in 1944, remarked bitterly that he had heard a man on a bus say, "If this war lasts for two more years, I'll be on easy street."

In the early war years an unfortunate public reaction caused the internment of Japanese-American citizens. War hysteria influenced many West Coast residents, fearful of a Japanese invasion, to publicly refuse to deal with the 110,000 Japanese living in that area. Americans refused to sell them food or cash their checks, and companies cancelled their insurance. Eventually, with no charges leveled at them and with no trial, they were herded off to "camps," usually on old Indian reservations known for having the worst land and being the most desolated locations. They were paid a pittance for their labors, yet the Japanese as a whole kept their spirit and family unity. The square of security and protection became a prison of fear and distrust, and America succumbed to her anxiety.

On August 6th and August 9th, 1945, the United States dropped atomic bombs on Hiroshima and Nagasaki and 106,000 Japanese died. The war was over.

After the war, returning GIs had to face another kind of reality: how to get a job and where to live, basics of the number 4. It turned out to be less of a problem than anticipated, for the public responded enthusiastically. Atlanta bought a hundred trailors to help their married GIs. In North Dakota, they converted surplus grain bins into housing units and Benny Goodman's band played a benefit requesting rented rooms instead of money. On the work front, government aid assisted veterans in setting up their own businesses, while others went back to old jobs or to college under the generous GI Bill of Rights. The readjustment was handled well in most cases, and America finished the decade in stable condition.

The country emerged as a world leader after the war, and even though the horror of the atomic bomb lurked in the background, we felt some sense of stability and security. The war was over, and we were the only one who had the A-bomb.

The 1950s

Number 5, the ruler of the 1950s, represents restlessness, freedom, change, curiosity, experience, travel, and choices. 5 is the central number in the 1 to 9 series and indicates a point at which one tends to look back as well as forward. An uneasiness arises. It is decision time. 5 needs information, all sorts of new experiences upon which to base its decisions. Therefore, all forms of communication are emphasized: socializing, travel, reading materials, culture, radio, television, and so on. It is a time of mental growth and versatility, wittiness, and enthusiasm, a restless seeking and experiencing. Since the nervous system is activated under number 5, drugs

and alcohol that stimulate the body should be avoided. 5
meets so many new and varied personalities in its seeking that
sexuality is an issue. Because there are four numbers on each
side of the 5, it is called "the keystone in the arch of the structure of life," and as such represents the five senses, which
dominate our lives and demand satisfaction. 5 is the number
of life, and it lives fully.

In 1951, Louis Kronenberger in *Company Manners*
stated: "The moving van is a symbol of more than our
restlessness; it is the most conclusive possible evidence of our
progress." I am not totally convinced that the moving van is a
symbol of progress, but surely it is a symbol of restlessness, a
perfect description of the number 5 and the 1950s. It was a
time of movement and experience, with life as the teacher.
Recreation seekers more than doubled, and the sale of camp-
ing equipment, braziers and lawn furniture soared. Alcohol
consumption in suburbia mushroomed along with the sale of
aspirin: gin, from 6 million gallons in 1950 to 19 million in
1960; vodka, from 0.1 million to 9 million gallons; and aspirin
from 12 million pounds to 18 million pounds.

"Suburbia was not only a *new* place to *live*, it was a *new*
way to *live*, with more *active* sports, more simple *fun*." I have
italicized (in this Time-Life book statement) keywords for the
number 5. Suburbia created more than a healthy cultural environment for the children; it also created a commuting problem for the family breadwinner, who was faced with
unreliable train schedules and crowded highways. People
were on the move—towards the cities to work and towards
the country to escape.

The decade's curiosity and eagerness for new experience
peaked in its search for cultural enrichments: encyclopedia
sales rose from 72 million in 1950 to 300 million in 1960,
musical instruments from 86 million to 149 million, and
juvenile books from 32 million to 88 million. Six major
magazines were born in the "once stable world of legitimate
magazine publishing": *Flair* (short-lived), *Playboy, Mad, Jet,
Sports Illustrated*, and, to the surprise of many, *T.V. Guide.*

Elvis Presley's nervous gyrations exemplified the decade's
mood in music, but TV dominated the entertainment field. It
came into its own with the premier of a half hour news show,
"See It Now," with Edward R. Murrow. Murrow took
"vigorous editorial stands," which eventually prompted a
simultaneous comment from the *St. Louis Dispatch* and the
New York Herald Tribune: "Television has come of age." This
program received twenty awards in 1954 alone.

To fill in the empty time slots on television, live drama
was introduced and won acceptance by the public—shows like

the "Kraft Television Theatre," "U.S. Steel Hour," "Philco Playhouse," and "Hallmark Hall of Fame."

The dark cloud on the horizon was the knowledge Russia now also had the atomic bomb. The USSR exploded its first A-bomb in the late summer of 1949 and stunned the world. America suddenly realized that the horror of Hiroshima and Nagasaki was on her doorstep. Nobel Prize winning chemist, Harold C. Urey, said: "There is only one thing worse than one nation having the atomic bomb—that's two nations having it." Part of the restlessness of the time was Russia's reneging on its wartime agreements. The Bear had devoured half of Europe and continued feeding its war machinery. By 1950, she had three times as many military planes as the United States, four times as many troops, and thirty tank divisions to our one. And she had the atomic bomb.

It was a time of uneasiness. The film, *On the Beach*, from Nevil Shute's novel depicting in horrifying detail the end of all life on earth as a result of nuclear war, dramatized the nation's fears. Jimmy Dean's portrayal of a lost teenager in *Rebel Without a Cause* further reflected the quandaries of youth. For most teenagers, it was also a time of desperate innocence, as if the lightheartedness and clean fun of their lilliputian world of beach parties, record hops, and hula hoops could erase the looming destruction of atomic war. It was a moment suspended between the sanity of the past and the madness of the future.

The 1960s

The 1960s decade was perfectly summed up in 1965 in Bert Bacharach and Hal David's best-selling song, "What the world needs now is love sweet love." 6 is the number ruling the need for love, balance, harmony, and justice. In 6 there is duty, service, responsibility, and commitment towards home and community, and a need to help others by establishing human rights, equilibrium, and peace. A deep appreciation of art and music emerges because of the 6's fine sense of balance. Beauty and adornment become important. The home, marriage, and intimate personal relationships are emphasized in order to bring greater understanding of universal love through the experience of personal love. 6 is the Cosmic Mother, sex and regeneration. On the 6th day, God created male and female and thus established the interrelation between humanity and divinity.

A wall poster in the Haight-Ashbury section of San Francisco in the 1960s read "Haight is love." It was the hippie generation of love children. "And love was indeed the dominant mood—not only physical love, though currents of eroticism hung like incense in the air, but a kind of indiscriminate love, all embracing brotherliness." To a reporter's inquiry as to who he was and why he was part of the scene a hippie responded: "God is. Love is. I am."

In the summer of 1969, on a rented 600-acre dairy farm in Woodstock, New York, 400,000 young people gathered for three days of music, talk, dance, drink and love. "Despite traffic jams, lack of food, shelter, and sanitation, and blustering rainstorms that turned the crowded hillsides to mud, there was not a single fist fight nor even a disparaging word. In fact, all was love."

Community families sprang up in the hippie communes and in the "retirement towns" exclusively for people over fifty. The need for love, companionship, and sharing reached both ends of the spectrum.

The Beatles beguilingly proclaimed the message of love. Their first hit, "She Loves You," swept the country and started Beatlemania. It was a time of feathers and bangles and baubbles and beads. Psychedelic experiences in color splashed across faces, across the model Twiggy, and over bodies, automobiles, posters and places of entertainment.

The drug cult emerged with Dr. Timothy Leary, a former professor at Harvard University, as its guru. LSD was said to bring a "new expression of love and freedom."

Though panned by critics, Jacqueline Susann's "raunchy sex novel," *Valley of the Dolls,* which brought the author more than one million dollars, dominated the 1960s. Her second novel, *The Love Machine* doubled that total. Helen Gurley Brown's *Sex and the Single Girl* was an overnight best seller in twenty-eight countries and seventeen languages.

The singles subculture was born: singles bars, resorts, publications, apartment houses, tours to Europe and cruises to the Bahamas. It began in 1962 when Grossinger's Hotel in the Catskills sponsored a singles-only weekend, the first event of its kind. And, when Mike O'Harro, on leave and lonely, threw a party for other singles as lonely as he, JOPA (Junior Officers and Professional Association) was created. Three years later it boasted 47,000 members and a million-dollar operation which promoted singles travel and entertainment.

The decade began with an energetic wave of idealism, a "spirit of commitment" exemplified by the Peace Corps. Young President Kennedy and his beautiful wife Jacqueline brought a "magical blend of elegance and vibrance" to the White House. It was a glamorous time; a time of Camelot, misty-eyed optimism, appreciation of beauty and the arts; a time when, as President Kennedy remarked in his inaugural

91

address, "America...will not be afraid of grace and beauty.

On November 22, 1963, Camelot crumbled: the president died by an assassin's bullet. Two days later, the assassin was also dead, the victim of another assassin. President Johnson took over with promises of a Great Society. But the need for human rights had not been answered, and the scales of justice were unbalanced. A routine commitment to defend Vietnam from communist aggression escalated into the third most costly war in American history. Skepticism arose during the 1960s as to the "justness" of the war, a war that (as televesion cameras showed) burned children with napalm, threatened prisoners with torture, chemically defoliated the landscape, and confirmed suspicions that over half of American aid was being siphoned off onto the black market. America was used to fighting "just" wars, wars that were clear and had a cause. No one knew when the war began or why. Antiwar protests began, and culminated with Mayor John Lindsay's campaign for reelection supporting the war protests.

Justice was demanded on another front. Blacks, historically deprived of voting privileges, subjected to segregation and menial jobs, emerged under the nonviolent leadership of Martin Luther King, Jr. "We shall overcome" rang across the land from ocean to ocean. In August, 1963, 200,000 people gathered in Washington to demand civil rights. Riots broke out in the black communities in cities across the nation—in Watts, Los Angeles, and in the black ghettos of Cleveland and Chicago. In Detroit in 1967 the worst race riot of the decade exploded with 42 dead and 386 injured in nine days of fire and looting. Civil rights workers were beaten, shot at, and killed. In April, 1968, Martin Luther King, Jr. was assassinated. Two months later, Robert F. Kennedy lay dead also, another assassination victim. And then, on July 16, 1969, the U.S. Apollo 11 piloted by Neil Armstrong, Edwin Aldrin, Jr., and Michael Collins (who remained in the command module) landed on the Moon. It is curious that the first step on the Moon, a symbol for lovers, would occur under a 6, a Venus and love decade. The 1960s began with a search for love, hope, and peace, and found instead hate, despair, and war. The scales had tipped and society set about to balance them once again.

The 1970s

During the 1970s the number 7 ruled. 7 represents rest, reflection, analysis, deep thought, and an inner search for answers. It is a time to retreat from the outer world, which, mysteriously, can take care of itself. (It is said God rested on the 7th day;

therefore, this is not a time to push external affairs, because illness can result: one is then forced to take it easy in a sick bed.) Events will climax on their own because the energy has already been expended. Now one should perfect what is already in motion. Corinne Heline says in *The Sacred Science of Numbers* (New Age Press, 1976) that 7 is not "the cessation of activity but emergence from chaos into a higher and more perfect order." Metaphysical, religious and philosophical topics are highlighted in conjunction with physical health. 7 avoids crowds and needs time to contemplate self through intuition, visions, dreams and spiritual realization. Mental analysis awakens knowledge, and knowledge is power. 7 is the reformer presenting ideas to the world. On the negative side, 7 becomes suspicious, cynical, aloof, and a law unto itself, demanding acceptance of its ideas.

In the first paragraph of an article from the January 7th, 1980, issue of *Time* Magazine which capsulized the decade of the 1970s, the third sentence read: "The American gaze turned inward." Social critic Tom Wolfe called the 1970s the "Me Decade." "Waves of self awareness disciplines," from Rolfing, est and Arica, to Transactional Analysis, Silva Mind Control and Transcendental Meditation, washed over the country. "The question uppermost in the collective consciousness of the 1970s was, Who am I?" We "set about fumigating, refurnishing and redecorating the inner space of the American psyche." It was a decade of "dreamily obsessive self-regard," a time to "soothe troubled psyches and spirits," "to get it all together." Part of getting it all together was the physical aspect of the 7, and the decade saw an exercise boom. Over forty million Americans, or one-fifth of the country's population, were jogging either part or full time. Sneaker sales soared and publications on running popped up everywhere. Running was not only an exercise, but also a drug, a religion. One writer stated that through running, "we can drain off tension and negative emotions, heighten creativity and enter altered states of consciousness . . ." Running made men and women feel very good about themselves.

Organized religion experienced a revival. Spiritual study groups sprang up all over the country and born-again Christians proclaimed the Gospel. Bumper stickers directed: "Honk if you love Jesus," and "May the *Force* Be With You." Sinister religious insanity surfaced in cults that kidnapped and brainwashed young followers, who were often "re-kidnapped" and deprogrammed by concerned parents. This religious insidiousness culminated at Jonestown, Guyana, where 911 followers of Reverend Jim Jones died in a mass suicide.

The shrinking dollar caused us to pause and question our

immersion in materialism. The Arab oil boycott of 1973 and the ensuing lines at the gas pumps presented the possibility that the United States' "astonishing material indulgence" might end. Gradually the nation was absorbing "the difficult lessons about the limits of its power and resources." In fact, in 1979, productivity actually decreased, showing the influence of the number 7's peaking and passivity.

On the negative side of number 7, a "new breed of self-righteous young assassins" formed secret organizations and used terror "to undermine political order around the world" spreading "fogs of fear" over governments. A decade of murder, kidnappings, bombings and hijackings emerged.

The number 7 brings issues to a head, issues that have been brewing from the beginning, in this case from the 1900s on. In the 1970s we had the "biggest women's protest marches since the days of the suffragettes." Songs like "I Am Woman" declared the female sentiment. In March, 1971, Indira Gandhi won a landslide victory in her bid for Prime Minister of India with two-thirds of the parliamentary seats. In 1979 Margaret Thatcher became Britain's first woman Prime Minister.

The oil issue culminated when Saudi Arabia took over their own oil wells from the United States-Arabian oil consortium. Suddenly the world's wealth fell into the hands of a few obscure people and created havoc with world economy.

The tax issue hit a peak when California voters approved Proposition 13, which cut property taxes in half. Antiwar sentiment came to a head when young students were killed at Kent State. Sixty percent of all Americans were then against the war in Vietnam—a pressure which helped to end U.S. involvement in the war in 1975. President Sadat of Egypt visited Israel in an unprecedented move towards peace, breaking twenty-nine years of hostility. Jimmy Carter, a dark horse candidate who proclaimed "a special relationship with God," became the president who would mediate in this peace settlement in the years ahead. "Blessed are the peacemakers" he said as the Middle East Peace Treaty was signed in September, 1978.

Moral issues emerged. Watergate revealed the hidden machinations of government leaders and resulted in the resignation in disgrace of an American president and prison sentences for a number of his aides. In 1974 President Nixon "found himself posturing in limbo." He waved the victory sign as a helicopter "lifted him away to exile."

Another moral issue surfaced in the enormous unknown risks of nuclear power. Three Mile Island became a symbol of the insanity and total destruction some people felt nuclear power would wreak on the world. Organized masses gathered at nuclear plants around the country to protest their construction. The issue of cloning touched off controversy over its morality and the responsibility to God and humanity.

On the brighter side, Hank Aaron broke Babe Ruth's record with his 715th home run, and Lou Brock broke Ty Cobb's standing record of 49 years by stealing his 893rd base. The racial issue culminated in the most celebrated book and subsequent television drama of the decade, Alex Haley's *Roots*, viewed by 130 million Americans.

The cinema touched the pulse of the nation with *"All the President's Men, The China Syndrome, Raid on Entebbe, The Godfather, The Deerhunter*, and *Boys From Brazil. Star Wars*, the biggest success in movie history, was an exercise in the mental reaching and philosophical needs of the decade; the forces of good versus the forces of evil. The blessing, *May the Force Be With You*, spoke an eloquent plea in our inner call for divine guidance.

What Will the 1980s Bring?

We have just begun a new decade ruled by the 8. Number 8 is karma, as ye sow, so shall ye reap; as it is above, so it is below; for every action there is an equal and opposite reaction. In other words, we are going to get exactly what we deserve. 8 is balance, strength, discipline, fortitude, intelligence and respect. It is practical, tough, fair, just and careful. Under 8, we move more cautiously, implementing big ideas and plans. It is a time of work, unity, organization and authority. The number 8 implies restriction and responsibility, a shaving down, a cutting of losses, a shedding of excess. The shape of the figure 8 implies a pinched waistline, a time to tighten our belts.

8, Scorpio, Pluto and Saturn work together changing the "Me Decade" of the 1970s to the "We Decade" of the 1980s. 8—two circles together. The rainbow, representative of the number 8 (see page 61), may become the decade's most popular symbol, now splashed over T-shirts, posters, advertisements, jewelry and business emblems. Because they relate to the number 8, areas such as taxes, birth, death, underground activity, the masses, insurance, sex, justice, money, business and finance will be key issues. The negative side of the 8 brings fear, loss and unnecessary restriction.

We are only three months into the decade (as of this writing, March, 1980), and I have just heard President Carter's first major address of the year. The nouns, verbs, and adjectives in his speech can be used as keywords for the number 8. His economic message to the nation was delivered on March 14, 1980, a 35/8 day, and the issue was inflation. Because of the

95

strain in the financial market, restraints will be imposed on the use of credit cards and on the lending policies of banks not with the Federal Reserve and on other money-lending institutions. Federal loans and guarantees will be cut by four billion dollars. A ten cents per gallon tax will be imposed on foreign oil (for gasoline use only), and the funds will be used to reduce the national debt. A team of experts will track and investigate increases in wage and price developments that are out of line. These are just the first tough measures to fight inflation in the coming 1980s. The budget must be balanced in this decade.

President Carter went on to remark that our excessive dependence on foreign oil, the price of which was doubled in the last twelve months (March, 1979, to March, 1980), must end. Increased conservation and production of home oil and other sources of energy must be instituted. "America's extravagant gasoline use" must be curtailed. He spoke of "long term structural changes" that will not be easy. The "New budget is very tight;" there are "some things we cannot afford." Balancing the budget is the first order of the day. Tax relief may follow to encourage the economy. He used words like "pain," "cost," "inconvenience," "discipline," "patience," all keywords for number 8. He warned that we should not look for massive changes next week, that we must "take control of the problem which means take control of ourselves," "that we must put aside fear, face the world as it is, be honest about hard decisions and with courage carry them out," and that we must build a strong America. His last sentence had 8 written all over it: "With the proper discipline, we will prevail in our fight against inflation."

Because we are no longer in the mood for extravagance and waste, the presidents we elect this year and in the coming two election years of this decade will be serious, strong, confident, older perhaps, and tough. We will want individuals who speak plainly and honestly, and who mean business. There will be few give away programs in this decade because we are ready for discipline. Like a spoiled child having a tantrum, we are demanding a hard hand.

The March 24, 1980 cover of *Time* Magazine read "Carter vs. Inflation...The President's demand: 'discipline... discipline...discipline.'" A major keyword for number 8 is discipline.

Numerous articles and news items now speak of the energy crises. The gasoline crunch will produce "fuel frugal vehicles" that will get many more miles per gallon. Companies are planning to trim down cars, reduce weight, build smaller engines with more efficient fuel management systems, and design "cleaner" bodies for lower wind resistance. Sources of fuel will change drastically in the 1980s. A southern university professor has produced, after fifteen years of research, a synthetic gasoline which is nonpollutant and which can be extracted from U.S. coal reserves. His work was inspired by the Germans who produced gasoline from coal during World War II. The cost is now $1.25 per gallon. This could eventually be reduced to eighty cents.

Garbage may be another fuel source. I envision receptacles built into kitchen counters, one marked paper goods, the other food refuse, into which homemakers can discard "garbage" items. These feed into a system in the basement that converts the garbage into fuel to heat the home. This process would eliminate unsightly dumps and free many acres of land for other uses; would do away with garbage collection (and strikes that leave garbage piled high on city streets), costly equipment, and maintenance; would free a labor force for other jobs, as well as relieve our dependence on other energy sources.

The 1980s may see nuclear disaster resulting from human error at a nuclear plant. Criminal plant takeover or hijacking nuclear wastes for extortion is possible. Disasters could cause mass evacuations. All this will turn the public away from the use of nuclear energy towards solar power as the safest, cheapest, cleanest, and most natural source of energy.

Total reliance on solar energy is feasible in the 1980s. Homes are being built right now that can store solar energy up to three days without the sun, and heat an entire home comfortably, efficiently, and inexpensively. The public will become aware of these methods, regardless of the efforts of vested interests to prevent it. The year 1980 is formed with four 0's; one in the 9, two in the 8, and one in the 0. The 0 is the God symbol, the Light; the Sun has always been a symbol for the God power. This is the decade of the God power, the Light, the Sun's energy. Businesses that produce and install proper solar energy systems will prosper, some becoming very wealthy.

Groups to fight taxes will continue to rise and gain power and will eventually bring about a complete overhaul of the tax structure in this country. The world of finance and our basic monetary system seems to be gasping its last breath. By the end of the decade we may not recognize our means of exchange. Gold, historically valuable, will always be so, but it will temporarily lose its value over the next decade, perhaps two. We cannot eat it, live in it, wear it for protection, or ride on or in it. Only useful commodities will be valuable. It is said there are built-in safeguards against another stock market crash, and that banks are insured; however, underground rumblings are shaking these foundations as well.

Marriage and "old fashioned morality" is back in style. Stricter ideas regarding matrimony will prevail, providing solidity to this now shaky institution. A new respect for sex and love relationships will surface. On the negative side, diseases of generative organs may appear in epidemic proportions, reflecting our misuse of the creative power and our basic resources. Changes in the law regarding prostitution may surprise many.

The legal system is ready for an overhaul. This has already begun with the publication of Woodward and Armstrong's best selling book. *The Brethren*, an expose of the Supreme Court. These judges are no longer sacred cows, and will be subject to new laws that require mental health checkups as well as ethical conduct.

Organized crime, a quietly powerful entity, will have internal conflicts along with public confrontations. Having already infiltrated many areas of public life, crime will emerge in the most shocking places, and mass confrontations may cause difficulty. Power struggles of great magnitude are possible. No institution, from organized religion to the banking community, will be exempt.

Underground insects, poisonous snakes, and scorpions may emerge as the decade's heroes, providing serums for the "social diseases," sterility, arthritis, paralysis and acne. They may provide a serum that will enable severed limbs and joints to regenerate themselves.

Archeological digs may uncover fabulous lost cities and civilizations, some unknown to us today. Many secrets of the ancient past may be revealed, perhaps through natural disasters that open or rearrange the contour of the earth.

Burial ceremonies will change drastically. Cremation may become the only plausible answer to crowded land conditions, and traditional burial procedures may be cast aside as people choose more meaningful methods. Death and birth will take on new meaning as the metaphysical aspects of both are revealed.

Work, organization, unity and respect for authority—all number 8 attitudes—are already evident. An article by Lance Morrow in the March 10, 1980, issue of *Time* magazine eloquently states: "A complicated impulse has stirred in America's thinking about their country and its place in the world. Patriotism has reappeared." He goes on to speak about "the emergence of a new patriotic impulse in America," that "the villains have moved overseas again," and how Americans now "find they are in an unexpected kinship of common interests." He speaks of America's finest feeling of patriotism as "uniquely difficult and valuable; it is a devotion...to a political and social vision, a promise and the idea of freedom—an idea not much honored elsewhere in the world or in history." This renewed patriotism should bring about a rise in the sale of American flags, military paraphernalia, and changes in hair and clothing styles that will reflect the military.

Athletics will become even more important in the 1980s as we feel the need to test our strengths. I see the martial arts as a rapidly growing area of interest as well as fencing, ballet and all esthetic athletic pursuits that stress balance and beauty, where mental and physical aspects of the self must work together. The athletic system itself will be tested as athletes and their managers undergo stressful relations.

Gardening may take on a new shape. The tiny square plots of land called victory gardens in the 1940s exemplified the productivity of the 4 and the square with its four sides. The four is even drawn much like a square, 4 . The number 8 is a solidified square, or double 4. Productivity is again important. Since the 8 is formed with circles we may discover that somehow growing foods in circular arrangements becomes important. A friend just last week told me about a woman who has come up with an idea for growing potatoes in a barrel (round) which can produce enough for a family for an entire winter. This same friend of mine has a relative who is growing her vegetables in a pail. Shapes have their own peculiar energies, and since the circle is the God energy, perhaps we will find we have been growing our food within the wrong outline, and that somehow even the seed will react to the circular shape as we do. All is consciousness. Who are we to define the limits of the God consciousness, especially when we are living under the 8 for a decade?

We are only four months into 1980 (as of this writing) and so far the rewards from this karmic 80 decade are not encouraging. Fifty American hostages are still being held by Iranian militant students at the American embassy in Iran and the Iranians are threatening to kill the hostages if America steps out of line. The United States promises retaliation if one American is harmed. Russia has invaded Afghanistan and set up a puppet regime threatening the borders of other oil producing nations; the world economy is in serious jeopardy; the Catholic church is attempting to silence its intellectual priests who are openly questioning certain church tenets, and although difficult international negotiations continue, war seems more imminent each day. We sit on a powder keg, waiting for one rash action to send the world into pandemonium. The negative thinking of the past years, constantly sent out from our minds into the environment, has accumulated into a heavy cloud which now surrounds the earth, disturbing the harmonious flow of the natural rhythm of things. We cannot expect the earth, or the elements, to remain silent. The earth in retaliation will speak most eloquently as she unleashes her power. Mt. St. Helens in Washington state has been rumbling and smoking for weeks as if parodying the rumbling and smoking of world leaders. Iran has suffered a number of earthquakes since the hostage situation began. We can expect more from the elements now and in the coming years. They will speak in the areas that are the most troubled.

It is apparent that we may all suffer because of the actions and ensuing results in a tiny section of the world. Events today are no longer isolated acts; they send repercussions around the world. We are all under the Universal Year Cycle 9 (1 + 9 + 8 + 0 = 18/9), and we must all clean house, let go of worn out ideas, be charitable, have compassion and be ready to change. It is time to act and we as a world know it, feel it, and must comply, or it will be forcibly enacted by Cosmic Law. We need to change—for the better. This could be the last chance before Armageddon.

In the latter part of 1982, an unusual perfect alignment of all nine planets on the same side of the Sun occurs in our solar system. In their book, *The Jupiter Effect*, John Gribbin, science editor of *Nature* magazine, and Stephen Plagemann of NASA's Goddard Space Center in Maryland, bring out interesting points which make one wonder if this effect is the Apocalyptic prediction of Revelations.

The authors point out that the planets have an effect upon each other and upon the earth. Earthquakes are one of the effects of certain planetary conjunctions. It has been noted that conjunctions of two or more of the planets Mars, Jupiter and Saturn cause sunspots which in turn are directly related to war, economic crashes and earthquakes. These three planets are in Virgo this year, and Jupiter and Saturn make a conjunction as well. Earthquakes have been hot and heavy since the fall of 1975, and certainly no one can deny the possibilities of economic depression and war (the Iranian-Afghanistan-Russian crisis). The authors go on to point out many possible effects of this total planetary alignment: firestorm activity in the Sun, a change in the earth's ionosphere, changes in wind, rain and termperature patterns, an altering of the rotation of the earth thus effecting the day's length and causing more earthquakes. The long predicted California quake may result from this 1982 alignment.

Pluto, the power of transformation, enters Scorpio late in 1983, retrogrades out and returns in 1984. (Do you recall

George Orwell's novel *1984*?) Pluto, the destroyer, was discovered in 1930 in the sign of Cancer. A slow moving planet, it will enter its own sign, Scorpio (the house of birth, death and transformation) in 1983–1984 for a fourteen-year transit. A planet is always the most powerful in its own sign. This is the first time since the discovery of Pluto that it has been in Scorpio. A brief examination of the planet Pluto and the sign Scorpio reveals what the possibilities are in the coming years. Pluto and Scorpio rule such things as atomic energy, plutonium, the masses, power struggles and mass destruction as well as rebirth and new life.

I am an optimist. I believe in never-ending life, in the continuance of our energy and the goodness of the Cosmic Force, God. I know that no matter what happens we will be alright, we will survive, we will learn, we will grow and be reborn—even if this process must occur upon the ashes of atomic warfare. We have probably done this before—with the terrible crystal in Atlantis (perhaps even before that in the shrouds of history long lost to us). But now, we have the awareness, we know what the possibilities are. We can see the trends, and there are many who pray and work every day to counteract the negativity in this world. Perhaps this time around the goodness will prevail, the positive energy will counteract and absorb the negative, teaching us that division is only an illusion. This game of life is just that—a game—and if we could see ourselves desperately struggling for power in this material world we would laugh at the emptiness of it all. Perhaps we will learn, this time around, that life is to be lived joyously, completely, with reverence and respect for all peoples and all ideas.

The Age of Aquarius

A final note on what is called the Aquarian Age might be appropriate here. Because of a phenomenon known as the Precession of the Equinoxes, during which the starting point of the zodiac of signs, zero degrees Aries, moves backward through the twelve zodiacal constellations of stars in periods called Ages (each lasting approximately 2,160 years), we are now entering what is called the Aquarian Age, having just finished the Piscean Age.

A cursory look through history reveals startling parallels between the overall emphasis of the Ages and the corresponding signs of the zodiac. Remembering that signs pick up their opposite polarities, or their opposite sign, let's examine a few Ages.

In Egypt, during the Taurean Age, approximately 4,000

101

to 2,000 BC (the Taurus-Scorpio polarity), the culture utilized the bull and eagle as symbols for their society. The bull (Taurus) representing the earth and its yield, was worshipped as the life-giving source for the people; and the eagle or the falcon, the higher side of Scorpio, adorned the headresses of the pharaohs.

When Moses brought the two tablets off Mt. Sinai, the Arian Age began, approximately 2,000 BC–33 AD (Aries-Libra). Moses scorned the worshipping of the golden calf (the baby bull, Taurus). The Taurean Age was at an end. His two tablets with the Law, the Ten commandments, represent Libra, the two scales of justice, law, and balance. His people then began to sacrifice rams or lambs (Aries) at the altar, purified through fire (Aries is a fire sign).

With the birth of Christ and his subsequent death and resurrection, the Piscean Age, 0–2,000 AD was introduced (Pisces-Virgo). Pisces is the fish, the early symbol for Christianity. Christ fed the multitudes with fish and bread. Virgo, its opposite polarity, symbolizes the Virgin, and rules bread and wine, used in the Christian sacraments. Pisces is a water sign, and Christians baptize in water.

We are now on the brink of the Aquarian Age, 2,000–4,000 AD (Aquarius-Leo). There has been much speculation as to the exact date that ushers in this new age. Some say the late 1800s, other feel it is this decade, the 1980's. Still others have differing ideas. But perhaps, after all this conjecture, the Aquarian Age has no exact point of change, no precise cut off between one age and another, as if a guillotine fell through time separating the ages irrevocably one from another. An Age of 2,160 years is a long time, and it seems to me that transition would take a little while. I propose that the turning point from the Piscean Age to the Aquarian Age is the entire 20th century, or from 1900–2000 AD. It makes sense that such a vast psychological and philosophical change would take 100 years. It is just possible that an Age, like a person, needs a full cycle to bring about a total change. Every nine years we go through a single complete change, solidified on the 10 or next number 1 cycle. As it is below, so it is above. Perhaps the Age needs one full cycle, from 1900 to 2000, to complete its change.

The 1900's ushered in a rebirth of metaphysics. Not for many years have there been so many and such prolific writers on this subject as we have had since the turn of the century. Their works are still being brought out of the dust of the past and reprinted. We delight in such authors as Mme. Blavatsky, Corinne Heline, Rudolph Steiner, Manly Hall, Evangeline Adams, Mark Edmund Jones, Leonora Luxton and Marie

Corelli. These and like individuals have revived the ancient wisdom and are ushering us into this new Aquarian Age. This century has produced fine metaphysical thinkers and writers: Faith Javane, Robert Pelletier, Robert Hand, Steven Arroyo, Marcia Moore, Isabel Hickey, Grant Lewi and more. We are immersed in the changing of the guard. The date line in the Great Pyramid, a 6,000 year line of history, ends with the year 2,001. The unusual film, *Space Odyssey: 2001*, also marked this year as significant. Coincidence? Perhaps. But perhaps by the year 2,001, we will truly have ended the Piscean Age and entered the Aquarian Age.

6

THE PRESIDENTIAL ORDER

AND TAROT KEYS

THE BASIC SEQUENCE of the numbers 1 through 9 operates in our universe from the most personal level to the greatest of cosmic events. Examination of the personal cycles in our lives and the events that fall within specific decades has shown that the consecutive numerical sequences are accurate. If a single year in our life responds to the number under which it is operating, and if these nine-year cycles are repeated over and over throughout our lifetimes, and if the decades themselves respond to the number by which they are known, it is then reasonable to assume that each century with its decades and each millenium with its centuries will respond the same way. In fact, everything operates within the 1 through 9 cycles, the rhythm of life.

Working within this concept and knowing that the appropriate events occur under corresponding numerical vibrations, I wondered if the numerical sequence of the presidents of the United States had significance. Although I knew instinctively that these numbers had to be important I approached my research with objectivity. Since the Tarot keys relate numerically as well, I thought it would be enlightening to include them along with the presidential information. Their symbology tells more than volumes could relate.

If you decide to research these Tarot correlations further, find a quiet corner, relax and hold the Tarot card before you. Let your mind flow freely. Insights and correspondences that I would never have thought of could come to you because your background of experience is different than mine. The symbology on these cards is so deep that many pages could be written on each one and still not cover the vast experiences the cards relate.

Before we go on, it is important that you understand the divisions of the Tarot deck. Basically, the Tarot is divided into three segments: Key 0, the Fool, which stands alone as the God energy; Keys 1 through 21, the Major Arcana, representing the entire evolutionary process in each lifetime; and Keys 23 through 78, the Minor Arcana, representing the earthly attitudes and experiences of each lifetime. There is no Key 22. 22 is actually Key 0, the Fool, after completing one cycle of experience. The Minor Arcana are made up of the Wands, 23 through 36, the element Fire, which is our drive and ambition; the Cups, 37 through 50, the element Water, which represents our emotions; the Swords, 51 through 64, the element Air, our intellect and thinking processes; and the Pentacles, 65 through 78, the element Earth, our money and possessions.

Notice how the presidents who fall within certain divisions of the Tarot deck fulfill the essence of that section. The first twenty-one presidents were responsible for setting the foundation of this country; presidents 22 through 36, under the Wands, were necessarily ambitious, driving individuals whose prime purpose was to establish this nation as an independent entity in the world. Our recent and future presidents, from 37 through 50, under the Cups, need the compassion, understanding, nurturing and somewhat passive attitude that this portion of the deck reflects. The powder-keg condition of international relations today certainly requires that America, the most powerful nation in the world, have compassionate leaders in the White House.

In this chapter I propose that the sequence of numbers within the presidential order sends out a call for the particular vibration needed at that time in history. The need is then filled by the person elected. We all react to our personal cycles, as shown in Chapter 2. Moreover, we all react to the numerical influence of the decades, as proven in the previous chapter.

Therefore, it is reasonable that we, as a group consciousness, would react to our country's needs by electing the appropriate president at the proper time. The sequence of numbers is not arbitrary, as has been proven, but has a deliberate structure oriented towards a specific goal. When our country needs to expand, it will elect a president who will take care of that need; and when our country needs to conserve, it will again elect the right person for the time.

We subconsciously understand that the number of the presidential term is important. Notice how we say "the 36th president" when referring to Lyndon Johnson or the 38th president when referring to Gerald Ford. We do not say "the ex-president" or "the president in 1974." We designate them by the numbers of their terms. We do this because we instinctively know the meaning of the numbers; and by expressing the number we are revealing much more about the president than we consciously realize. If, in talking with an individual who knows absolutely nothing about the meanings of the numbers, you ask him or her to speak the first words that come to mind when you give a single or a double number, you will find that the individual describes the number accurately. We know at deep levels of mind the true meanings of all things, and even though we are not always consciously aware of our knowledge, we speak these truths every day.

Just as we as individuals have our four personal numbers, so does a nation have its own four peculiar vibrations. In the following presidential analyses we will need to have the personal numbers of our nation on hand. They are calculated here. We are known as "The United States of America." We will include "The" because it is part of our country's name. We do not say "The England" or "The Africa," but we do say "The United States." We also commonly call this nation "America," and, although this is merely a nickname, it has been used often enough to qualify as a necessary part of the analysis. Our birthdate is July 4, 1776.

```
      5   3   9   5       1   5     6     1   5   9   1 =50/5 Soul
     THE  UNITED  STATES   OF   AMERICA
     2 8       5   2   4   1 2   2   1    6      4   9   3  =49/4 Outer Personality
                                                      99/18/9 Path of Destiny
```

```
          1   5   9   1 =16/7 Soul
        AMERICA
          4   9   3   =16/7 Outer Personality
              32/5 Path of Destiny
```

July 4, 1776: $7+4+21(1+7+7+6)=32/5$ Life Lesson Number

Notice that in America, the Soul and Outer Personality Numbers are identical. Whenever I see this in a chart I say "What you see is what you get." In other words, the inner and outer personality are the same. There is no falseness in the impression you receive from the individual.

Notice that America's Path of Destiny and Life Lesson Number are the same. This intensifies the Life Lesson and indicates that America must walk a straight and narrow path embodying the principles "for which she stands."

America's chart looks like this:

	The United States of America		America
Soul	50/5	or	16/7
Outer Personality	49/4	or	16/7
Path of Destiny	99/9	or	32/5
Life Lesson	32/5		

32/5 is a very important number in our destiny. It is a number that influences nations and peoples. Charles Darwin, Abraham Lincoln and Thomas Jefferson are just a few who had a 32/5 Life Lesson Number, and their works have influenced millions throughout history.

With this information as a basis, we will examine the presidencies to determine if their numerical order drew the kind of man needed at the time, and if the ensuing decisions, events and legacies of their offices correlate with their number sequence.

The following list of the American presidents by birthdate and astrological sign should prove helpful in the presidential analyses.

Aries: March 29 - John Tyler
April 2 (O.S.)
April 13 (N.S.) - Thomas Jefferson*

Taurus: April 23 - James Buchanan
April 27 - Ulysses Grant
April 28 - James Monroe
May 8 - Harry Truman

Gemini: May 29 - John Kennedy

Cancer: July 4 - Calvin Coolidge
July 11 - John Quincy Adams
July 14 - Gerald Ford

Leo: August 10 - Herbert Hoover
August 20 - Benjamin Harrison

Virgo: August 27 - Lyndon Johnson
September 15 - William Taft

Libra: October 1 - Jimmy Carter
October 4 - Rutherford Hayes
October 5 - Chester Arthur
October 14 - Dwight Eisenhower
October 19 (O.S.)
October 30 (N.S.) - John Adams*

Scorpio: October 27 - Theodore Roosevelt
November 2 - Warren Harding
November 2 - James Polk
November 19 - James Garfield

Sagitarrius: November 23 - Franklin Pierce
November 24 - Zachary Taylor
December 5 - Martin Van Buren

Capricorn: December 28 - Woodrow Wilson
December 29 - Andrew Johnson
January 7 - Millard Fillmore
January 9 - Richard Nixon

Aquarius: January 29 - William McKinley
January 30 - Franklin Roosevelt
February 9 - William Harrison
February 11 (O.S.)
February 22 (N.S.) - George
Washington*
February 12 - Abraham Lincoln

Pisces: March 5 (O.S.)
March 16 (N.S.) - James Madison*
March 15 - Andrew Jackson
March 18 - Grover Cleveland

The dates of the presidents' terms are calculated from election year rather than inauguration year.

---

*Footnote: The Gregorian calendar was adopted by England and her colonies in 1752; this added eleven days to the calendar. The New Style (N.S.) calendar birthdays attributed to historical persons reveal how history views them. The Old Style (O.S.) calendar birthdays are an indication of what they were here to learn in their lifetimes.

1 KEY 1: THE MAGICIAN consciously fixes his attention on a specific goal and through sheer will, using his body as a channel, directs the divine life force into the material world where the goal becomes a reality. The Magician's conscious mind has perfect control over earthly things. As tools, he has the four elements: Fire (wand), Earth (pentacle), Air (sword), and Water (cup) representing spirit, body, mind and soul. Number 1 is a strong, independent vibration requiring the exercise of will to direct the future course of the cycle.

George Washington: First President. Born: February 11, 1732 (O.S.). Life Lesson Number: 26/8. February 22, 1732 (N.S.). Life Lesson Number: 37/1. President: 1789-1796. George Washington was not "the man who would be king," to quote Kipling, but the man who could have been king. He was offered this position but declined, stating it was the very thing he had fought against. Seen as a leader, under a Life Lesson Number 1, he was well over six feet tall with fiery red hair and a temper to match. It is said that it was the sheer force of his personality that held the tattered Continental Army together that bitter winter at Valley Forge. No one dared desert. After the war, he was the only man for the presidency. He had proven himself on the battlefield and had won not only the war but also the loyalty of his people. He was "first in war, first in peace and first in the hearts of his countrymen." Thomas Jefferson, urging Washington to run for a second term, spoke for the nation when he said, "the confidence of the whole Union is centered in you...North and South will hang together if they have you to hang on." When Washington died, Jefferson wrote: "Never did nature and fortune combine more perfectly to make a man great, and to place him in . . . an everlasting remembrance."

America wanted a flawless hero, and despite the political slander and the difficulties that marred his two terms, he emerged as a demigod, a Magician who united the country, who used himself as a channel, taking the power from above and directing it into earthly affairs. Historian W.E. Woodward may have been correct when he wrote that "people think they do not understand Washington because they can find in him nothing that is not within themselves." "It was this quality that contributed to his greatness. He was the American common denominator, the average man deified and raised to the nth power."

George Washington was the Magician, the only power in his day who could have transformed a disorganized people into a great nation.

THE HIGH PRIESTESS

2 KEY 2: THE HIGH PRIESTESS represents the subconscious mind where all memory is recorded. The curtain behind the High Priestess connects the two columns of light and darkness, and as such indicates pairs of opposites which must be kept in balance. The scroll on her lap is partially hidden because God has more to reveal. Number 2 represents hidden, secret workings, division which can lead to dissension, balance, and mediation. Elements are at work that are not always obvious on the suface. 2 is the peacemaker who can see both sides.

John Adams: Second President. Born: October 30, 1735 (N.S.) Life Lesson Number: 56/11. October 19, 1735 (O.S.). Life Lesson Number: 45/9. President: 1796-1800. John Adams, a brilliant intellectual with a unique character, was "haughty, condescending, self-righteous, and cantankerous." He was so aloof that even those he joined were not always sure he was on their side. When he was, however, they were elated, because he was "incorruptible and extraordinarily intelligent, and he had the courage to stand by his convictions at any cost." Another outstanding trait was his introspectiveness. "He could be unusually objective about himself . . ."

After Washington, Adams had a tough act to follow right from the beginning. He tried to take Jefferson and Hamilton into his confidence, but failed to do so. The Adams-Hamilton conflict was a thorn in the side of the administration and eventually caused the downfall of Adams.

John Adams found himself to be the "man in the middle" in the French-English antagonisms. He was biased against aristocratic England and unsympathetic towards the French revolutionists. Underground chicanery by the French resulted in Adams' publicizing the XYZ Affair, an anonymous label given to the three agents sent secretly by Talleyrand to Paris to blackmail Adams' diplomats who were on a mission of peace. Eventually, however, good relations were restored, and Adams, so valuing his role as peacemaker, soon after composed his own epitaph: "Here lies John Adams, who took upon himself the responsibility of the peace with France in the year 1800."

Secrecy and suspicion surfaced in the Alien and Sedition Acts passed by the Federalists. The Alien Act gave the president power to expel foreigners he considered dangerous. And the Alien Enemies Act gave him the power to expel or imprison citizens of any nation at war with the United States.

John Adams' "introspectiveness," his role as a "man in the middle," the passing of the Alien and Sedition Acts, and his own epitaph as the person responsible for the peace with France all qualify him as the Number 2 president.

Just as the High Priestess sits in the shadow between the Magician and the Empress, the cards on either side of this number, so did John Adams preside between George Washington and Thomas Jefferson. He was overshadowed in his day by both great men—literally a man in the middle. The balance of the High Priestess was exemplified in Adams' pride in his role as a peacemaker.

3 KEY 3: THE EMPRESS is that part of the subconscious mind that responds to the memory of the High Priestess and produces growth through imagination. She is pictured as pregnant; the landscape around her is blooming as well. She has combined the will of the Magician, Key 1, with the memory of the High Priestess, Key 2, and brought forth life, Key 3. Number 3 is the activity behind all manifestation. It is growth, expansion and freedom; self-expression, extravagance and luck. Many talents and interests unfold under a 3, and freedom and growth are the keywords.

Thomas Jefferson: Third President. Born: April 13, 1743 (N.S.). Life Lesson Number: 32/5 (same as U.S. Life Lesson Number and Path of Destiny Number of America). April 2, 1743 (O.S.). Life Lesson Number: 21/3. President: 1800-1808. Thomas Jefferson, author of the Declaration of Independence, had a range of skills that was almost unbelievable: politician and statesman, writer, lawyer, inventor, farmer, musician, philosopher, scientist, surveyor, linguist and botanist. Books were the "greatest of all amusements," he said.

Without a doubt, the purchase of the Louisiana Territory, which doubled the size of the United States, was the most important event of Jefferson's first term. He was also responsible for the Lewis and Clark expedition, which mapped the Missouri River and added to the public knowledge of the American West.

While still a delegate to the Virginia House, he introduced the Act for Establishing Religious Freedom, a classic bill guaranteeing that "all men shall be free to profess, and by argument to maintain, their opinions in matters of religion, and that the same shall in nowise diminish, enlarge or affect their civil capacities." While in Europe, he observed the inequality in French society and wrote, "There is not a crowned head in Europe whose talents or merits would entitle him to be elected a vestry man by . . . any parish in America." He maintained his philosophy of freedom all his life. Ten days before he died he wrote that America should be to the world "the signal of arousing men to burst their chains," and "that the mass of mankind has not been born with saddles on their backs, nor a favored few, booted and spurred, ready to ride them legitimately by the Grace of God."

In later years, Abraham Lincoln would say, "The principles of Jefferson are the definitions and axioms of a free society."

The Declaration of Independence, the expansion of America through the purchase of the Louisiana Territory and Jefferson's constant emphasis on individual freedoms graphically brought out the influence of the Number 3.

On the Tarot card, the growth, abundance, and freedom of life that Thomas Jefferson expressed is obvious in the Empress's pregnancy and all the "growing things" about her.

THE EMPEROR.

4 KEY 4: THE EMPEROR symbolizes reason, which is a function of the conscious mind. In his wisdom, he handles the affairs of the material world in a systematic manner. This card brings a cohesion of the first three keys, producing concrete results. In Key 4, the Emperor is the Magician, now older, having gained wisdom and authority. Number 4 is stability, solidity, work, organization, and foundation.

James Madison: Fourth President. Born: March 16, 1751 (N.S.). Life Lesson Number: 33 (Master Number). March 5, 1751 (O.S.). Life Lesson Number: 22. President: 1808-1816. James Madison, called a "giant in the history of the United States," was Father of the Constitution, a congressman, "chief organizer of the Democratic-Republican party, Secretary of State and President." He was described as knowledgeable, witty, satirical, and earthy. He could converse on Greek philosophy with Thomas Jefferson but was "quite capable of making small talk" with less erudite guests. Long an advocate of strength through solidification, Madison arrived in Philadelphia for the Constitutional Convention in 1787 with his own two documents which "presented example after example of nations gaining strength and longevity under a central authority" but failing and dissolving when ruled by individual elements. His willingness to work, his ability to organize, and his inclination to compromise made him the "Father of the Constitution." Madison's two terms were troubled by the War of 1812, the Creek War, and the burning of Washington in 1814, but nevertheless, when he retired to Virginia in 1817, he handed President James Monroe "the leadership of a strong and proud United States, beginning an 'era of good feelings.'"

The Emperor is the Magician grown older, the solid father figure. Madison's position as "father of the Constitution" and "chief organizer," and advocate of solidification through strength, qualify him as Number 4 and as the Emperor.

5 KEY 5: THE HIEROPHANT represents true intuition, inner hearing, based on reason, Key 4, the Emperor. After all the facts have been gathered by the conscious mind and fed into the subconscious, the subconscious assimilates, sorts and sends back, in a flash of intuition, the correct analysis. The Hierophant's triple crown represents the conscious, subconscious, and superconscious minds. The first two fingers of his right hand, raised in blessing, represent the conjunction of Jupiter and Saturn, or the perfect union of the two halves of the brain, one of which rules the analytical reasoning side (Saturn), the other, the creative sensitive side (Jupiter). Number 5 as the central digit in the series 1–9, represents a centering. It rules communication, new interests, change, decisions, versatility, adaptability, excitement and freedom.

James Monroe: Fifth President. Born: April 28, 1758. Life Lesson Number: 53/8. President: 1816-1824. James Monroe, after a thirteen-state goodwill tour at the beginning of his presidency, wrote to Jefferson, "In principal towns the whole population has been in motion, and in a manner to produce the greatest degree of excitement possible." On July 12, 1817, the Boston Columbian Centinel declared that Monroe's visit ushered in an "Era of good feelings . . ." He was popular with the masses and with political adversaries as well. Even John Quincy Adams, who would remain silent rather than say anything nice about anyone, wrote that Monroe's term would "be looked back to as the golden age of this republic." Thomas Jefferson said, "He is a man whose soul might be turned wrong side outwards without discovering a blemish to the world." *The American Heritage Book of the Presidents and Famous Americans* states: "The times were just right for James Monroe to assume the presidency." Monroe was honest and trustworthy, and could maintain his friends even in the midst of political disagreements.

During his first term, Monroe sent a team of negotiators to London to settle the dividing line between the United States and Canada. The Convention of 1818 established the border at the 49th parallel.

The Bank of the United States, established in 1816, failed in 1819 and brought a few years of depression; but the "Era of good feelings" prevailed and no one blamed Monroe. Missouri requested admission to the Union in 1819. At that time, there were eleven free and eleven slave states. The North wanted Missouri admitted as a free state, the south as a slave state.

Debate was intense. Monroe wrote: "I have never known a question so menacing to the tranquility and even the continuance of our Union as the present one." Finally, Maine was admitted as a free state, and Missouri as a slave state, thereby maintaining the balance.

The need for internal improvements arose: post offices, interstate highways, canals—all means of communication. President Monroe was in favor of these bills, but felt that the Constitution did not give the government the power to legislate such issues. Sidestepping the problem, he ordered the Department of War to repair certain damaged roads in New York under the pretense that their proper maintenance was essential to the defense of the nation.

And finally, the Monroe Doctrine, as a protective measure against foreign expansionism in American territory, stated that "The American continents, by the free and independent condition which they have assumed and maintain, are hence forth not to be considered as subjects for future colonization by any European power."

The major events of Monroe's presidency qualify under the Number 5: the president's affability and acceptance by almost everyone, the "era of good feelings," important decisions such as slavery under the Missouri Compromise and the establishment of the U.S.-Canadian border, the issue of internal communication improvements, and the Monroe Doctrine that established the boundaries of a free American continent.

The Hierophant blesses the state of perfect balance just as Monroe presided over an era of harmony. His concern with improvements within the Post Office Department, and the highways and canal systems in the country relate to the Number 5 keyword, communication.

THE LOVERS.

6 KEY 6: THE LOVERS represent the union of opposite but complementary elements. The keyword assigned to this card is discrimination, that quality necessary to discern the innate differences between two things. Discrimination separates the true from the false. The male and the female represent the positive and the negative, the conscious and the subconscious minds. The conscious mind (male) looks to the subconscious (female) who in turn looks to the superconscious (the angel) for proper guidance, unity, and wholeness. The serpent in the tree behind the woman is the kundalini or life force that lies coiled at the base of the spine and must be raised up the spine through resisting temptation to the higher God centers in the head. Number 6 represents marriage and family unity, responsibility to home and community, beauty, harmony and balance, innate analytical ability, keen perception, honesty, and fairness.

John Quincy Adams: Sixth President. Born: July 11, 1767. Life Lesson Number: 39/3. President: 1824-1828. John Quincy Adams was restrained, ethical, extraordinarily industrious, and, although devoted to his nation, maintained an air of apparent detachment. He considered the frequent attacks upon his character as personal affronts, being "practically paranoid about the family name."

During his political career, there was only one political party, the Democratic-Republican party, and it gave the presidential nomination to the Secretary of the Treasury, William Crawford. By election day, however, three others were on the scene: Senator Henry Clay, General Andrew Jackson, and John Quincy Adams. None of the candidates received a majority of electoral votes; therefore the House of Representatives was called upon to vote. Andrew Jackson beat John Quincy Adams 99-84, but when Henry Clay finally decided to turn his devoted followers over to Adams, 37 more votes were tallied on Adams's side, deciding the outcome of the election.

Upon becoming president, Adams poured his energy into the "internal improvement of the country": large federal funds for roads and canals were established; a department of interior was set up to watch over the use of natural resources; and government funds for education were provided, as was a naval academy and astronomical observatories. "Development of the land and education of the people" were major concerns. His "conscience-stricken plea for justice for the American Indian" and his antislavery views cost him dearly. After his presidency, Adams became one of a few Americans to risk his reputation by publicly declaring the conflict with Mexico "a most unrighteous war." He was an ardent advocate of educational availability for all Americans.

John Quincy Adams' unyielding devotion to justice and equality, his fierce defense of his family name, and the emphasis of his presidency on domestic improvement in our nation exemplify his term as a Number 6 vibration.

Adams' attention to "internal improvement of the country," his ardent advocacy of educational opportunities for all Americans, his devotion to justice and equality, his "conscience-stricken plea for justice for the American Indian," and his antislavery views all tie him to Key 6. Key 6 is the Lovers, whose discriminatory powers are exemplified by the conscious mind looking to the subconscious, which looks to the superconscious for unity and wholeness.

THE CHARIOT.

7 Key 7: THE CHARIOT The charioteer is the soul directing the Chariot, the body. It is through receptivity, the

Chariot's keyword, that control of the sphinxes, the negative and positive senses, is maintained. Only through a quiet and receptive state can we find the primal force within and control the outer world of manifestation through mental means as the Charioteer controls the sphinxes mentally without the use of reins. Number 7 is rest, reflection, a turning inward for analysis, solitude, health, physical completion without effort, issues coming to a head, a time to maintain control, wait and listen, and to avoid pushing affairs. 7 is a number "in the world but not of the world."

Andrew Jackson: Seventh President. Born: March 15, 1767. Life Lesson Number: 39/3. President: 1828-1836. "All that is necessary for you is to be still and quiet," Senator John Eaton advised presidential aspirant Andrew Jackson in 1826. "Say nothing and plant cotton." But late in 1826, venomous attacks against the matrimonial history of Rachel Jackson began, and Jackson as well was accused of being the son of a prostitute and a mulatto. The Jackson group, against his wishes, insinuated "premarital impropriety" between President Adams and his wife. The campaign was vile. President Jackson won handily but the victory was hollow. His wife, a victim of slander, had just died, and the new president was bitter.

Anny Royall, a journalist at the inauguration, recorded that President-elect Jackson was "thin and pale, and his hair...was almost white, and his countenance was melancholy." He was the head of the country, but his heart was gone; he was "in this world but not of it."

John Randolph wailed, "The country is ruined past redemption." Of course, this was not true, but the country had changed. Jackson was a complete turnabout from his genteel, intellectual predecessors. Under the first six aristocratic presidents the country had prospered. A large middle class emerged and declared their birth by electing a man who embodied their struggle up from poverty, Andrew Jackson, a poor backwoodsman who achieved success through his iron will and strong convictions. A schoolmate, who claimed he threw him three times out of four, complained "he would never *stay* throwed."

Jackson's health was impaired for life in a duel over allusions to Rachel's matrimonial past. A bullet lodged so close to his heart that it could not be removed. Nevertheless, he went on, ignoring his pain in a feat "short of incredible."

Jackson took control of the presidency and completely altered the course of American government. He did not trust paper money, and was convinced that the Bank of the United States created an alliance between government and business which benefited a few at the expense of many. He vetoed the Bank's request for recharter, which had already been passed by both the House and Senate.

In 1832 South Carolina, in opposition to oppressive tariffs, passed the Ordinance of Nullification, declaring the tariff not "binding upon the State, its officers or citizens." Jackson reacted quickly. "No state or states has a right to secede...Nullification therefore means insurrection and war, and other states have a right to put it down." He then introduced a bill authorizing the president to use force to maintain governmental authority. South Carolina knew he was prepared to send an army to back up his conviction, and his will overcame that of his opponents. A compromise tariff was passed as a token gesture.

Jackson's anti-Indian sentiment constituted a blot on his career. Hundreds of Indians died in The Black Hawk War. In Georgia the peaceful Cherokee had won a Supreme Court decision; but it was ignored, and so they too like other tribes embarked on that long journey west called "the trail of tears."

Andrew Jackson's iron will controlled the country in the midst of the climactic events that had been building for years: decontrol and destruction of the Bank of the United States, the tariff affair, and the betrayal and relocation of Indians to less useful lands. Slanderous attacks on his wife and her subsequent death three months before his election to the presidency removed him emotionally from the world. Jackson played his role with an iron fist but an empty heart. His posture reminds us of the Charioteer, a figure removed from the world yet still controlling it through mental will. The solitude, health aspects, control, and culminating issues of Number 7 held sway during his reign.

8 KEY 8: STRENGTH Through suggestion we direct the life force into the world of manifestation. Key 8 depicts the subconscious mind (the woman) controlling the physical body and its functions (the lion). She receives and acts upon suggestions sent from the conscious mind. Her power over the lion is gentle and mental. The chain of roses about the woman and lion show that cultivation (roses need care) of our desires sets up a chain reaction which eventually produces tangible results. Number 8 is responsibility, strength, power, discipline, intelligence, solidity, business, money, finance, justice, karma, respect and unity; or financial loss, restriction and heavy burdens.

Martin Van Buren: Eighth President. Born: December 5, 1782. Life Lesson Number: 35/8. President: 1836-1840. Martin Van Buren was the "prime architect" in electing Andrew Jackson to the presidency. Arthur M. Schlesinger, Jr., wrote: "Van Buren's understanding of the new functions of public

117

opinion, as well as of Congress, furnished the practical mechanism which transformed Jackson's extraordinary popularity into the instruments of power. . . ."

On his rise to power, Van Buren discovered the value of a friendly press. Without support from "a sound, practicable and above all discreet republican," he once admitted, "we may hang our harps on the willows." He became the most powerful man in government under Andrew Jackson. Both he and Jackson agreed on a strong political party. Van Buren used his office to tempt and allure politically undecided peers.

In his inaugural address in March, 1837, "on the eve of one of America's worst depressions, he assured the nation that prosperity was now perfectly secured.' " Days later, the Panic of 1837 broke over the nation because of Jackson's hard money policy, as citizens withdrew their money in large amounts. In 1836 the wheat crop had failed and cotton prices fell by one half. Food and fuel prices soared; and banks and businesses collapsed when England and Europe demanded payment of short-term loans. Van Buren's solution was an independent treasury which would take control away from the moneyed establishment. The Independent Treasury Bill finally passed in 1840, his last year in office. He claimed it to be the "Second Declaration of Independence."

Although Van Buren believed that government did not have the right to meddle in the economy, he issued an Executive Order in March, 1840, that limited the work day to ten hours for federal workers. However, the nation looked upon Van Buren as a manipulator afraid to take a stand. And when he opposed Andrew Jackson and Sam Houston on the annexation of Texas, he lost points with Jackson, his former supporter. His ambivalence was partially due to the restricted presidential and federal roles he advocated, as well as his "fundamentalist approach." He agreed that Congress had a right to collect taxes but disagreed that Congress had the constitutional authority to spend the money.

Van Buren was conservative, disciplined, and structured in his handling of the chain reaction that ensued in the Panic of 1837—a perfect example of the powerful financial emphasis of Number 8. His focus on the Treasury and the working hours of the labor force also qualify him as Number 8.

Key 8 depicts control over the animal impulses and the material world through gentle means. Martin Van Buren's subtle dispensation of power and his "highly limited views of the presidential and Federal roles in the life of the nation" qualify him as the figure in the card who administers power in unsuspecting ways.

9 KEY 9: THE HERMIT represents achievement standing on the mountain of attainment. He has made the arduous climb and now turns to show his light (of wisdom) to those who would follow. Through discrimination he has discarded the useless and unnecessary elements on his path and has achieved mastery of himself. Number 9 is a transitional number representing ending, completion and charity.

William Henry Harrison: Ninth President. Born: February 9, 1773. Life Lesson Number: 29/11. President: 1840-1841. William Henry Harrison, inaugurated as President of the United States on March 4, 1841, spoke for one hour and forty minutes despite extremely cold weather. The 68-year-old president was tired and worn, and the campaign had been taxing. On March 27 he came down with pneumonia and died on April 4, one month after becoming president. He was the first American president to die in office.

Perhaps his role in the presidential sequence pointed out and brought to an end two naive attitudes on the part of the American public: (1) That a president is immortal during his tenure of office. Therefore, not much attention was paid to the character qualifications of the vice-presidential candidate, John Tyler. Adams's diary contains the following words: "No one ever thought of his being placed in the executive chair." And (2) that succession had been attended to by the forefathers. But had the succession of office been spelled out? Was John Tyler actually president or only an acting president?

As the ninth president, William Henry Harrison fulfilled the 9 vibration by bringing an end to the complacency with which vice-presidential candidates were selected. His death reminded the nation that it must be prepared for sudden changes in government, and that the government must have the strength and flexibility to handle those transitions smoothly. Harrison's death began a twenty year death cycle which has hounded every president up to this present writing (March 1980). The president elected every twenty years since 1840 has died in office (see accompanying chart). This series of tragedies coincides with the conjunction of Jupiter and Saturn in earth signs (Taurus, Virgo and Capricorn) every twenty years since 1840. Will this cycle continue for the president elected this year, 1980? No one is sure, because the Jupiter-Saturn conjunction moves into an air sign, thus breaking the pattern of elements for the first time since 1840.

1840: Harrison — an Aquarian ♒ , February 9.
1860: Lincoln — an Aquarian ♒ , February 12.
1880: Garfield — a Scorpio ♏ , November 19.
1990: McKinley — an Aquarian ♒ , January 29.

1920: Harding — a Scorpio ♏, November 2.
1940: Roosevelt — an Aquarian ♒ , January 30.
1960: Kennedy — a Gemini ♊ , May 29.
1980: ?

At present it appears that the presidential contest is between Ronald Reagan, an Aquarian ♒ conservative Republican, and President Carter, a Libran ♎ Democrat. Since the country is apparently going conservative in the '80s, we might expect a conservative nominee to win. Ronald Reagan, an Aquarian, fits the bill. We have had four Aquarian presidents. They have all died in office.

When President Harrison died, the country awoke to the fact that a single heartbeat could change her destiny. The Hermit's lantern of wisdom depicts the light of understanding shining on a nation that suddenly realizes a president is not immortal, and selection of an able vice-president is vital.

WHEEL ⟨of⟩ FORTUNE.

10 KEY 10: THE WHEEL OF FORTUNE represents the flux of life—rotation and cyclicity are the keywords. Everything is in the process of change; change is the only constant. The Wheel of Fortune's symbol is the closed hand, which indicates comprehension. When we "grasp" something, we understand it. The symbols in the four corners represent the four fixed signs of the zodiac, or the immutable fixed laws of the universe. The human body with the animal head indicates that humanity has not gained true understanding yet, understanding which is symbolized by the elevated sphinx, again a combination of the four fixed laws. The Number 10 is called a turn for the better, a new cycle, innovative ideas resulting from past experience, an initiation period in which decisions are made, and luck.

John Tyler: Tenth President: Born: March 29, 1790. Life Lesson Number: 49/4. President: 1841-1844. When John Tyler opened his door early on April 5, 1841, to hear Daniel Webster's son, Fletcher, deliver the fateful message that the president was dead, Tyler was without precedent to resolve "the immediate constitutional problem of his status in the government."

Despite his distaste for the office of vice-president, Tyler seemed as destined to hold it as he was destined to become the tenth president of the United States. He refused the offer of the vice-presidency a number of times. Later he accepted, and was nominated on a number of losing tickets, before he was chosen by the man who would be president for only one month, William Henry Harrison.

Although the succession clause was not clear, Tyler,

determined to become president, was sworn in fifty-three hours after Harrison's death. At fifty-one, Tyler was the youngest man to become president up until that time. Argument about presidential succession ensued but Tyler won out, and the precedent was set for the future.

Internal problems set in when Tyler refused to vote with the Cabinet, as agreed by Harrison. And Henry Clay, having extracted from Harrison a promise to run for only one term, wanted to be the next president. Now he was unsure about Tyler's future presidential plans. Clay and the Congress subsequently passed bills and Tyler vetoed them. In fact, he vetoed a total of ten bills, earning the nickname "Old Veto." Eventually the entire Cabinet, with the exception of Daniel Webster, resigned.

Tyler's dream was finally fulfilled when, four days before he retired, Congress agreed to annex Texas. From the beginning of his term in office, it was important to him that "he be remembered favorably." And the annexation of Texas became the symbol of "assuring himself a respected place in history."

Perhaps his need to be remembered favorably stemmed from his oblique occupation of the presidency. To be the first vice-president, a nonelected official, to take over the highest office in the land, may have required, in his mind, a legacy of worth and accomplishment. Tyler seemed to have "grasped" the significance of his place in history and the precedent he was setting. His refusal to blindly follow the policies set up by his predecessor and his determination to leave a positive image and something of value qualify him under the Number 10. The element of luck was evident when he narrowly escaped death twice within a short time during his presidency. On board the steam frigate "Princeton" he was about to witness the firing of a newly designed bow gun, which had been successfully fired earlier that day, when he stopped below board to listen to his son-in-law sing a song. Before the song was over, an explosion rang out. The gun blew up and killed eight people. One person killed was Secretary of State Abel P. Upshur, who had just moments before left the president's side when he had stopped to listen to the song. Then, on the day of the funeral, Tyler's horses bolted and ran some distance before they could be brought under control. He again was unhurt.

The Wheel of Fortune card depicts a series of events culminating in and producing a result. Luck is an element here as well. John Tyler refused the vice-presidency several times, ran on a number of losing tickets, yet accepted the vice-presidential nomination with the man who would eventually become president. Fifty-three hours after President Harrison's death, although there was some argument, Tyler was sworn in

as president, setting a precedent. He narrowly escaped death twice, exemplifying the luck element.

11 KEY 11: JUSTICE The figure on the throne holds the sword of discrimination which cuts through outer form to reveal inner truth. The scales represent balance through justice. Present conditions must be weighed and balanced through elimination of error. 11 is the first Master Number and as a Master Number demands much. It is a testing and challenging vibration emphasizing legalities and decisions. Great inspiration is available for those who can tap their inner source. Sudden recognition and public acclaim are possible.

James K. Polk: Eleventh President. Born: November 2, 1795. Life Lesson Number: 35/8. President: 1844-1848. "Who is James K. Polk?" was asked laughingly and often in 1844, when he became the first "dark horse" presidential nominee. Suddenly he was there and elected. After his inauguration he immersed himself in the work that marked his single term as one of the most active in presidential history. By 1848, everyone knew who James K. Polk was. He knew what he wanted to do, said he needed only one term in which to do it, and went ahead and did it.

America's interest in expansion was a crusade, a "manifest destiny," and in this "ambitious, cocksure, destiny-enraptured" frame of mind, she elected James K. Polk. His contemporaries maligned his importance but his reputation has grown steadily, continuing even up to our own time. He persevered because he was an excellent taskmaster who kept a finger on the pulse of every government department. In himself, he created the example for others to emulate. He was a moderate "in the midst of radicals and reactionaries," winning the "enmity of both sides and the admiration only of history."

President Polk stated four goals for his administration: "one, a reduction of the tariff; another, the independent treasury; a third, the settlement of the Oregon boundary question; and lastly, the acquisition of California." These were also the goals of the nation, and in his four-year term, he accomplished all four, becoming "one of the country's most effective Presidents."

Bernard Devoto's description of Polk as a man whose "integrity was absolute...no one bluffed him, no one moved him with direct or oblique pressure...he knew how to get things done...and he knew what he wanted done...the only 'strong' president between Jackson and Lincoln."

The Justice card depicts a figure who sees the issues clearly (the sword of discrimination) and is determined to set right any imbalance (the balanced scales). Polk set four goals for his administration and stated he only needed one term in which to accomplish them. He did so, becoming "one of the country's most effective presidents." He knew what he had to do and no one could fool or divert him. His position as a "moderate in the midst of radicals and reactionaries" qualifies him under this Master Number.

12 KEY 12: THE HANGED MAN The crossed legs of the Hanged Man form a figure 4, indicative of Key 4, Reason. The keyword for this card is reversal. The Hanged Man is a person in control, poised on an inner level, centered in peace. Although the world about is in chaos, the figure maintains serenity. For this reason, The Hanged Man is set apart from the world, seeming different, upside down, as it were, to others who do things differently. He has reversed the usual way of living and found contentment. Number 12 represents a pause, a listening time to observe things as they really are and not as they seem on the surface. Some affairs will culminate but decision-making should be suspended. Absorption in physical matters brings loss of friends and finances. Sacrifice follows. The best method of operation is passivity, sympathy and tact, and a centering within. Tolerance is the key here. You appear to walk contrary to the world, yet your philosophy frees you from the physical.

Zachary Taylor: Twelfth President. Born: November 24, 1784. Life Lesson Number: 55/1. President: 1848-1850. General Zachary Taylor was respected for his ability to lead and for his courage and ableness as a frontier commander. However, he was inexperienced in government, although he had "a native political sharpness that stood him in good stead." After a string of military successes he was finally convinced to run for the presidency. However, he eschewed political deals and, on the whole, stuck to the middle ground on most issues. In speeches to the public, he promised that "if elected I would not be the mere president of a party—I would endeavor to act independent of party domination, and should feel bound to administer the government untrammelled by party schemes..."

It is said that he maintained his perfect record of never voting in a presidential election by not even voting in his own election. On the surface "an utterly apolitical figure," he nevertheless had an interest in government and, once elected, made his opinions known. The major issues in his short term were his offers of statehood to California and New Mexico.

Slavery was still an issue, and the North and South fought over the slavery positions of these potential new states.

On July 4, 1850, the Clayton-Bulwer Treaty, smoothing out problems in preparation for the digging of the Panama Canal, was signed. That same hot day President Taylor returned to the White House, after attending ceremonies at the Washington Monument, and ate raw vegetables or fruit, while consuming "large amounts of cold milk or water." He came down with acute gastroenteritis and died suddenly on July 9th.

It was "common to think of him...as a naive, goodhearted tough old man..." but President Zachary Taylor "was more his own man than even many of his contemporaries realized." He lacked the practical experience his job required but, even so, "he held his own in the central conflict of his presidency."

Zachary Taylor was a man set apart from the world in many ways. His appearance alone marked him. His large head and upper body dwarfed his extremely short legs. For a uniform, he wore "baggy cotton pants, a plain coat bearing no insignia and a farmer's wide-brimmed straw hat." One might have thought him a "weirdo." However, his lined face emanated deep-seated spiritual powers. He looked at life forthrightly, giving his full attention to immediate affairs.

The Hanged Man is seen as an oddity because his ideas are so different, ideas which stem from deep understanding. Taylor was "his own man," surprising many of his contemporaries who described him as "merely an eccentric." This ties into the Hanged Man.

DEATH.

13 KEY 13: DEATH The death card suggests reproduction and birth through its symbol the fish, fish's mouth, or mouth of the uterus (see Paul Foster Case *The Tarot*). The birth may be into this plane of consciousness, changes within this plane, or birth into a higher plane. The skeleton astride the horse brings transmutation to all regardless of station. The Sun in the background promises that the life force does not die but merely changes its outer form. Number 13 is is a number of constant change that reminds one of the transitory nature of the material world. Here changes are wrought that will bring an end to conditions that have outlived their usefulness. It is a period of change and transformation, and release from the past.

Millard Fillmore: Thirteenth President. Born: January 7, 1800. Life Lesson Number: 17/8. President: 1850-1852. On July 10, 1850, the day after Zachary Taylor died, Fillmore became president. The major issue during Fillmore's term was the increasingly intolerable situation of slavery, which divided the Southern planters from the Northern industrialists. When, upon Taylor's death, the Cabinet resigned and all stumbling blocks to the passage of the Compromise of 1850 were eliminated, President Fillmore signed the bill, "convinced that he had no constitutional alternative." The bill abolished slave trade in the District of Columbia, admitted California as a free state, and New Mexico and Utah as territories open to "popular sovereignty," maintained the current status of slave states, and ordered all free states to return runaway slaves to their masters. Fillmore hesitated before signing the bill for "political as well as moral reasons," but finally sign he did, hoping the compromise would settle the issue. What he seemed unable to understand, as did his heirs to the presidency up until Lincoln, was that "the country was compromising on an issue that defied compromise." The bill satisfied neither the North nor the South. The South was convinced that this bill was the precursor to other bills concerning slavery, which they considered the right of the state. The North found the included Fugitive Slave Law demanding return of runaway slaves intolerable. Harriet Beecher Stowe's popular *Uncle Tom's Cabin* kept the fires kindled, and Fillmore threatened to use force to enforce the law.

Through Fillmore's efforts, federal grants for railroad construction were procured, and the Erie Railroad was completed in 1851. His letters to the Japanese Mikado resulted in the breaking of the Japanese barrier, and relations and trade were eventually established.

The death knell tolled for slavery under Fillmore's administration. Paradoxically, the establishment of certain states as slave states through the signing of the Compromise of 1850 and the ensuing punishment of offenders of the Fugitive Slave Law brought about the eventual death of slavery thirteen years later under Abraham Lincoln.

The discovery of gold in California, and the admission of California to the Union, established our "sea to shining sea" boundary once and for all. President Millard Fillmore unwittingly became the tool through which the seeds of some major issues for our country were planted—the size of our nation and the abolition of slavery—yet he sank into virtual obscurity. We might say that the outer form died (Millard Fillmore is hardly remembered) but the energy lives on (our boundaries remain secure and human rights are still emerging).

The Compromise of 1850 was the Death card in Fillmore's term. It was the beginning of the end of slavery. Because of the passage of this bill, the North and the South began to realize that compromise on a moral issue was impossible. The flag in the Death card was waved for those with the vision to see the eventual demise of this issue.

14 KEY 14: TEMPERANCE It is through verification
and wrath (strong anger, not temper), keywords for
Temperance, that the desire for truth rises from within. This
process tempers the soul and brings about balance. The angel
is a blending of male and female forces, an angel of the Sun, or
life force, maintaining perfect balance between the subconscious (one foot on water) and the conscious (one foot on
land) minds. Under the 14, lessons are learned through varied
experience. Social and family obligations can cause peculiar
circumstances. Balance is very necessary, and much can be
gained through tact and diplomacy. Unless the body and emotions are tempered, the health can suffer. Strengths will be
tested.

Franklin Pierce: Fourteenth President. Born: November 23,
1804. Life Lesson Number: 47/11. President: 1852-1856.
Franklin Pierce entered the White House a sad man. His third
child, an eleven-year-old son, had just been killed in a railroad
car accident. Two other sons had died previously, one at three
days and another at four years, from typhus. Mrs. Pierce
thought the death of their last child was a sign from God that
her husband was to be freed from family responsibility so that
he could focus his attention on the presidency. She rarely
made appearances in public from then on.

The president took over the office in deceptively calm
times. Thomas Benton of Missouri told the newly arrived
Senator Charles Sumner from Massachusetts: "You have come
upon the scene too late, sir. There is nothing left to settle except petty sectional disturbances over slavery." Many felt that
the Compromise of 1850 had settled the slavery issue, and
Pierce, like many others "dedicated to the preservation of the
Union," never understood what the abolitionists stood for, or
that slavery was not settled but was merely fermenting.

That section of the Compromise known as the Fugitive
Slave Law only served to arouse the moral indignation of the
North and encouraged the abolition movement. The reaction
of the North increased resentment in the South, thus multiplying the problem.

In 1854 Senator Stephen Douglas tried to territorialize the
Great Plains so a transcontinental railroad might be built there
(he owned lands around Chicago). The bill he proposed, the
Kansas-Nebraska Bill, repealed the Missouri Compromise and
opened the northern states to slavery—a move to gain the support of slavery interests for his bill. The president was furious
but signed the bill because he feared losing the support of the
South. Kansas soon became a battlefield and Pierce's party
began to crumble because of the pressures of the situation.

It seemed that Pierce favored compromise over conflict.
In fact, his four-year term saw a "record number of treaties"
signed. As 1856 approached, he began to think about another

term, but "Bleeding Kansas" had ruined him and he could not muster the support he needed.

Senator Clement Clay's wife recalled that "before Franklin Pierce became president of the United States she had 'seen him bound up the stairs with the elasticity of a schoolboy. He went out after four years,' she added, 'a staid and grave man, on whom the stamp of care and illness was ineradicably impressed.'"

Number 14 seems to show in his family situation and in his efforts toward compromise, which in a few major instances failed to bring the necessary balance; thus setting a scene for a heartrending conflict.

The Temperance card depicts the process of tempering or blending opposite forces. The angel with one foot on the ground and one in the water seems balanced. When Pierce took office, times were "deceptively calm." Many thought the issue of slavery had been settled with the Compromise of 1850, but others realized the balance was precarious (not on solid footing). The Nation was being tested, put through the fire (tempered), in a search for human equality.

THE DEVIL.

15 KEY 15: THE DEVIL The Devil is God upside down, or misconceived. Lack of discrimination produces illusion which holds one in invisible bondage. The Devil represents the mistake of judging only outward appearances instead of inner truths. The two humans could easily slip off the loose chains about their necks, but they seem unaware of this truth. They are bound by half truths (represented by the half cube). The inverted pentagram and torch indicate wasted energy, inverted power. Number 15 implies indecision and bondage. Old views should be carefully examined. The candle burns at both ends. Contracts or agreements should be signed with care. With discrimination, one should look beneath the surface for the real truth.

James Buchanan: Fifteenth President. Born: April 23, 1791. Life Lesson Number: 45/9. President: 1856-1860. James Buchanan came to the presidency in 1857 a winner of the electoral college but with less than half the popular vote. Considered charming, gentle, and diplomatic, he was a fanatical record-keeper and knew where his every penny went. As a result he became quite wealthy. His contemporaries were exasperated by his caution but nevertheless respected it.

The slavery controversy had been raging for some years. Under Buchanan's administration, the issue culminated in the Dred Scott case, in which a slave, taken to Wisconsin and Illinois by his master, sued for his freedom on the grounds that his new residency in a free territory allowed him that privilege. The court's decision was: that Scott was a slave, not a citizen, and could not therefore sue for anything; that the Missouri Compromise, which denied slaveowners the "right to take their property wherever they wished," was unconstitutional; and that the court had no jurisdiction and therefore could not legislate over a territory until it became a state.

Buchanan had a part in this decision and felt the issue was settled. Known as a conservative and a man of compromise, he said, "I am not friendly to slavery in the abstract (but) the rights of the South, under our constitutional compact, are as much entitled to protection as those of any other portion of the Union." But the decision settled nothing; on the contrary, it fanned the flames higher.

Whether to admit Kansas as a free or slave state stirred the controversy even more. Buchanan vacillated, and the long and bitter debate ended in a refusal to admit Kansas as a new state. Kansas was admitted a few years later, in 1861.

Then, in late 1859, John Brown and a handful of blacks and whites seized Harpers Ferry, Virginia, the federal arsenal, in a protest against slavery. Brown was soon captured, tried, and hanged; thus he became a symbol of freedom for the abolitionists.

Slavery was not the only issue in Buchanan's term, but as it turned out it was the major one. The president, however, "stood curiously disconnected from the realities." His lack of discernment was evident when even in the midst of the chaos he could say, "The prospects are daily brightening. From present appearance, the party will ere long be thoroughly united." Buchanan inherited a difficult situation. He tried to play both sides until a solution could be worked out. Before Christmas of 1860, South Carolina, Florida, Alabama, Georgia, Louisiana, and Texas had seceded. Lincoln was elected in November of 1860.

All along, Buchanan labored under the false impression that the slavery issue could be compromised, that steps were leading to a peaceful settlement, that "the prospects are daily brightening." His adherence to the old views, his indecisions as to how to act on some key bills, and his lack of discrimination on the slavery issue helped stoke the fire. On the slavery debate, however, he was no different from his predecessors who could not understand that compromise over slavery was impossible.

The Devil card represents bondage to false ideas. The slavery controversy had been raging for some years, and in Buchanan's term it peaked in the Dred Scott Case. The president and perhaps half the nation were in bondage to the false idea of slavery. The chains were about to be slipped off.

THE TOWER.

16 KEY 16: THE TOWER The keyword for the Tower is awakening. A flash of lightning (understanding) out of the blue (the subconscious) strikes the Tower (the house of God, the body). The crown (or thoughts from the head) is toppled. This picture represents the forceful removal of erroneous thoughts. Number 16 brings sudden, unforeseen events that overthrow existing material conditions. Losses in business and finance are possible, as are scandals and bankruptcy. It is a time to be careful of accidents and conflicts. Obsession with ownership of things material must cease.

Abraham Lincoln: Sixteenth President. Born: February 12, 1809. Life Lesson Number: 32/5. (Same as Life Lesson of U.S. and Path of Destiny of America.) President: 1860-1865. Abraham Lincoln was the first president to be assassinated. Every school child is familiar with his story—his humble birth in a log cabin, studies by the firelight encouraged by a loving stepmother, his law practice and eventual rise to the highest office in the land, and his assassination on April 14–15, 1865, by John Wilkes Booth.

Abraham Lincoln was called by John Hay, "The greatest character since Christ." He remains today an "American messiah, murdered on Good Friday, a martyr to assaulted truth." Lincoln, with his homespun simplicity and virtues of honesty and thrift, has become "the embodiment of American idealism," grown beyond himself by assassination and circumstance. Although he despised slavery as much or more so than any abolitionist, he did not plan to change the status quo where it already existed. His main concern was always the preservation of the Union. When Lincoln became president, the Confederacy had captured all federal forts and Navy yards in their states except Fort Pickens and Fort Sumter. And when the first shot was fired on Fort Sumter at 4:30 AM on April 12, 1861, the war that would kill 600,000 Americans had begun.

Lincoln did vacillate on slavery. He knew that the signing of a document could not change a basic institution, and he knew that after the war, slavery would still be an issue to deal with. Border states were requested to gradually free their slaves, and Congress passed bills freeing slaves of "disloyal" masters. In July, 1862, Abraham Lincoln called his Cabinet together for a discussion of an emancipation proclamation.

Richmond finally fell on April 3, and at 4:00 PM on April 9, 1865, General Grant accepted the surrender of the South from General Lee at the Appomattox Court House.

Abraham Lincoln was re-elected president in 1864, and died April 15, 1865, the victim of a bullet from the gun of John Wilkes Booth, a twenty-six-year-old proslavery extremist. Lincoln's Emancipation Proclamation was signed into law eight months after his death. Lincoln was the second president to die in office as a result of the 20-year death cycle which began in 1840 (see page 119).

The fermenting slavery question finally caused the decay of this one-hundred-year-old institution in America. Under the sixteenth president, events caused the overthrow of conditions long existent. Because it was internal, the Civil War was the worst conflict in our history. Number 16 brought about the demise of the ownership of human life.

The Tower card represents the destruction of the long-held erroneous ideas. The Civil War, the result of long years of dispute over slavery, erupted and plunged the nation into a terrible, internal war. Subsequently, Lincoln's Emancipation Proclamation finally tore down the long-held ideas on slavery.

THE STAR.

17 KEY 17: THE STAR The keyword for the Star is "fish-hook," suggesting an angling, groping, or fishing for something that is not yet realized. Through meditation, the Star's function, truth can be gleaned from the depths of the subconscious. This card represents the beginning stages of mental development, the beginning of ideas. The large star is the cosmic energy which radiates through the seven smaller stars, or the 7 "interior stars," the chakras in the body. The woman symbolizes Mother Nature who keeps "the imperishable record of the memory of nature." She is supported by earth and balanced by water (physical sensations reinforce meditation but the subconscious balances the results). Number 17 bestows hope, faith, and courage in the face of problems. There is compassion, and a desire for peace and love among all people, which stems from deep understanding. Intuition is developed. In difficulty, going within aids in finding truth.

Andrew Johnson: Seventeenth President. Born: December 29, 1808. Life Lesson Number: 58/4. President: 1865-1868. Andrew Johnson had no political ambition to live in the White House. When he was elected to the United State Senate, he said, "I have reached the summit of my ambition." Thrust suddenly into the presidency by Lincoln's death, however, he was immediately faced with the reconstruction of the South. The only southern Congressman or Senator to do so, he pleaded with Congress to prevent secession of the southern states, and so was branded a traitor to the Confederacy. He held a unique position as both a Southerner and a staunch Unionist, pledging "my blood, my existence" to maintain the Union. As the new president after the war, he had a fight on his hands: The Radical Republicans sought to trample the South. They had much to gain. A loss of southern seats in Congress would eliminate many Democrats. And northern industrialists had their eyes on southern land for industrial development. Johnson, following in Lincoln's footsteps, simply wished to heal the nation. "If a State is to be nursed until it again gets strength," he said, "it must be nursed by its friends, not smothered by its enemies."

The battle was on: the Constitution-breakers versus the Constitution-defenders. Congress passed bills that gave them power over the South; Johnson vetoed them; and Congress passed them again over his veto. The situation resulted in the impeachment of Andrew Johnson, the only American president to be impeached. (To impeach means to indict, not to remove from office.) The House of Representatives impeaches; the Senate conducts the trial. In 1867 when Andrew Johnson vetoed a radical civil rights bill, the House set about to determine impeachment grounds. Was the president guilty of trying "to overthrow, subvert or corrupt the government of the United States?"

The Senate trial was vicious and unrelenting. The Radicals knew they needed just one of the remaining uncommited seven senators, all radicals, to convict the president. Soon it was clear that six of the seven, choosing conscience over party," were going to vote to acquit Andrew Johnson. The decision would ultimately be made by freshman Radical, Edmund Ross. When his name was called in the final vote, a hush fell over the packed room. All eyes were focused on him. Quietly, with mute expression, he said, "Not guilty." His vote saved the president and probably the Constitution of the United States. "I almost literally looked down into my open grave," he recalled. "Friendship, position, fortune, everything that makes life desirable to an ambitious man were about to be swept away by the breath of my mouth, perhaps forever." And he was right. His political career was finished.

Ex-president Andrew Johnson returned to Washington as a United States Senator. When he entered the chamber for the first time since leaving the presidency, "a great burst of applause" greeted him. Flowers covered his desk. He had been vindicated.

Andrew Johnson was not a bitter man. He had been aided by seven courageous political opponents whose careers were brutally destroyed because they had the same convictions and conscience that the president displayed. And Johnson accepted the handshakes and good wishes of those same men who had once tried to impeach him. He showed the compassion and true understanding of the Number 17.

Key 14, the Temperance card, depicts an internal tempering as the angel pours from one cup to the other. The nation was in the process of being tempered. Now, in the Star, the process is completed. Universal healing (the star overhead) is poured on the emotions and physical body of the nation (the cups poured into the pool and onto the earth). Johnson's job of reconstructing the South was the beginning of mental healing. The one vote that saved the president during his impeachment trial, and perhaps also saved the United States of America, destroyed the political ambitions of Edmund Ross; but he, like the Star card, represented truth and understanding.

THE MOON.

18 Key 18: THE MOON Organization and sleep are the keywords for the Moon. It is during sleep that waste is eliminated from the body and new cells are produced. Our hopes and wishes are built in as well. Our daily thoughts are woven into our cell consciousness at night. The crayfish, shaped like a scorpion, represents the creative force starting out on the path of attainment. The dog and the wolf, of the same species, symbolize the domesticated and wild side of human consciousness. The towers are the material structures we build through effort. The Sun's light reflected by the Moon indicates the goal of complete attunement of the inner and outer selves. Number 18 brings great activity and intense emotion. The subconscious is extremely active creating sensitivity, and perhaps nervous habits. Deception in business and difficulty in personal affairs are strong possibilities. These conditions can bring on war. Pisces, ruler of this number, may cause escapist tendencies through alcohol and drugs, a negative use of these energies.

Ulysses S. Grant: Eighteenth President. Born: April 27, 1822. Life Lesson Number: 44/8. President: 1868-1876. Ulysses Simpson Grant never wanted to be a soldier. He went to West Point at the insistence of his father and was "an indifferent scholar." He was constantly redressed for his slovenly appearance, tardiness and lack of soldierly bearing. He preferred drinking at the local pub to dancing and other social niceties. His drinking became more obvious when he was transferred to Fort Vancouver and was financially unable to bring his wife and children west. A friend recalled that Grant did not drink much, but when he did it caused his tongue to wag. Furthermore, it did not take much liquor for Grant to appear inebriated. On May 1, 1854, after a public display of drunkenness, Capt. Grant was forced to resign.

But the Civil War and its call for experienced leaders thrust Grant into the limelight, and he distinguished himself as a soldier on the battlefield. Abraham Lincoln eventually appointed him Lt. General in charge of all the Union forces. The South surrendered to Grant, who went on to become the eighteenth president of the United States.

President Grant's two terms in office were saturated with scandal, intrigue, deception and graft. He had no comprehension of the give-and-take of politics and could not compromise, therefore he lost support where he might have found it. One Senator claimed that the Republicans were "the (most) corrupt and debauched political party that ever existed." Two major limitations bound Grant: his unwillingness to consult with those persons who were informed and could have bailed him out of the rising flood waters; and his "consuming awe of the world's rich and influential."

During Grant's presidency the North attempted through legislation to establish northern interests in the South, sometimes under the pretext of aid to the newly freed black people. Some bitter Southerners reacted forming the Ku Klux Klan.

Although Grant was urged to run for a third term, the House deterred him by voting that another term would be ill-advised and set a precedent that would imperil America's institutional freedoms. Financial troubles plagued the Grant family thereafter until Ulysses' death on July 23, 1885. His memoirs were to bring $450,000.00 to his heirs within two years.

The intrigue and deception rampant throughout Grant's two terms, and his own succumbing to alcohol, bear out the implications of the Number 18.

The Moon is a card of the evolutionary process that occurs unbeknownst to the conscious mind. Growth occurs mysteriously in the dark hours; hidden forces are at work. The creative power here can be used, as always, in a positive or negative way. The president preceding Grant, Andrew Johnson, began the Era of Reconstruction in the South. The president after Grant, Rutherford Hayes, ended the Era of Reconstruction. Grant's term was depicted by the road going off into the distance between the two towers (the beginning and the end of the reconstruction era). There was a subtle, evolving process during Grant's term which was not so visible on the surface. The Moon card depicts the dark struggle of Grant's administration.

THE SUN .

19 KEY 19: THE SUN is the crucible of all life's energy. The Sun, or face, or head, bestows leadership The keyword is regeneration. When we regenerate our minds, we transform our bodies and our environment. Historically, the Sun has symbolized the light and the life power, the great divinity. The Sun is not only a physical entity in our solar system but a living power, a representative of the great spiritual power. The nude child symbolizes the naked truth which has subjugated the animal desires. The four sunflowers—mineral, vegetable, animal and human—always face the Sun, drawing their power from this source, as does all life. Number 19 brings new beginning, promising liberation. Future plans should be laid carefully. Obstacles can be overcome because "luck" shines upon you. A positive image reflects the leadership qualities underlying this number. Number 19 is known as the love vibration, and marriage here can be very happy.

Rutherford B. Hayes: Nineteenth President. Born: October 4, 1882. Life Lesson Number: 27/9. President: 1876-1880. As president Rutherford B. Hayes put an end to the blight of Reconstruction and took steps to pull the country together again. His equanimity and devotion to the Union pervaded his entire life. Even today he is regarded as a capable, level-headed man of integrity whose presence in the White House relieved a dangerous national condition.

His rise as lawyer, city official, army officer and governor finally placed him in the position of a nominee for the presidency. The Republican party needed a presidential candidate who embodied the principles of resilience and just government. Hayes had a reputation for "clean and progressive leadership," while remaining a loyal Republican and a "capable politician."

The election was close, and rumors spread that votes were being bought. Congress finally had to decide the outcome. In a bitter dispute, Rutherford B. Hayes was declared the victor over Samuel J. Tilden. In his diary Hayes pledged "the firmest adherence to principle against all opposition and temptation...(and that) I shall show a grit that will astonish those who predict weakness."

True to his word, he laid the groundwork for reconciliation. His 1877 tour of the South helped to achieve his goal. He declared that the spoils system "ought to be abolished. The reform should be thorough, radical and complete." When the Democrats tried to block government enforcement of the 15th Amendment allowing the black vote in the South, he effectively maintained leadership by rebuffing Congress's attempts to encroach on presidential authority. His efforts finalized Reconstruction and changed the politics of the past.

Rutherford Hayes, his wife Lucy and their children enjoyed a happy life. Lucy Hayes was the first president's wife to have a college degree. She was clever, cheerful and kind, and their years together were quite devoted ones.

Hayes exerted the leadership qualities of Number 19, maintaining his integrity and authority in the face of obstacles. He ended the Reconstruction of the South with some semblance of peace, and brought about a new era of unity. His happy family further exemplified this number vibration.

The Sun card represents regeneration. The Sun bestows new life, hope and faith. Hayes, a determined, capable president, was the Sun as he "created a favorable atmosphere for reconciliation," ending the reconstruction era and binding the country once again into a happy, healthy, whole.

20 KEY 20: JUDGEMENT The ancient symbol for this card is serpent, tooth and fang. The keyword is realization. An adept was called a serpent—"Be ye wise as serpents," Matthew 10:16. The serpent's fang conveys the poison that instantly attacks every cell in the body. Truth instantly eats away everything false. Judgment day is that time when we have reached the ability to discern true from false. In this card, Gabriel calls those who are ready to hear the truth and be freed from the stone coffins of ignorance. Number 20 is a number of decision and awareness. Resistance to necessary change causes restlessness and uneasiness. Sudden events make it mandatory that decisions be made.

James A. Garfield: Twentieth President. Born: November 19, 1831. Life Lesson Number: 43/7. President: 1880-1881. James Abram Garfield was the third president elected in twenty-year spans since 1840 to die in office. (These twenty-year cycles coincide with a Jupiter-Saturn conjunction in earth signs in the heavens. See page 119.) William Henry Harrison, elected in 1840, died of pneumonia while in office; Abraham Lincoln, elected in 1860, was assassinated.

James Garfield was born poor, and spent his childhood working a farm with his widowed mother and her three other children. He eventually received a degree from Williams College, which made him "a person of consequence." Garfield's oratorical talents as preacher and defender of the faith brought him nationwide fame when he debated evolutionist John Denton for five days before a capacity audience of 1,000 people. He was evangelical but charming, using God and the Bible to fend off Darwin.

When the Civil War broke out, Garfield held a strong Republican leadership position in the Senate. A Milwaukee newspaper remarked that he "is exceptionally clean for a man who has been engaged for twenty years in active politics." Garfield was nominated and won the presidency by a comfortable margin.

In his four months as president, two issues demanded his attention. The feud between the Stalwarts (conservatives) and the Half-Breeds (moderates) in the Republican party was rekindled; and an investigation of the Post Office Department resulted in an expose of fradulent use of funds, called the Star Route Frauds. Even though high-ranking Republicans were involved, Garfield "to his credit, instructed the Post Master General to continue to release the findings."

On July 2, 1881 at a Washington train station, about to embark on a trip to New England, President Garfield was shot twice by Charles J. Guiteau, a man frustrated in his attempts to gain political office. One bullet grazed Garfield's arm; the other entered his back. For two months, doctors probed with unsterile instruments trying to find the bullet, and spread infection throughout his body. On September 19, 1881, he died a needless death. If he had been left alone, he would have lived since a cyst had engulfed the bullet, protecting his body.

As an orator and preacher, his concern with the truth as he saw it, and his integrity, were fitting qualities for the Judgement card and the Number 20. But a "sudden event" terminated his life. He could have lived, but fate obviously had decided otherwise. Judgment had been passed on him and on the nation. One may well wonder what turn of events might have occurred, had he lived.

On the Judgement card, the angel Gabriel calls those ready to hear the truth, just as Garfield did throughout his life.

THE WORLD.

21 KEY 21: THE WORLD The cross with equal arms is the symbol for the World. Cosmic consciousness is the final mark, or X (a cross with equal arms), of our work on the material plane. Perfect balance of the Yin and Yang is represented by the perfectly balanced androgynous (both male and female) figure in the center. The four fixed signs, or fixed laws, of the universe are indicated by the figures in the four corners. 21/3 rules a potent period in which the old order changes, making room for a new order. New plans should be implemented because the chances for success are high. There is growth and protection here, as well as talent, charm and luck.

Chester A. Arthur: Twenty-first President. Born: October 5, 1830. Life Lesson Number: 27/9. President: 1881-1884.

Chester Alan Arthur, "The Gentleman Boss," was handsome, intelligent and refined. His outstanding quality was total honesty. A struggling lawyer before the Civil War, he became wealthy after the war handling cases dealing with war claims.

As vice-president under James Garfield, he found himself in limbo, as was the nation, during the many weeks the wounded Garfield slipped back and forth between life and death. When President Garfield finally succumbed Chester Arthur became president and was suddenly faced with a bad situation he had, in part, caused: because of certain resignations Arthur was presiding officer, acting as the Senate President pro tempore. He had refused to relinquish this position because of a Democratic majority in the Senate. Now, as the new president, there was no one to succeed him in the event of his death. In a letter he sent to "the President," instructions were to call an emergency session of Congress if anything should happen to him. 1881 was a tense year as the country worried over the lack of legislative measures to insure a smooth presidential succession.

Arthur was responsible for the Pendleton Bill, which created the Civil Service Commission, a body with supervision over one-tenth of the government jobs. Examinations were required for government jobs under this bill, and kickbacks became illegal. Formerly accepted standards of the spoils system, repaying favors through government appointments and kickbacks, were no longer acceptable. This bill was a turning point in governmental politics.

All in all, Arthur's performance was acceptable, contrary to the expectations of many Americans who felt he was merely a spokesman for political boss Roscoe Conkling. Chester Arthur fulfilled his presidential duties forthrightly, honestly and ably.

Under 21/3, old orders passed away with the establishment of the Civil Service Commission, which eliminated the "spoils system," and the realization that the line of presidential succession must remain secure and apolitical.

The figure in the center of the World card represents completed balance in accordance with the fixed laws of the Universe (the symbols in the four corners of the card). Under Arthur's term, it was time to eliminate outworn institutions and establish a new order. Elimination of the spoils system and the establishment of the Civil Service Commission qualifies this term as a transitional point in American History. The precarious balance of the presidential succession was also tested under this card.

THE FOOL.

22 KEY 0 (22): THE FOOL The Number 22 is not included in the Tarot deck. The Major Arcana consist of 21 keys (1-21), and the Minor Arcana run from 23-78. The Fool, Key 0, stands alone. 22 was the number ascribed by the ancients to the circle, or a complete cycle. It seems fitting that the Fool, as Key 0, represents the life force before incarnation, whereas, Number 22 (indicative of cyclicity) would be the Fool after incarnation, having completed the 21 keys or 21 steps of growth, as exemplified in the 21 Major Arcana keys of the Tarot. The Fool is the superconscious about to step off into another cycle. The Sun has not reached its zenith, indicating that we never reach the limit of our potential. The dog represents the lesser forms of consciousness on the path of evolution. Number 22 focuses on wealth and power on a grand scale. There is a genius here for breadth of thinking and practical solutions. Number 22 bestows hard work, honesty, and above all, ethics. Wisdom and strong opinions are always used in practical ways. Marriage and relationships provide a firm base.

Grover Cleveland: Twenty-second and Twenty-fourth President. Born: March 18, 1837. Life Lesson Number: 40/4. President: 1884-1888 and 1892-1896. Like the Number 22, Grover Cleveland, as the 22nd Chief Executive, holds a unique position in the line of presidents. He is the only president to serve two nonconsecutive terms, as the 22nd president from 1885-1889, and as the 24th president from 1893-1897. Not only was his Life Lesson Number a 4 (40/4), but so was his first term (22/4), thus emphasizing hard work and practicality. Grover Cleveland was a good looking outdoorsman who enjoyed a beer and a cigar, but was also a tireless worker. He was also known for his strict honesty. When, during a presidential campaign, he was attacked over the possibility of his fathering an illegitimate child, Cleveland directed his aides to "tell the truth"—a statement considered "unique in the history of politics." He was the only Democratic president between 1861 and 1913, a man of rigid independence and character. He astonished friend and foe alike by keeping his record untarnished, so much so that he eventually alienated his own party, and became known as "His Obstinacy."

His career, legal and political, was one of fiercely independent honesty, bucking the established procedures for election and political machinery such as that of John Kelly of Tammany Hall in New York State. Yet it was his "stubborn opposition" that excited the voters and brought him into prominence. He was quick to own up to errors and once remarked "I desire to acknowledge that my action in the matter was hasty and inconsiderate. A little examination and reflection would have prevented it."

During his first term he recovered thousands of acres of land held by the railroads in a loose interpretation of land grants and offered them to homesteaders. He returned 500,000 acres of land to the Indians. He focused on two major issues of the 1880s: maintaining the gold standard and lowering the tariff.

Cleveland won the next election by 100,000 popular votes but lost the electoral college to Republican Benjamin Harrison. Tammany Hall took New York State from him.

Cleveland's marriage at forty-nine, to twenty-one year old Frances Folsom, took some of the sting out of his abrasive personality.

Cleveland's focus on the monetary standard, his honesty, strong opinions and unyielding morality are perfect representations of Number 22. He left a United States treasury "swollen with a large surplus," bringing in the powerful material aspect of the Master Number.

23 KING OF WANDS The King looks to his right, towards the future. He has the power, indicated by the lions on the background screen and the living wand of spiritual power in his right hand, with which to make decisions about future courses. The card depicts a mental attitude of preparing for coming events. 23/5 supplies power and influence. Money and material property can be inherited. Contracts could alter lifestyles. Changes occur here that may turn the tide of affairs.

KING of WANDS

Benjamin Harrison: Twenty-third President. Born: August 20, 1833. Life Lesson Number: 43/7. President: 1888-1892. Benjamin Harrison received 100,000 fewer votes than did incumbent Grover Cleveland, but he won the electoral college. The Republicans won the election through a "combination of good organization and corruption." They bought votes in many states and surreptitiously gained the support of New York's Tammany Hall, which had no love for reformer Grover Cleveland. This era has been called 'The Period of No Decision." The nation was rapidly changing from an agrarian culture to an urban-industrial nation. Neither party faced the farmer discontent and labor problems, and the American people were becoming apathetic and cynical from long years of political injustice.

Harrison was honest but colorless, a constant Republican who was sometimes unpredictable, however. Once in the White House he found himself bound by favors. So many debts were accumulated on the way to the presidency that Harrison found the clean slate he promised to begin with was full of smudges. Cleveland's civil service guidelines were temporarily suspended while Republican officials removed Democratic workers from civil service posts to be replaced by loyal Republicans. The rules were then reinstated. Harrison recalled, "When I came into power, I found that the party managers had taken it all to themselves...They had sold out every place to pay the election expenses."

President Cleveland had left the treasury with a large surplus which the Republicans, during Harrison's four-year term, managed to deplete. The "Billion Dollar Congress" spent more in peacetime, over one billion dollars, than any other Congress before it. Such extravagance shocked the nation, and they overwhelmingly re-elected Grover Cleveland in the next campaign.

The tremendous surplus inherited by Harrison's administration, and the powerful influence of those in the government at that time (albeit used negatively) reflect the 23/5 vibration. Perhaps the nation's reaction to the corruption in politics peaked during this administration's extravagance, turning the tide of public apathy. Cleveland's overwhelming victory could support this theory.

The King of Wands represents a power card. Obviously, under Harrison's term, there were too many kings and too much corruption. The wands represent the energy expended in any action. A King card indicates a term under which great good could be achieved; however, those in power chose to bestow the good amongst themselves, thereby setting the country up for bankruptcy in the following term. The King looks at his wand, the emblem of his power, as if it is newly found, and he is unsure how to use it; just as Harrison seemed unable to exercise his power as president.

QUEEN of WANDS.

24 QUEEN OF WANDS The Wand, or power in action, is held in the Queen's right hand suggesting conscious use of the power. She is sustained by the subconscious power (the sunflower, which always faces the Sun, in her left hand). Her clairvoyant powers are evidenced by the black cat, and her strength is symbolized by the carved lion (Key 8, Strength). The three mountain peaks in the background to her right indicate she has attained conscious harmony on three planes of consciousness. 24/6 centers on relationships. Financial gains are possible from people in authority. Sound practical judgment is needed in business dealings. Understanding the feelings and emotions of others is very important now. Generosity and patience must be exercised. Negatively expressed, stubborn, domineering qualities surface.

Grover Cleveland: Twenty-fourth and Twenty-second President. Born: March 18, 1837. Life Lesson Number: 40/4. President: 1892-1896 and 1884-1888. When Grover Cleveland was returned to the White House after the intervening presidency of Benjamin Harrison, he was greeted by a depleted treasury and gold reserves at a dangerously low level. Harrison's "Billion Dollar Congress" had managed to spend over a billion dollars in a single session, a feat unheard of in peacetime. J.P. Morgan went to Washington. He had "offered to raise $62,000,000 in gold for the government." He also knew that less than $9,000,000 in gold remained in the New York Sub-Treasury, and that the government had an outstanding note of $12,000,000. He confronted Cleveland: "Mr. President, if that (note) is presented today; it is all over." In order to save the country from bankruptcy, the proud, stubborn Cleveland had to give in. Americans were frightened more by the "unrestricted power of J.P. Morgan" than by the nation's financial condition.

Cleveland mishandled labor problems. The worst case was the mishandling of the Chicago Pullman strikers and the unemployed protestors of "Coxey's Army," which marred his exit from office. During his term, his valiant effort to keep the gold standard went unappreciated.

Before he died, however, he had "completely regained the country's veneration." An overwhelming ovation from a St. Louis crowd in 1903 was, as biographer Allan Nevins said, "the apology of the West to a man of courage."

The influence of the 24/6 brought about a most difficult financial relationship with J.P. Morgan, in order to save the country from bankruptcy. Cleveland did the only thing he could have done. His misunderstanding of the emotions and feelings of the laborers also reflects this number, although on the negative side.

The Queen of Wands looks away from the firmly-held wand in her right hand. She knows her power and is comfortable with it. Grover Cleveland knew his power and handled a very difficult situation in the only way possible, saving the country from bankruptcy.

25 KNIGHT OF WANDS The Knight, dressed in a suit of armor, has set out on a holy quest. Thoughts are stirring about new enterprises which his crusade will bring to light. Forces are active and growing. 25/7 indicates trials and difficulties which demand vigorous attention. Conflicts can arise if plans are not made carefully. The mind, positive and alert, must be used constructively.

KNIGHT of WANDS.

William McKinley: Twenty-fifth President. Born: January 29, 1843. Life Lesson Number: 46/1. President: 1896-1901. William McKinley was the fourth President to die in office in the twenty-year death cycle that had stalked every president since 1840 (see page 119). His assassination on September 6, 1901, less than a year after his 1900 re-election, at the Pan-American Exposition in Buffalo, New York, by a twenty-eight-year-old anarchist named Leon Czolgosz, ended the term of a man loved by the American people, a man who was cordial, attractive, and confident—without being self-absorbed. The president died on September 14th.

During his administration, the collapse of the Cuban sugar market presaged events that would lead to the Spanish-American War. When, in February 1898, the battleship Maine paid a courtesy call on Spanish-controlled Cuba and was mysteriously sunk, killing 260 men, American newspapers fanned the flames of suspicion with their headlines: "Remember the Maine and to hell with Spain!" Teddy Roosevelt's Rough Riders charged up San Juan Hill in a costly assault. But by July 3rd, the war was over. President McKinley proclaimed that "When the war is over, we must keep what we want." Cuba was given her independence and the United States took Guam, Puerto Rico, and the Philippines. Hawaii was annexed in 1898 and Wake Island was formally declared occupied. The Washington Post proclaimed, "The taste of Empire is in the mouth of the people even as the taste of blood in the jungle."

In 1900, William McKinley ran for re-election with Theodore Roosevelt as his vice-presidential nominee. He continued to monitor, direct, and, from all appearances, lead public opinion—especially when it took its own course. Republican Joseph Cannon once said that "McKinley's ear was so close to the ground that it was full of grasshoppers." An assassin's bullet ended his life.

Expansionism under the 25/7, the Knight of Wands, was a prime issue under McKinley. The Spanish-American War was the conflict that provided new territories for the United States. And President McKinley's ability to feel the pulse of American opinion showed his constructive use of his mind under the 25/7.

The Knight of Wands represents energy sent forth in conquest. During the 25th presidential term five territories were added to the United States, and the Spanish-American War took place. The Washington Post headline, "The taste of Empire is in the mouth of the people," further exemplifies the expansionist trend of this card.

26 PAGE OF WANDS By fixing his attention on the flowering wand before him, the young Page appears to be contemplating his power. He knows his inner strength but has not yet been called upon to exercise it. 26/8 is a karmic number. There are 26 letters in our alphabet, the extent of our ability to communicate verbally and through the written word. 26 is the number of the cube, an ancient symbol for the human body, and the world of form. Salt crystalizes in cubes, and we are said to be "the salt of the earth." A 26-degree angled hallway leading to the Queen's Chamber in the Great Pyramid revealed, upon its first opening, walls mysteriously encrusted with up to a half-inch of salt. 26/8 brings events with karmic implication. Powers of expression and communication develop gifted speakers under this number. Good judgment is necessary. Stressful situations and varied experiences help develop self-confidence. There is enthusiasm, courage, and power here.

PAGE of WANDS.

Theodore Roosevelt: Twenty-sixth President. Born: October 27, 1868. Life Lesson Number: 59/5. President: 1901-1908. Upon President McKinley's death, Theodore "Teddy" Roosevelt became the 26th president of the United States. In Roosevelt, a "brash new breed of political activists" was epitomized. "Never sit still." Roosevelt declared, "Get action, do things...take a place wherever you are and be somebody." He was an eruptive, dynamic person who molded the office of President into its modern form. He forged the idea of national one-ness, that the country as a whole was larger than its individual parts.

As a child, his frail, asthmatic body drove him to build his strength. He lifted barbells at home and boxed, "boxed hard," in the college gymnasium. It was a "triumph of will over trauma." T.R. was a tough, hardhitting man of action, who was at ease in buckskins or the library, at a formal party or a court of law. When he was suggested as a running-mate for President McKinley, Mark Hanna, GOP National Chairman, asked, "Don't any of you realize there's only one life between this madman and the White House?" When, at 42, Teddy Roosevelt succeeded President McKinley, Hanna cried, "Now, look, that damned cowboy is President of the United States."

Teddy Roosevelt earned a reputation for being a man who lived his principles. His motto, a West African hunting proverb, "Speak softly and carry a big stick; you will go far," became world known. As a man, he was eternally young. One observer commented, "you must always remember that the President is about six."

Perhaps the karmic situation calling for Teddy Roosevelt as the 26th president was the nation's embroilment in a time when, as never before in America's history, progressive movements were demanding an end to cruel abuses of the laborer by spectacularly indifferent industrialists. Would the conservative McKinley have been able to strike out against the "criminal rich" as Teddy Roosevelt did, declaring that "of all forms of tyranny, the least attractive and the most vulgar is the tyranny of mere wealth, the tyranny of plutocracy." It was hard to say, but history seems to have proven that Teddy Roosevelt was the right man at the right time. As said above, he "(shaped) the Presidency as we know it today."

The enthusiasm, courage, power, and persuasion of the man cannot be denied. He was a giant in a time when gigantic deeds were necessary. He shaped the destiny of the American presidency and ushered in a new century. The karmic 26/8 had been fulfilled.

Teddy's motto, "Speak softly and carry a big stick," is pictured by the Page of Wands, who stands quietly observing his wand (his stick). Although his posture is reserved, he knows his inner strength and is ready to use it when necessary.

ACE ✦ WANDS.

27 ACE OF WANDS A living wand is offered by the hand of God. Some of the leaves in the shape of yods—the creative spark—fall to the earth bringing new energy, ideas, and movement. Life is dispensed everywhere. 27/9 indicates great spiritual strength, deep understanding and insight. The inner self should be listened to rather than the advice of others. There is mental strength which allows individual action. This is a fertile, creative period. Unwise use of this energy creates confusion and indecisiveness.

William Howard Taft: Twenty-seventh President. Born: September 16, 1857. Life Lesson Number: 45/9. President: 1908-1912. William Howard Taft's father, Alphonso, had been Secretary of War, Attorney General, and Minister to Austria-Hungary and Russia under two presidents. He imbued his children with a sense of self-restraint in all areas except for hard work. When William came fifth in his class, his father commented, "Mediocrity will not do for Will." Later at Yale, a fellow classmate recalled that Taft was "the most admired and respected man not only in my class but in all Yale."

When William's father died, William's wife Nellie took over Alphonso Taft's ambitions for his son. She had vowed she would marry a man who would someday become president.

Taft's ambition was to sit on the Supreme Court, but

destiny would have it otherwise for a while. He proved himself to be a hard, efficient, able, and compassionate worker under Teddy Roosevelt. As the first American civil governor of the Philippines, he twice refused to return home to accept the long-awaited appointment to the Supreme Court, because he felt duty-bound to bring some semblance of comfort and education to the Filipinos. Finally, Roosevelt made him Secretary of War, a position that would allow him to have jurisdiction over the Philippines.

A great friendship built up between Taft and President Roosevelt. Taft was a prudent, capable administrator, faithful to Roosevelt, whose energy, enthusiasm, and tenseness caused him to get carried away at times. The two men's varied personalities complemented one another.

Roosevelt backed Taft for the presidency and Taft won handily. But in the next few years, President Taft's decisions would come to infuriate Theodore Roosevelt. When Roosevelt finally came out with extreme, "socialistic" stands, Taft knew he had to fight for re-election to keep Teddy out of office. Roosevelt made accusations against Taft, exaggerated at times and sometimes entirely false, but Taft refrained from answering—until April 25, 1912, when his political advisers insisted he must. A reporter found him after his speech, sitting alone, his head in his hands. "Roosevelt was my closest friend," he said, and then burst into tears.

He lost the election, and as a private citizen once again, he was happy. His weight went down—at 350 pounds he was the heftiest president we have ever had—and his wife's health improved. In 1921, his lifelong wish was fulfilled. President Harding appointed Taft Chief Justice of the Supreme Court. He administered the presidential oath to Calvin Coolidge and Herbert Hoover. When he died in 1930, he had become "one of the most beloved Americans."

Taft's deep inner strength and his stand against his dear friend, Teddy Roosevelt, indicate his need to listen to his own inner voice rather than to the advice of those about him—27/9 qualities. His battle with Teddy Roosevelt left him confused and saddened, as he was about his place in American history and his own capabilities at times. But history wrote a different epitaph and remembers him fondly, as a capable, compassionate man.

As with all Aces, the hand of God is extended in offering. There is a tremendous creative energy here tied into the higher self. Taft, throughout his career, exemplified a man tied to his inner convictions regardless of the outward consequences. He left a fruitful legacy which has grown steadily since his death.

145

28 TWO OF WANDS The figure, holding the world in his right hand and the living power in his left, looks out over his domain. He is surrounded by power (the two leaf-ed wands). The garden behind him shows he has done the work necessary to place himself in a position of power. He is lord of the realm. 28/1 is ambitious, progressive, and willing to take the lead, hoping to improve conditions. There is good judgment and an ability to translate ideas into reality. Unusual and unexpected events occur. The competitive aspect (this number is Aries ruled) suggests conflict which can bring loss. Events can arise that will test one's ability to judge fairly.

Woodrow Wilson: Twenty-eighth President. Born: December 28, 1856. Life Lesson Number: 60/6. President: 1912-1920. Party bosses should have known by the rigidity of his face alone that Woodrow Wilson was not a man who could be handled. He answered to himself throughout his political career.

In his college years, he was a superb debater and orator. While at John Hopkins University, he wrote and published his first declaration of political philosophy, *Congressional Government*, which received "enthusiastic reviews." In his lifetime, he wrote nine erudite volumes and thirty-five articles.

In March, 1909, before a St. Louis audience, he said, "We must now stop preaching sermons and come down to those applications which will actually correct the abuses of our national life, without any more fuss, and without any more rhetoric." He was a no-nonsense man in a period of "noisy campaign."

During the presidential campaign, Wilson met Louis D. Brandeis. It proved to be a fateful event. Brandeis's philosophy of government regulation in the competitive market as a control over monopolies resulted in the shaping of the "New Freedom," under which tariff reform, progressive income tax, and banking and currency reforms were major issues dealt with.

It seems that Woodrow Wilson enjoyed being president. He had the self-assurance and dedication of a "man who felt himself not uniquely endowed but perhaps divinely ordained" to be the Chief Executive of the land.

Wilson tried to keep America out of war, convincing Germany to suspend their "unrestricted warfare" policy. But when, some time later, Germany's ambassador, his eyes filled with tears, announced that his country would "resume unrestricted warfare the following day," Wilson was forced, on April 2, 1917, to declare war against Germany. His wisdom showed in choosing John J. "Black Jack" Pershing as commander of American forces in France. Likewise, Wilson's acumen was displayed in insisting that Pershing's unit fight independently of the Allies.

Woodrow Wilson fought valiantly to establish a League of Nations. He did not have the support of the Senate, so he appealed to the nation. He traveled 10,000 miles touring the Midwest and West, delivering forty speeches in thirty cities. On September 25th, at Pueblo, Colorado, he tripped on his way up to the stage. But he persevered and gave an emotion-charged speech that had both himself and the audience in tears. That night he had a stroke.

Although ill, Wilson wanted a third term; however, America was tired of war and Wilson's demands for leadership in the world did not set well. America wanted to rest, and so she elected a gentle man, Warren G. Harding.

Wilson was a man of sound judgment, willing to take, actually relishing, the responsibility of leadership. His career saw him move from conservatism to progressivism. Although desperately trying to avoid war, he would be remembered as the man "who lost the peace" rather than won the war. His very stature reminds one of the figure in the Two of Wands.

The Two of Wands depicts a man supported by wealth and endowed with power. He holds the world in his right hand. It was said that Wilson had "the self-confidence and dedication of a man who felt himself not only uniquely endowed but perhaps divinely ordained" to be president. He held the world in his hand with respect to his role in the first global war.

29/11

THREE OF WANDS The wands, or living spiritual power, are placed behind the figure. He looks away from the power. The barren foreground shows that much work is needed. He seems preoccupied with inner thoughts to the exclusion of outer advantages, although he firmly holds one of the wands for security. 29/11 is a Master Number requiring much. One needs to be alert to the opportunities that are presented, and be able to use them wisely. Be open to business ventures and partnerships with reputable individuals. A negative 29/11 causes fear and uncertainty. Friends cannot be counted upon as they may be dishonest or unreliable. Those who offer help should be scrutinized carefully.

Warren G. Harding: Twenty-ninth President. Born: November 2, 1865. Life Lesson Number: 33. President: 1920-1923. Warren G. Harding, elected in the fateful year 1920, was to die before his tenure was up, the fifth victim of the twenty-year death cycle since 1840 (see page 119). His death was surrounded by rumour and suspicion: one source implied Harding's death was a suicide; another claimed the Attorney General had murdered him; still another rumor was that Mrs. Harding had done it. Biographer Samuel Hopkins Adams wrote: "Few deaths are unmingled tragedies. Harding's was not. He died in time."

As president, Harding surrounded himself with political friends, and he trusted them. They were a tight group, each member liking and helping out the other. The Teapot Dome Scandal that would break a year after Harding's death would reveal just how corrupt this administration had become. If Harding had lived, he most likely would have stood by his friends. Although he was regarded as a poor president, he was known to be a good friend. He was handsome, friendly, passive, a good speaker, and the "most popular man in the legislature." He never forgot a name or a face, a "regular he-man." These qualities combined to make him the ideal peacemaker in the trouble-ridden Ohio Republican party in his early political career.

When Harding was elected, Harry M. Daugherty, the shrewd political adviser who had advanced Harding's career, became Attorney General. And the intrigue began. President Harding was "baffled by the job." He would listen to one side and think they were right, then listen to the other side and think they were correct. He once admitted: "I knew that this job would be too much for me."

The major achievement of the Harding administration was accomplished by Secretary of State Hughes, who, placed in charge of an international conference on naval disarmament, settled several old disagreements. Nine separate treaties were signed. Japan, England, France, Italy and the United States agreed that no ships would be built in the next ten years and some would be scrapped.

Rumors of wrongdoings began to circulate late in 1922. Charles Cramer, a lawyer who worked on the Veterans Bureau Frauds, left a suicide note to the president and shot himself to death. Jesse Smith, Daugherty's associate, committed suicide or was murdered. The president, frightened, sent his mistress and their child to Europe, and toured the United States with Mrs. Harding. During this trip he died from cardiac or gastrointestinal difficulties, or pneumonia or food poisoning—or utter exhaustion. He suffered from each of them, although no one knows which did him in. Rumors sprang up immediately but there was little evidence that he had died of anything but a natural death.

Harding's administration was fraught with unstable and dishonest friends. Nine treaties were signed, a supreme accomplishment albeit due to Secretary of State Hughes (however, if another man had been president, Hughes might not have had the power to do so), emphasizing the legal side of this Master Number 11, and the need to bring about agreements. It would seem that President Harding, a gentle fun-loving man, unequipped to handle the presidency, responded to the negative side of this number vibration.

The Three of Wands depicts a figure looking away from, perhaps totally unaware of, his power residing in the wands. The foreground is barren. President Harding was given the power, but he was confused by it; therefore, he was unable to use it. He turned his back on the power. The figure in the card looks out over the water as the ships sail by. Curiously, the nine naval treaties encouraged by Secretary of State Hughes were the outstanding achievements of the Harding administration period.

30 FOUR OF WANDS Garlands, garnished with fruit and flowers, the results of hard work and well planned effort, adorn the living wands. Victory and prosperity have been achieved. The two figures, the yin and the yang, are in perfect unison holding aloft three victory bouquets, the three parts of mind. The well-built tower in the background represents the accomplishment of a perfected consciousness. 30/3 working with God Power 0, provides protection while seeking perfection and security. The mind is active, creative, superior, interested in philosophy and/or metaphysics. Activities begun in the past will begin to peak in this period. Rewards are received for past efforts and prosperity reigns.

Calvin Coolidge: Thirtieth President. Born: July 4, 1872. Life Lesson Number: 29/11. President: 1923-1928. Calvin Coolidge, pale, thin and painfully shy, was a sharp contrast to the handsome, genial Warren G. Harding, whose position he took on the morning of August 3, 1923, after Harding's death.

When Calvin Coolidge had been nominated for the vice-presidency in Chicago in 1920, a colleague of H.L. Mencken was overheard proclaiming to a group of reporters, politicians, and policemen that President Harding would be assassinated. Some in the group admonished him but he persisted. "I don't give a damn what you say. I am simply telling you what I know. I know Cal Coolidge inside and out. He is the luckiest_____in the whole world." This journalist was just one of many political pundits who found Coolidge's greatest asset to be luck. But there was more to it than luck. Coolidge was thrifty, not showy, a complete, equitable, self-denying man of honesty—a man who meditated over the role of government. Dedicated to maintaining the good of the community, Coolidge was trusted by the electorate. Because of this trust he was repeatedly elected to political office.

Coolidge was cautious and conservative through and through. "If you see ten troubles coming down the road," he said, "You can be sure that nine will run into the ditch before they reach you and you have to battle with only one of them." He believed that good government arose from peace and prosperity, with the result being "Coolidge Prosperity."

His policy of watch and wait was partially responsible for his failure to take decisive action when the stock market began to falter. He had been warned by experts but he felt the government had no jurisdiction over the regulation of the New York Stock Exchange.

During Coolidge's presidency, sixty-two nations signed a treaty to outlaw war. After Coolidge left office, Mencken capsulized America's feeling when he said, "His failings are forgotten; the country remembers only...that he let it alone. Well, there are worse epitaphs for a statesman." But the country gained more from Calvin Coolidge. After the Harding scandals, the presidency was losing its prestige. Coolidge brought new dignity to the White House with his public honesty. Alice Longworth commented that the White House had changed. "The atmosphere was as different as a New England front parlor is from a back room in a speakeasy."

In 1920 Calvin Coolidge was not sure that he could handle the duties of the vice-presidency; yet, upon Harding's death, when he was handed the presidency, he "felt at once that power had been given me to administer it." The peace, prosperity, protection and philosophy of the 30 surfaced in the man and the events of the period.

The Four of Wands is a picture of stability, contentment and prosperity. President Coolidge, after Harding's scandalous and corrupt four years, ushered in a period called "Coolidge Prosperity." He brought reassurance and stability back to America, thus fulfilling the vibration of this card.

31 FIVE OF WANDS Five young men seem to be battling one another without organization or unity. Each one seems to be intent on doing things his own way. Cooperation is needed here if balance is to be accomplished. 31/4 indicates a need for adjustment, reassessment and cooperation; or obstacles can bring difficulty, isolation and loneliness. It is essential that balance is maintained in business, financial speculation and legal dealings, or much suffering can result.

Herbert Hoover: Thirty-first President. Born: August 10, 1874 Life Lesson Number: 38/11. President: 1928-1932. Herbert Hoover, reserved and impersonal, was a hard-working, thrifty, self-reliant man who, in his rise up the political ladder, saved the country many dollars by "eliminating bureaucratic inefficiencies" and attacking waste. Despite a poor beginning, he accumulated great wealth, which was not, however, a political liability. He was a prime example of rugged individualism. His policy of "strictly limited federal intervention: and his "intellectual rigidities" allowed no room for compromise. When "General Prosperity" suddenly failed on Black Thursday, October 24, 1929, 12,894,650 shares of stock were sold, many at prices that pulled the rug out from under the owners. Government handouts in the form of federal relief programs were not in Hoover's philosophy, and his conservatism allowed no experimentation. He asked for voluntary cooperation from farmers and business and continued to veto bills that would raid the treasury. He was at odds with the people because he could not demonstrate compassion nor a humanitarian understanding of their plight. Instead of a president with high ideals, the people saw a stone-faced intelligence.

In later years, when the national debt had doubled in the eight years after Hoover left office, he commented on the decimal point as "wandering around among the regimented ciphers trying to find some of the old places it used to know."

Under the 31 influence, business and the financial world suffered greatly because of the inability of the president and the nation to come to terms. Each faction in the country seemed at odds with the other, and all seemed at odds with Hoover. This resulted in difficulty for the country and isolation and loneliness for Hoover, who left office under the darkest cloud that had ever hung over any United States president.

The five of Wands portrays panic, confusion and isolation with each figure battling independently and without organization. Hoover presided over one of the most difficult periods in American history. A thrifty, hard-working man, he could not agree to federal relief programs or government intervention in the independent New York Stock Exchange. The Panic of 1929 ensued, certainly perfectly portrayed by the Five of Wands card.

32 SIX OF WANDS A figure crowned with the laurel wreath of victory, rides his horse triumphantly to the accolades of the surrounding throng. He is the returning warrior, the conquering hero, standing for right and responsibility. This is a card of victory, a victory of the will (the rider) over the physical world (the horse). 32 is a special number that has mastery over nations and peoples. It is the Life Lesson and Path of Destiny Number of America. Thomas Jefferson, Abraham Lincoln and Charles Darwin are just a few famous personalities whose lives have changed the destiny and thoughts of the world. 32 brings good news, the settlement of difficulties and disputes. This number bestows an ability to persuade, influence and counsel. Excessive pride and an overbearing nature can alienate some who may then delay plans and upset goals.

Franklin D. Roosevelt: Thirty-second President. Born: January 30, 1882. Life Lesson Number: 50/5. President: 1932-1945. A cursory examination of Franklin Roosevelt's presidency gives positive proof of his identification with this Number 32. He was elected to an unheard-of fourth term in office, only to die some forty days later, the sixth president to die in the 20 year death cycle. He "aroused a loyalty and an opposition un-equaled in American history," although he won decisive victories in all four elections. He championed the poor and minorities, and stuck up for labor while defending American capitalism from the vogue of communism. He marshalled the Allied victory over the Axis and was "prophet of a new world order under the United Nations." His "New Deal," the "alphabet soup" programs—AAA, PWA, FERA, TVA, NRA, HOLC—put to work "15 million American who had no jobs in 1933." Immediately upon taking office, he restored financial stability through a series of quick legislations. He was truly the conquering hero to many Americans. And when he died, the world said, The President is dead. No one had to ask who the president was. Wands depicts the conquering hero amongst his cheering worshipers. F.D.R. was surely this—the savior of a nation as he instituted new laws and programs to rescue the country from a terrible depression. He was worshiped by most of the world. A generation of children grew up thinking he was the king, or at the very least, president for life. He represented the very essence of this card.

33 SEVEN OF WANDS This is sometimes called the martyr's card. A man is prepared to defend his place. He seems to care little for the material world. His dress is simple, his shoes mismatched and he stands on a barren hill. But he defends the very basics in his life—his principles. 33 as a Master Number is called the Christ vibration. It requires sacrifice, responsibility and courage. Assistance will be required by others; strength and energy will be needed. There are strong pioneering instincts and leadership abilities here.

Harry Truman: Thirty-third President. Born: May 8, 1884. Life
Lesson Number: 34/7. President: 1945-1952. Harry Truman
was the "average man." When Eleanor Roosevelt called him to
the White House, placed her arm around his shoulders, and
said, "Harry, the President is dead...you are the one in trouble now," he did not know then if he could handle the job. But
Truman surprised many. Averell Harriman talked with
Truman for "only a few minutes" when he first took over, on
Soviet tensions, and "began to realize," he recalled, "that the
man had a real grasp of the situation. What a surprise and
relief this was!"

Truman's presidency began with the explosion of the
atomic bomb over Nagasaki and Hiroshima and ended with a
police action in Korea. In between, labor bucked him, Congress rose up angry, and members of his cabinet turned on
him. The Truman Doctrine and U.N. Charter would be signed, and McCarthyism would terrify many Americans.
Truman wrote later, "Charlie Ross said I'd rather be right than
President, and I told him I'd rather be anything than President."

Truman was a determined man. He stood his ground and
eventually proved himself right on many unpopular issues.
Sam Rayburn, Speaker of the House, commented that
Truman had been "right on all the big things, wrong on all the
little ones." Winston Churchill visited President Truman during his last year in office and admitted, "the last time I saw you
and I sat across a conference table was at Potsdam. I must con-
fess, sir, I held you in very low regard. I loathed your taking
the place of Franklin Roosevelt. I misjudged you badly. Since
that time, you more than any other man, saved Western
civilization."

As time passed Truman's reputation increased as the
minor events of his term were forgotten in favor of his larger
accomplishments.

Truman's stubborn stand on his principles exemplify
Number 33, as did his plain, everyday, "average-man" image.
He was not concerned with frivolities. When it was suggested
that his dismissal of MacArthur had been an act of courage, he
said, "Courage didn't have anything to do with it. General
MacArthur was insubordinate and I fired him. That's all there
is to it." Perhaps he remains a martyr in the sense that he is the
only president, the only person in the world as a matter of
fact, to use the atomic bomb in warfare. This must have caused him great anguish.

The Seven of Wands portrays a simply dressed figure

standing his ground against a concerted effort to depose him. Certainly Truman qualifies here. As the new president, everyone appeared to gang up on him—the Cabinet and Congress, foreign dignitaries and the American people—as if he were solely responsible for F.D.R.'s death and now had the audacity to try and replace him. He battled tremendously serious problems: the use of the atomic bomb, McCarthyism, and the firing of a national hero, Douglas MacArthur. Through it all he stood his ground, like the figure on the card. The Seven of Wands is the martyr's card, or the Christ vibration. No other president has ever had such an enormous responsibility as that involved in ordering an atomic weapon dropped on a nation of people.

34 EIGHT OF WANDS The eight living wands move uniformly and freely through the air towards the earth and water, showing that the three parts of mind (the three groupings) are united with the four elements—Fire (the wands), Earth, Air and Water. There is "orderly growth, with much cosmic help." Number 34 indicates a coming completion. It is an active period when messages are exchanged and settlements made. The wheels are in motion and travel, perhaps by air, is likely.

Dwight D. Eisenhower: Thirty-fourth President. Born: October 14, 1890. Life Lesson Number 42/6. President: 1952-1960. One of six sons of David and Ida Eisenhower, Dwight deeply believed in honesty and justice. During his presidential campaign, he promised "to go to Korea and end the war there . . . 'This promise clinched what was probably already a certain victory.'" A few months after he was elected president, on July 26, 1953, the Korean War ended in an armistice. The McCarthy "witch hunts" were finally condemned by the Senate, and McCarthy died three years later, a shattered and pitiful man.

The Supreme Court decision, on May 17, 1954, that "racial segregation in public schools was unconstitutional" resulted in picketing and riots. In September, 1957, Orval Faubus, Governor of Arkansas, commanded the National Guard to keep Negro students out of Central High School in Little Rock; Eisenhower sent in federal troops to enforce the law.

And then, on October 4, 1957, the Russians launched Sputnik I into orbit around the earth, and the race for exploration of space began.

Many historians feel that the Eisenhower years were indifferent and rudderless. But it is also true that Eisenhower's terms gave the nation a chance to recover from the violence and deprivation of the past while redefining itself to face the real fears of a future clouded by nuclear holocaust.

Eisenhower guided the country through a frightening period in a calm, friendly and detached manner. Some important issues were settled, and a completely new form of air travel was introduced, but it was Eisenhower's competence in his orderly steerage through troubled times that qualifies him under this Number 34.

It is amazing that this card, the Eight of Wands, depicting wands moving uniformly and freely through the air, would coincide with the period in which the race for the exploration of space began. It is the only wand card, with the exception of the Ace of Wands, the hand of God (which, however, is stationary), that is not earthbound. This card represents flight; it also represents an orderly, steady, smooth advancement towards a goal. Eisenhower's administration exemplifies this. Although some classify these years as indifferent ones, they should not be dismissed. These were years in which Eisenhower guided the nation calmly through a frightening period in its history.

35 NINE OF WANDS The figure, bandaged and weary from battle, stands ready to defend his position once more if necessary. He holds the living power in his hands in readiness. He is strong, both physically and spiritually. Inherited strength is implied by the planted wands in the background. Number 35 denotes "a period when almost anything can happen." Preparation and strength are necessary for oppositions that can arise. Pressures and worry can affect health. But there is tremendous vitality here. Charm and attractiveness to both sexes come under this number.

John F. Kennedy: Thirty-fifth President. Born: May 29, 1917 Life Lesson Number 52/7. President: 1960-1963. John Kennedy was the seventh victim of the cycle of death which has struck American presidents every twenty years since 1840. (see page 119). He was the youngest man ever elected. America loved watching John and his wife, Jacqueline, who embued the White House with their zest, vitality and elegance.

During the war Lt. J.G. Kennedy saved the life of one of his men as their PT boat sank in the Pacific. With the drowning man's life-preserver strap clamped between his teeth, Kennedy stayed afloat for four hours. During his years in Congress he was bothered with a bad back; after two unsuccessful operations, he decided it was something with which he had to live.

On January 20, 1961, Kennedy became the 35th

president—elected by a narrow margin in November of 1960. He told his audience, "Now the trumpet summons us again—not as a call to bear arms, though arms we need—not as a call to battle, though embattled we are—but a call to bear the burden of a long twilight struggle year in and year out..."

His New Frontier doctrine summed up "not what I intend to offer the American people but what I intend to ask of them."

The Peace Corps, first suggested by Senators Hubert Humphrey and Richard Neuberger, was formed on March 1, 1961 during Kennedy's administration. The Bay of Pigs and the building of the Berlin Wall surprised many; as did Kennedy's assassination on Friday, November 22, 1963.

Kennedy exemplified the strength of the Number 35; so did the policies he encouraged—strength to "bear the burden of a long twilight struggle..."; and the strength he required when he told Americans to ask of themselves what they could do for the country, not what it could do for them. His charm and vitality were contagious; Assistant Secretary of Labor Daniel P. Moynihan's comment capsulized the sadness of the nation in mourning: "We'll laugh again. It's just that we'll never be young again."

The Nine of Wands depicts a figure who, although battle-worn, exudes strength and ability. He holds the wand of power firmly in both hands. John Kennedy exuded the same strength, determination and purpose. The firmly planted wands behind the figure in the card exemplify the organization and support—both familial and political—behind Kennedy. His request that the people do for the nation, rather than ask of it, further suggests the posture of this card. A curious coincidence?—The figure has a bandaged head, the only card pictured this way. President Kennedy was shot in the head.

36 TEN OF WANDS The figure, heavy laden, has bound his spiritual power and walks behind the wands with head bowed to the city of consciousness. He has gathered his power, and rather than hide behind it or deny it, he now plans to consciously use it. Number 36 may present heavy burdens that will require determination to resolve. Fix attention upon the goals, and use inner strengths and talents to reach them. There is energy, common sense, wisdom and persistence here.

Lyndon B. Johnson: Thirty-sixth President. Born: August 27, 1908. Life Lesson Number: 53/8. President: 1963-1968. "No man in American history became president with a greater relish for power or with more experience..." wrote Rowland Evans and Robert Novak about Lyndon Johnson. Upon Kennedy's death, Johnson assumed office with a confidence and ability that eased the doubts of a nervous nation. He was responsible for the Civil Rights Act of 1964, as well as educational bills, new tax laws, and his famous "war on poverty." After a landslide victory over Barry Goldwater in the 1964 presidential election, he continued to push "with shrewd strategy and relentless drive," legislation through Congress that brought about more innovations than any other president in a single Congressional session. His "Great Society" policies covered many areas. "I am a compromiser and a manipulator," he said.

The Vietnam War brought dissension from all sides. When the United States stepped up its bombing, the doves screamed. Antiwar protests sprang up. North Vietnam, encouraged by the peace demonstrations, continued its aggression. The hawks were enraged and complained that the bombing was too limited. On May 19, 1967, American planes bombed Hanoi for the first time and American casualty lists soared that month. On March 31, 1968, Johnson announced a partial end to the bombing in North Vietnam and set about to negotiate. On October 31 all bombing of North Vietnam ceased.

Lyndon Johnson was a man born to rule—upon Johnson's birth his father announced that a U.S. Senator had been born—and he had the feel for it. He fixed his attention on that "big white house" on the highest hill in every town, the house where the people in power live. And through his political shrewdness, talent and ability—and destiny—he became president of the United States.

The Ten of Wands depicts a figure who has gathered all the experience from the wand portion of the Tarot deck and is petite for power and the means to keep himself full. Johnson was born to rule: he had the qualifications and the feel for it. He was ready, and he took office bent beneath a heavy burden, as is the figure on the card.

KING of CUPS.

37 KING OF CUPS The seated King seems firm in his power—holding the scepter in one hand and the cup of controlled emotion in the other. His floating throne indicates that his subconscious mind (water) supports him. The ship in the background involves him in the material world. He will prevail as long as he maintains emotional stability and balanced power. Number 37 brings influence, friends and financial benefits. This is a reserved number, a calm exterior covering a deep need to rule. If threatened, militant and defensive attitudes arise. Travel overseas as an important personage is possible. Negatively, "A calm exterior...conceals a dishonest, perhaps violent nature. You use all forms of trickery to gain your ends."

Richard M. Nixon: Thirty-seventh President. Born: January 9, 1913. Life Lesson Number: 24/6. President: 1968-1974. Campaigning on a promise to bring an end to the Vietnam War, Richard Nixon won in a close race over Hubert Humphrey and George Wallace. And in August, 1972, the last combat unit left Vietnam. Nixon visited many European countries in 1969 and became the first president in nearly 25 years to visit a Communist nation, Romania. Nixon's visits to Russia and China in 1972 were marked as historic moments in American diplomacy.

A year after his re-election in 1972, the Watergate scandal broke. Richard Nixon finally resigned in disgrace after many of his former top assistants were accused of obstruction of justice and he himself was an apparent accomplice.

Nixon, true to Number 37, showed a calm exterior that covered an intense desire to lead. His overseas travels brought great prestige to the United States and promoted good feelings between formerly antagonistic nations. But as Watergate broke and mushroomed, he became defensive. Lost tapes of White House conversations and a labyrinth of political intrigue and deception finally forced his resignation.

The King of Cups represents a transition from the wands to the cups in the Tarot deck. A transition is the introduction of some element that has not been considered or experienced. Cups represent the emotions. Nixon's resignation, the first in American presidential history, and the emotionality surrounding the entire Watergate affair, tie his term to the King of Cups. The ships in the background on the card indicate communication with foreign countries: Nixon's visits to Russia and China were marked as historic moments in American diplomacy. In addition, his visits to many European countries in 1969 were the first by an American president to communist nations in nearly twenty five years. This is the only Cup card picturing a ship. A curious aside: The term "Watergate" could apply to this card as well. This card is the gateway into a new segment of the Tarot deck, the Cups (water; emotions). This first Cup card is the "water gate" to the emotional division of the Tarot deck.

38 QUEEN OF CUPS In her hand, the Queen holds the cup of vision. In it, she can see the events of the future. The cherubs carved on her throne represent divine protection and guidance. The water and earth, and the red and blue of her robe, indicate her balanced conscious and subconscious minds. Number 38 reduces to a Master Number 11. "People in high position not only offer you assistance but may bestow some sort of recognition on you." Rewards are promised now. Advantages and powerful spiritual forces are present.

QUEEN of CUPS.

Gerald Ford: Thirty-eighth President. Born: July 14, 1913. Life Lesson Number: 35/8. President: 1974-1976. Gerald Ford holds a position unique in the history of the American presidency. He was elected neither as president nor as vice-president, but was appointed vice-president under a new constitutional amendment, when vice-president Agnew resigned in disgrace. Ford then became president when Nixon resigned. Ford seemed the unanimous choice of both parties. He was moderate, unassuming, reasonable and well-liked. As vice-president, he candidly offered to make all his assets and personal information available, as a step in regaining the public's confidence. And a year later, his calm, guileless and earthy demeanor restored trust and dignity to the office of the presidency. He was a stabilizing center, a cornerstone of virtue, upon which we all focused in a moment of despair, hopelessness and frustration.

In May, 1975, when a United States merchant ship was captured by the Cambodians, Ford immediately ordered the Marines to attack which resulted in the rescue of the ship and its crew, and the world was once again reminded of the enormous power of the presidency.

Gerald Ford seems a fine representative of the well-balanced 38/11. He was given the recognition of this Master Number by his peers. And its divine protection was in effect when he narrowly escaped assassination twice during his short term.

The Queen of Cups depicts a female figure with the gift of vision and insight. She knows and understands present circumstances and future possibilities. She is calm, passive and sure. Gerald Ford, the unanimous choice of both parties, ushered in a period of passive acceptance and calm deliberation. His quiet insight and wisdom in pardoning ex-president Nixon calmed an hysterical nation and healed the wounds of Watergate. Ford depicts this quiet, passive figure who, because of insight into the future, knows what has to be done and calmly sets about to do it. The divine protection indicated by the cherubs on the throne of the Queen of Cups shielded him from two assassination attempts.

159

39 KNIGHT OF CUPS The Knight and horse appear calm and gentle, moving leisurely over an open plain offering the cup of love to humanity. As a knight, he has a holy quest; however, he approaches it with serenity and unhurriedness. Number 39 brings warmth, friendliness and love, and a need to share these qualities with everyone. This draws good will. Partnerships are offered. Good feeling prevails. Negatively, propositions can be deceitful and fraudulent. Delays under this number are always for the best. An unhurried attitude should prevail.

KNIGHT of CUPS.

Jimmy Carter: Thirty-ninth President. Born: October 1, 1924. Life Lesson Number: 27/9. President: 1976-   . Jimmy Carter's campaign for the presidency depicted him as an open, friendly, warm individual with a homespun quality. Certainly unhurried, and highly spiritual, he set out on a holy quest of peace. One of his early acts as president was to pardon almost all Vietnam draft evaders.

In foreign affairs he acted boldly, presenting a moral posture to American foreign policy that had been missing for some years. He surprised everyone by announcing that "after a lapse of almost thirty years, the United States and Mainland China would resume full diplomatic relations."

He has been a forthright champion of human rights, and spoke openly in defense of Soviet dissidents. He was the motivating force and mediator in the peace agreement between Egypt's President Anwar Sadat and Israel's Prime Minister Menachem Begin in September, 1978.

On November 4, 1979, student militants seized the American embassy in Iran and fifty Americans have been held hostage inside the building since that time—as of this writing 158 days. Carter has shown unbelievable restraint, trying to negotiate a peaceful settlement without giving in to the irrational demands of the militants. How long this will continue, no one knows.

As a peacemaker, humanitarian and moral and religious figure, showing compassion and an unhurried attitude, Jimmy Carter has portrayed the Knight of Cups, Number 39, in every way.

The Future

As I write this in the spring of 1980 I wonder if in the fall we will elect a 40th president or stay with our 39th, Jimmy Carter, for another term. If we re-elect Carter, the 39th vibration will continue. If, however, we elect a new president, that person will come under the Number 40, the Page of Cups.

40 PAGE OF CUPS The Page is dressed in a costume decorated with the symbol of eternal life, the lotus, a plant which contains both male and female parts and thus renews itself. He contemplates the cup containing the fish, a divinity symbol. He appears calm and confident but also ready—backed by the surety of divine protection. Number 40 has the God 0 behind it. Wisdom backs up the dealings in the material world. There is a firm foundation here from which to proceed in all earthly matters. Inner guidance is accessible; therefore, this is a good period in which to make plans. Money is handled wisely, budgets are constructed and adhered to, and order prevails. Old habits are discarded as a new lifestyle commences; therefore, certain separations and isolations are necessary. There can be obstacles to orderly growth but the solutions found now will point out where the errors were made that brought about the problem. A strong foundation is then built.

PAGE of CUPS.

As we look at the 40 we feel a sense of wisdom and security. The 4 and the 0 have much in common. 0 is the God symbol, the Spirit, the life force. As it becomes manifest in the material world it moves through the numbers in an orderly fashion. The 1 is the spark of life exerting itself away from the God source, seeking experience; in geometry, the point (•). 2 is the seeking for oneness that it just left, or the awareness of division and separation; in geometry, the parallel lines (||). 3 is the coming together or the first perfect form made with straight lines, the triangle (△). 4 is solidity and form that result from the coming together of the 3, or the second perfect form made with straight lines, the square (□).

Now, the 0 has 360 degrees—unity, wholeness. The triangle has only 180 degrees, but the square has 360 degrees—the same as the circle! 360 = 360, or ○ = □ . In the square, the number 4, we find God's perfect expression in the material world.

In this sense, the 40 conveys wisdom and security, a wholeness, a unity, a faith that cannot be shaken regardless of the tempests that toss. The 40th president should bring these attitudes into office and subsequently convey them to the country and the world.

So, will the election determine that we stay with the 39th president, or go on to the 40th? All indications at this moment point to a Ronald Reagan–Jimmy Carter contest in November. Of course, that could change in the intervening months if either one dies or makes a serious error; however, as things go now, these two seem the likely nominees.

In the last chapter we talked about the 1980s decade as one that will require discipline, strength and responsibility—certainly a much more conservative trend than the 1970s when we "let it all hang out." 1980 is also part of the fateful cycle that sees a president die in office every twenty years—with one difference however. The usual Jupiter–Saturn conjunction that seems to bring about this fated event will no longer be in earth signs as it has since 1840, but will move into an air sign, Libra, for the first time. Will this end the death cycle for the presidents? We all pray that it will.

Jimmy Carter is a Libran. At the beginning of this chapter, on page 108, you will find that, with Jimmy Carter's election, we have had more Libran presidents than any other sign. All the planetary activity in Libra this fall and next year certainly heightens his chances.

However, Ronald Reagan is a conservative; a tough-talking, no-nonsense man. The country's conservative trend may swing the election towards him. He is also an Aquarian. We have had four Aquarian presidents, all of whom have died in office. No Libran president has been elected in this twenty-year death cycle, therefore no Libran president has died in office during this phenomenon. Reagan is in his late sixties. If he is elected, and the change of the Jupiter–Saturn conjunction into another element has no effect upon the death cycle, will the strain of the office be too much for him?

These are all questions no one can answer today. If I had to guess, I would probably say Ronald Reagan will win the presidential election in 1980, not because of any personal political affiliations—both seem like fine men and I both agree and disagree with each of them on different subjects—but because the evidence points towards a strong, abrupt swing to the right, the yin and the yang in action, as always. We might look at the decade numbers—or any sequence of numbers—as the swing of a pendulum: i.e., 1 to the left, 2 to the right, 3 to the left, 4 to the right, 5 to the left, 6 to the right, 7 to the left, 8 to the right, and 9, time to change everything. We are in the 8 decade—the '80s—and the pendulum has swung to the right; the yin will prevail.

Regardless of whom we elect, I have trust and confidence in the subconscious powers of the mind, and the blending of those powers with the cosmic cycles. The American consciousness has, throughout history, been so tuned in to her presidential candidates that she has almost consistently elected the right person at the right time. So many honest, ethical, moral individuals have been elected during times of corruption, men who stood their ground against all opposition, and who usually paid a high price for their loftly ideals. Others have risen to the demands of the office, often to the surprise of the political bosses who nominated them thinking they were controllable. Some have seemingly failed, but perhaps in that failure they laid the seeds of new growth. All in all, the American people have been amazingly insightful in their selection of presidents.

And when the 1990s decade arrives, a time to change everything, who knows—we may elect a woman!

You may want to do some research on your own about future numerical sequences and what they may hold for the American presidency. More information about the double numbers and their corresponding Tarot keys can be found in *Numerology and the Divine Triangle* by Faith Javane and Dusty Bunker.

7

THE EFFECT OF CALENDAR

MONTHS' NUMBERS

The calendar has a long and complicated history. In the beginning, certain natural phenomena probably gave rise to the division of time. The apparent revolution of the Sun around the Earth every twenty-four hours was the basis of the division into days, and the phases of the moon recurring about every twenty-nine days suggested the monthly divisions. A longer measurement of time, the year, was supplied by the apparent north and south motion of the Sun through the seasons.

Some claim that the division into weeks is attributed to God's commandment to Moses to observe the Sabbath (meaning "seventh") day and keep it holy; and other authorities ascribe the number to the original seven planets whose names were given to the days. The weekly division could also relate to the seven-day quarters of the moon, e.g., there are approximately seven days from the new moon to the first quarter

to the full, from the full to the third quarter, and from the
third to the next new moon. Since agrarian cultures placed
much emphasis on planting by the moon's phases, they were
well aware of these seven day quarters of the month.

In 4236 BC, the civil calendar was introduced in Egypt.
When Julius Caesar was in Alexandria, Egypt, in 46 BC, he met
Sisogenes, an Egyptian astronomer, who showed him how the
Egyptian solar calendar, based on 12 months and 365 days,
worked. The Roman calendar, based as it was on 12 months a
year with an extra month thrown in now and then, was
eighty-five days wrong at that time. Caesar decreed that this
new calendar be adopted, with the addition of a leap year
every fourth year, to make up for a slight inconsistency in the
365-day year. It was named the Julian calendar in his honor.

But by 1582, because the year was then too long and spring
was ten days early, Pope Gregory XIII proclaimed that ten
days be dropped between October 5th and October 15th to
correct the calendar. To keep time more accurately, those centuries divisible by 400 (e.g., 1600, 2000) would be leap years
while the intervening centuries would ignore leap year.

(divisible by 400) - 1600-366 days-leap year
                       1700-365 days
                       1800-365 days
                       1900-365 days
(divisible by 400) - 2000-366 days-leap year
                       etc.

January 1 became the legal beginning of the new year
rather than March 25th, which was formerly used. The new
calendar, slightly different from the Julian calendar, was named
the Gregorian calendar in honor of Pope Gregory.

Catholic countries adopted the change readily, but it was
not until the 18th century that the Protestant countries converted. By the time England and the American colonies
adopted the Gregorian calendar, eleven days had to be added
instead of ten. Today, the Jews, Moslems, and Chinese are still
using their own calendars.

We know that we respond to personal cycles in our lives,
as discussed in the early chapters, so we must consider that
calendar changes throughout history reflect the consciousness
changes of the people who changed and adopted them. The
Gregorian calendar adopted in 1582 is now used almost
universally, which stresses an important point. The consciousness of the world is beginning to fall into one cycle of
thinking: e.g., since we use the same calendar, we are in the

same Universal Year Cycles. A Universal Year Cycle is any given calendar year reduced, such as 1980 is $1+9+8+0=18$. $1+8=9$. 1980 is an 18/9 Universal Calendar Year. Because we are all in the same cycle, we feel the same way at the same time about the same things in a general sense. This is a wonderful beginning towards universal understanding. Those nations that use a different calendar; e.g. the Moslems, Jews, and Chinese, might be the peoples who find it difficult to, or do not want to, break into the mainstream of current thought. They may still be struggling with tribal ideas, trying to enforce them within their nations and on their people, in a world that is fast becoming of one mind. Because the world is united in its use of one calendar does not mean there will be no conflict; however, the points of dissension lessen, or at least come to a point where we can understand why another nation feels the way it does at a given time, because we are feeling the same energies.

We are presently in an 18/9 Universal Year Cycle. This applies throughout the entire world; even, in a sense, to those countries that use a different calendar, because on an international basis they too use the Gregorian calendar. 1980 is an 18/9 Universal Year Cycle, and 1981 is a 19/1 Universal Year Cycle. This is a transitional period worldwide, from a 9 cycle to a 1 cycle. As we know from the number delineations, a 9 cycle indicates a time of endings, a period of cleansing, when old ideas and possessions that are no longer useful must be discarded. It can be an emotional period because we may not want to relinquish our hold on some things; but if they have served their purpose, then we must let go. 9 is a period in which we must be charitable, help others, and give back part of what life has given us in the previous eight cycles. 9 is the final culmination, the pot of gold at the end of the rainbow, or the pot of sludge that can bring physical and mental suffering. We should look carefully at the events around the world this year and next to discover what Cosmic Consciousness is showing us and what we have reaped as a result of our previous acts up to this point.

With the majority of the world using the same calendar, we as a nation will find that the energies expressed by the numbers of the calendar year, or the Universal Year Cycle, will be felt universally. When we are in a 3 Universal Year, everyone will be in a 3 Universal Year, and we can therefore understand why another nation feels the need for freedom, expansion, and self-expression—because we have the same emotions and needs. When the world experiences a Universal Cycle 7, we will comprehend another country's need to rest, withdraw, and contemplate, and we will not be offended by the lack of diplomatic exchanges simply because we will not be in the mood for talk either.

If we respond to the number of the Universal Year Cycle, would we respond to the number of the calendar months? This question led me to consider that each month, because of its special number, causes special reactions from us. January is a 1 month, February a 2 month, and so on up to December, which is a 12 month. When we abbreviate dates, we use these numbers to identify the months of the year; e.g., March 15, 1980, is written 3/15/80, and November 18, 1982, is written 11/18/82. Therefore, through constant repetition, the months have taken on the particular vibration and meaning of the number assigned to them.

Recently I purchased a copy of *Crockett's Victory Garden* and have been diligently reading it as my husband and I prepare the vegetable garden for the year—planting asparagus and peas and melons and corn. I suddenly realized that James Crockett's monthly divisions of gardening activities were a sound parallel to my own investigations of the meaning of the calendar months, in connection with the patterns of the activities of the numbers. Nature follows the natural sequence of things, the rhythm of life, just as we do—although we are not always aware of our role in the cycles around us. We watch nature with her seasons and changes and feel somehow immune from it all, without considering that we are part of this cosmic sequence. And yet in the spring we feel energetic, in the summer lazier, in the fall energetic once more and through the winter withdrawn and more subdued. We respond to the seasons and the weather as well as to all other phenomena that affect this planet. Nature is a teacher that we often overlook.

I quote from *Crockett's Victory Garden* in the following pages because I find that Mr. Crockett's descriptions of the gardening activities for each month describe the meaning of the month's number and the effect that this all has on the consciousness of the world. Amazing!

We will now examine how the months of the calendar year respond to their number assignments. First, you might want to refresh your memory as to the numbers' meanings by rereading their delineations in Chapters 10 and 11.

1 JANUARY THE 1ST MONTH: In Roman mythology, Janus was the god of doors, archways, gates and all beginnings. His symbol was the key that locked and unlocked, opened and closed all doors. The Romans prayed to him each morning before honoring any other god, and he was especially honored on the first day of every month. The greatest of all his celebrations occurred on the first day of the new year. It was at this time that he was asked to bless the year ahead. It is said he helped with the creation of the world, and that daybreak came under his domain. As a result, all initiative and new enterprises are ascribed to him.

He is pictured as having two faces, each looking in an opposite direction, one observing the interior and one the exterior of homes and public buildings.

As always, mythology tells truths through hidden implications if one will look beyond the symbology. The doorway represents stepping from the past into the future. Janus's two faces gazing in opposite directions indicate a time of the year when we reflect upon the past and look forward to the future.

Crockett says that January is "a good month to undertake indoor construction projects that are too time consuming for the busier garden months." Those indoor construction projects could very well be in the New Year's resolutions we make. And in January we must make time for these resolutions before we become too busy later in the year to spend time on number 1, ourselves, and our own needs. We must be in good shape mentally and physically before we can be any good to others.

January, the beginning of the new year, the start of a new cycle, is a time for resolutions. We are imbued with a new energy, zest, and determination to make this new year better. No matter how difficult the past year has been, we are inspired with the hope and promise of new life, knowing that we must take the initiative and make our own plans. Experiences from the past year are now history, part of that store of wisdom from which we will draw the necessary information to handle future decisions. Conscious decisions are made as we sit alone, making mental notes or working with a pen and paper. We take stock of ourselves in those solitary moments as we look in two different directions—the past and the future. Perhaps we, like the Romans, should examine the beginning of every month and every day of the month (pray to the god Janus) and ask how well we did yesterday and how can we do better today. We could make each day and each month a new beginning by making New Day's resolutions and New Month's resolutions. The first of anything is overseen by the god Janus who watches and observes, ready to supply us with the energy and initiative to make the affirmations and enforce them.

2 FEBRUARY THE 2ND MONTH: February seems to come from the Etruscan god Februus who was connected with Dis Pater, the Roman god of riches. Dis Pater is the equivalent of the Greek Plutus (*pluotos,* meaning "riches").

Their wealth came from the unceasing number of subjects who came to them through death. The month of February, the month of the dead, was dedicated to Februus.

February, or *Februarius mensis*, means expiatory month. The *Random House Dictionary* defines expiatory as "able to make atonement," Febra is the Italian word for fever. The purpose of a fever is to purify the body, "putting an end to" an infection.

As the second month, February implies a need for cooperation, balancing, setting things straight. It is time for peace and mediation. Standing in the shadows, in the wings, out of the limelight—number 2 stances—February sees hidden forces at work beneath the ground and within the barren trees.

Of all the months of the year, February is the one people seem to dislike the most, although it is the shortest—28 or 29 days. It seems to be a "down" month, a depressing time for many. We are caught between the "dead of winter" and the "birth of spring." James Crockett says, "In the Victory Garden, February is the bridge month between winter and spring."

In February it seems we have to face our failings. Some of our New Year's resolutions may have failed by now and we are beginning to feel the guilt of unkept promises. While we wander around in the darkened labyrinths of our minds, hidden forces are at work beneath our feet, under the ground, and within all life forms that seem to be dormant. Life is still active, although it may appear otherwise. We work within ourselves to find a balance, to seek harmony, to find that other part of ourselves that seems missing somehow. Perhaps that is why we have chosen February to celebrate Valentine's day, when we send a special card to a special person who fills that void within us.

3 MARCH THE 3RD MONTH: March, the third month of the calendar year, comes from the Latin *Martius mensis*, or month of Mars. Some experts feel that the name is connected with the root word *mar* or *mars* which represents the generative forces. Originally an agricultural god, Mars was in ancient times the god of vegetation and fertility; but these duties were eventually transferred to other gods, and Mars became primarily the god of war.

The word march also means to "walk with regular and measured tread, as soldiers." On the march means moving ahead. The word martial also refers to warlike attitudes.

Mentally, we tend to feel more aggressive in March. We know winter is over, the darkness is past and before the month is through, the spring equinox will announce the season of resurrection and rebirth. Easter falls at the end of March or early April, telling us that life is "moving ahead," it is "on the march." New shoots aggressively battle chunks of ice to poke their tiny heads up into the sunlight. All life begins to battle its way up into the light.

Gardeners look forward to March as the first month of the year when planting begins. I can still remember the first time I planted baby marvel peas on a wet March day in soil splattered with patches of snow. As a novice, I was skeptical about their survival. Some weeks later, and I still remember the thrill, I looked out over the garden to see a faint threadline of green shoots emerging from the barren soil. No wonder March is the month of miracles.

Appropriately, Crocket's Victory Garden begins with the month of March. He says that "it's a month of promise as well as progress," a month when he can plunge his hands into the soil for the first time since winter began.

4 APRIL THE 4TH MONTH: *Aprilis mensis* was the second month in the Roman calendar that began in March. It probably comes from the Latin verb *aperire* meaning "to open."

April 1st, commonly known as April Fool's Day or All Fools' Day, is a day for pranks and practical jokes. It became a custom in France in the 1500s after the Gregorian calendar was adopted. Previously, April 1 had been the day to celebrate the New Year with gifts and visits. When January 1 became New Year's Day, people began sending mock gifts and making pretended ceremonial visits to those people who objected to the new calendar.

Some pranks backfire however. When my two daughters, April and Melanie, were four and two years old, they planned a trick to play on their father on April 1st at the breakfast table. As he sat unsuspectingly drinking his coffee, April said, "Look daddy. There's a robin on the lawn." My husband looked through the picture window and April laughed, "April Fools!"

Melanie beamed. It was her turn. "Daddy, look. There's a 'quirrel in the tree."

Playing the game, my husband looked out once more, whereupon Melanie giggled, "Melanie fools."

April as a 4 month is a time when we feel the need to organize on all fronts. Spring cleaning fever hits and we charge into those dark forbidding places—the attic, cellar, closets, under the kitchen counters, and then to the garage. We take down curtains, take up rugs, take out furniture, scrub, wash, clean, and then put everything back again. Well, not quite everything. Some of the odds and ends land on picnic benches and folding tables out on the lawn and in driveways as garage sale items. Eventually, however, they end up in someone else's attic, cellar, or garage as fodder for next years lawn sale.

James Crockett says that April is perfect planting weather, and it's almost as busy as May. So, we attack our gardens with hoe and rake and shovel, battering the earth until it unwillingly begins to yield. We then sprinkle—using the proverbial coffee can—cow manure, lime, and compost until the ground is an organic quilt. Turned over, the soil is finally ready for seeds, which we place so carefully in their tiny pockets. Hours later, a quick trip to the chiropractor tops off the expenses for the weekend's activities.

Less appetizing organizational chores await us, however, on April 15th—the income tax deadline. Heaven help the unorganized now. 4 is a money number as well as an organizational one. 4 is a square which has 4 sides. Notice where certain individuals end up when their money situation is not organized according to the standards of the Internal Revenue Service—in a square, boxed in, in jail!

April is a month of work—another keyword for number 4, and we all seem to be supplied with the energy and drive to accomplish the various organizational tasks it brings.

5 MAY THE 5TH MONTH: The etymology of May is somewhat uncertain, although some feel it comes from the Greek goddess of spring, Maia, mother of Hermes, the messenger god.

May as the 5th month is a time for release, change, and communication; a zesty, full-of-life, busy, curious month. We want to be rescued from the labor of the previous month. We have had it with clotheslines, rubbish, and dirty fingernails. Now we want to enjoy what we have done. We are free to leave our homes—now that they are so clean and organized!—and investigate the countryside and Mother Nature's handiwork.

For the gardener, May is the busiest month of the year. April laid the groundwork; it was the month for soil preparation and back-breaking toil. May is planting time for most seeds. *Crockett's Victory Garden* states: "May is the bridge month between the cool spring and the hot summer, and often its early days offer a little of both." The gardener is busy in the most enjoyable way possible—the organization is over, the month that all gardeners love arrives, and the planting begins.

Warm weather is mostly upon us in May. We feel like kicking up our heels, getting out the convertible, taking walks in the woods or by the seashore. In 1889, "Socialist party leaders at an international conference set aside May Day as a world wide labor holiday." The world consciousness recognizes the need to be rescued temporarily from the 4 month of April that brought so much work.

Even the term "Mayday," the international radiotelephone distress signal, used by ships and aircraft, is a call to be rescued, a needed release. Memorial Day sees us lay flowers on the graves of those who have already been released.

May flowers are a carry-over from the ancient Roman celebration of spring. The May pole was used during the Middle Ages as the central focus of dancing and sports, a gay festive period.

6 JUNE THE 6TH MONTH: Juno, queen of the Roman gods, was married to Jupiter, the king. She was the "most queenly of all the goddesses," and the Roman women celebrated her each year. She had her marital difficulties, however, keeping tabs on her philandering husband who had an eye for a pretty girl.

June is traditionally the month for weddings. All family and social activities—graduations, recitals, school awards, community banquets—are emphasized. School ends in June, and we all seem to recognize the need to honor those deserving persons and tie up loose ends before July sets in.

James Crockett states that in June, because the sun is so hot, he plants his June seeds "deeper than the early spring crops, putting the seeds in twice as deep as I do in April and May." Our June feelings run deep, just as do the June plantings. Feelings of love, pride and family unity are never stronger or deeper than those moments when we watch our child pirouette in the Swan Lake recital, receive a high school diploma or a community award at graduation, or get married. Children at June banquets receiving Little League, 4H, and Scout awards are a source of joy, as are the awards we adults receive from our own organizations.

Summer plants can be set out after Memorial Day, May 30th, because even the evenings in June are now fairly warm. Summer officially begins this month. We feel warmer, more loving, and generous, along with the earth and all of nature. We want harmony and beauty around us.

As the month of the summer solstice, June sees the culmination of the solar year. 6 is the number of love and perfect harmony, and it is in this month with the start of the summer season that "nature attains to the very peak of perfection."

We respond to the universal vibration of love and harmony in June by planning our most intimate and meaningful
family and community events during Juno's month

7 JULY THE 7TH MONTH: Julius Caesar, who adopted
the solar or Julian calendar in 46 BC, was honored by
having his birth month, Quintilis, renamed Julius. July comes
from Julius.

James Crockett says, "By the time July arrives...the soil
has been hard at work for four months and it may begin to
show some signs of wear."

7 is a number of retreat, rest after work well done, a time
for inner repair. July is the month for vacations. We have been
through the good intentions of January's New Year resolutions, the mental machinations of February's psychoanalysis,
the stirrings of March, the April work syndrome, the May
release, and June's festivities. Now we want a vacation. We
are ready for it and we feel we have earned it. The children are
out of school, we have scheduled our two weeks in July, so we
pack up and go off to the seashore or the mountains for those
two blessed weeks when there is nothing we have to think
about. No telephones, no appointments, no bills to worry
about—yet. No pressures. Just feet up, body out, and hand
clasped around a tall cool lemonade.

The mind, however, never rests. And it is now, when we
have set aside the outer world, left behind and temporarily
forgotten the noises and distractions, that we do our best
thinking and soul searching. Physical activity may slow but
mental activity increases in a transference of energy. Perhaps
that is why we do some of our best thinking and problem solving when we daydream and remove ourselves from a situation. July is that kind of month—a little lost, removed from
"reality" as the material world sees it, but extremely active
mentally.

8 AUGUST THE 8TH MONTH: The month of August is
named after the first emperor of Rome, Augustus
Caesar (63 BC to AD 14). Augustus means noble or venerated.
Augustus Caesar brought much culture to Rome. He built
libraries and schools, patronized the arts, and enacted just
laws. That period is called the Augustan Age of literature.

"August is the cornucopia month of the year," according
to James Crockett, "a payoff month. But not a month for
resting on laurels."

In August, under the Number 8, we reap what we have
sown. Our seeds have reached full maturity and we can see the   173

tangible results of our efforts. But 8 brings responsibility. We know we have more work to do. The 7th month of July gave us plenty of time to think about ourselves and our place in the sun, to rework those areas that "begin to show some signs of wear." Now, in August, it's time for action. Summer is fast ending and boats must be put up and summer camps closed. Children are restless, not knowing what to do with themselves. They also sense the need for organization under this 8 month. Financial pressures arise. School clothes must be purchased, college fees paid, and we need to take "daily trips through the garden, basket in hand," getting things done and cleaning up loose ends while we work with the results of our harvest.

Crockett says that he takes advantage of the spaces left by the harvest in August to plant cool weather crops that will produce in the fall. In this 8th month, we should look at the bare spots left as the result of our harvest, and determine how we can best re-plant those spots, always remembering that we reap what we sow.

9 SEPTEMBER THE 9TH MONTH: The Julian 12-month calendar fashioned on the Egyptian's solar year calendar was adopted in Rome January 1, 45 BC. Prior to that time, the Roman calendar began in March, making September the 7th month, October the 8th, November the 9th and December the 10th month of the year. Their names are derived from the Latin for these numbers. September comes from the Latin *septem*, for seven. When the Gregorian calendar was adopted in 1582, it was decided that these names would be kept, even though they were misnomers.

Labor Day, celebrated on the first Monday in September, is a national holiday in the United States. It originated in New York on September 5, 1882, when the Knights of Labor held a parade "to demonstrate the strength and enthusiasm of labor organizations." The idea spread and Labor Day soon became a national holiday in honor of labor.

On Labor Day, we celebrate the work we have done. We honor the effort to produce. It is curious that in the 5th month, the number of release and fun, May Day celebrates a day off from labor, whereas in the 9th month, the number of harvest, Labor Day honors the work well done.

Speaking specifically of gardening, James Crockett says that "September is a good time to record the year's successes and failures." We follow the same cycles as nature does, and September is our month to record the year's successes and failures. It is a month of endings, the transitional period. The harvest is in, vacations are over, fall is here and winter is close behind. We try not to notice that the season is over, especially when we experience a few weeks of beautiful, warm, Indian summer; however, gardeners keep their ears open to the weather forecasts through September, just to be sure, and to be prepared for freak frosts.

Number 9 is transitional, a letting-go period when we still try to enjoy the fruits of our past labors, knowing that their demise is imminent, and knowing that we must eventually let go.

10 OCTOBER THE 10TH MONTH: October is from the Latin *octo*, meaning 8. It was originally the 8th month in the old Roman calendar. It is presently the 10th month in the Gregorian calendar.

In the 10th month, a full cycle is completed (10 = 1+0 = 1). October is the month depicting the unceasing cyclicity of life.

Hallowmas, or All Saints' Day (Halloween) has been a Catholic celebration since the ninth century; a day when all saints were honored. The trick-or-treat custom of today probably originated in Ireland in the 1600s, when peasants went from door to door requesting money to buy food for celebration.

The *Encyclopedia Americana* has attributed Halloween to the Druids in England centuries before Christ. It is said they believed that on October 31, "the lord of death gathered together all the souls of the dead who had been condemned to enter the bodies of animals. He then decided which animals the dead souls would enter the next year." This tradition reflects the truth that is so embedded in our consciousness: that life is unending—our energy goes on. Death brings only disintegration of the physical body, while life is transformed and reborn.

October as the 10th month, the only month with the God 0 symbol, suggests the completion and cyclicity of each lifetime, and speaks eloquently for many lifetimes.

October brings the first real frost. With our heavy sweaters on, we watch piles of leaves smolder in the streets and admire the mounds of pumpkins by the side of the road; we know that summer is over and fall is solidly here. October is a point of awareness. As James Crockett says, "the first frost usually hits the victory garden at the end of the month (October), so October is the time for chilly weather preparations." In October, a month of awareness, we take note of the transitional process. Has the past cycle of nine months brought us a "trick" or a "treat" as we prepare for the chilly weather ahead? In cosmic terms, will our present attitudes and actions create,

175

for our next lifetime, negative circumstances to overcome (a trick) or positive tools with which to work (a treat)?

11 NOVEMBER THE 11TH MONTH: As the 9th month in the Roman calendar, November is so-called after the Latin word *novem*, meaning 9. It is the eleventh month, the only month with a Master Number. As an 11, it also reflects the 2 base digit (11=1+1=2).

"I would have to argue that November is the most important month in the gardener's calendar," James Crockett declares, "because it's the month the soil should be prepared for the next spring's plantings." Strange that we prepare our home soil by holding presidential elections in November—in preparation for next year's planting when the new president is sworn into office. Our November decisions determine the quality of the following year's leadership.

As a Master Number 11, November has to be a very important month in our calendar year. 11 rules sudden and sometimes upsetting decisions and conditions that bring about much needed balance. It is an exciting period filled with surprises. Expect the unexpected is the slogan here. Presidential elections in the United States, a country with so much influence and control over the destiny of the world, qualify as one important major event under Master Number 11.

Certainly, some of our election results have been sudden and upsetting in that they were unexpected. Remember the newspaper headine declaring Dewey the winner over Truman? More than one presidential candidate has gone to bed on election eve thinking he would be the next president, only to awake to the reality that he had lost. A few presidents have won the electoral college but lost the popular vote. But one thing we can usually be assured of, presidential elections are exciting and surprising.

Thanksgiving as an American national holiday reflects the camaraderie and sharing of the number 2 base digit side of the Master Number 11. The need for companionship and getting together is evident by the miles people will travel to share the bounty of the Thanksgiving table with their family. We celebrate Thanksgiving as an acknowledgment of our thankfulness for life's bounty. 11 as a Master Number brings a greater awareness, an attunement with the infinite, with the truth that lies in the cornucopia symbol—ever full and unceasingly producing.

12 DECEMBER THE 12TH MONTH: December comes from the Latin *decem*, meaning ten, since it was originally the tenth month in the old Roman calendar, prior to the Julian calendar introduced by Julius Caesar.

With the 12, we complete a mystical cycle—a combination of the 7 original planets and the 5 senses, 7 holes in the head and 5 in the body, 7 white keys on the musical scale and 5 black keys. 12 reflects in Jesus' 12 disciples, the 12 sons of Jacob, and the 12 tribes of Israel from which all nations sprang; the 12 months of the year and the 12 "planets" (Vulcan, Mercury, Venus, Mars, Earth, Jupiter, Saturn, Uranus, Neptune, and Pluto, plus the Sun and Moon, which are not planets but are called so for simplicity's sake).

7 is a physical cycle, 9 a psychological cycle and 12 a spiritual cycle. 12 is a moment of suspension, a pause, when the winter solstice sees the death of the Sun; at its farthest point below the equator, plunging us into the depths of winter.

"We leave the garden to rest for the winter and move indoors," says James Crockett. December is that month when we leave the garden, the hustle and bustle of growing and producing, and move indoors, within ourselves. It is a pause in the process of living, when feelings of compassion and love rise up the world over, regardless of religious affiliations. There is a respect for the moment, a time of temporary truce, when the entire world feels the essence of the holy season; the true religious reverence and awe at the process of conception, gestation and birth of the Christ child that resides within us all. The Christ child is not specifically one religious symbol, but that high self that resides in us all. The reverence we feel is for the miracle of life and the promise that, even through our darkest moments, the winters of our discontent, the Christ child lies cradled within us waiting to be born.

One last note about the calendar months: Could there be a relationship between the month in which we are conceived and the type of person we turn out to be? It would seem that the energies surrounding our conception should have some bearing on the final product, because it had a bearing on the thinking of our parents at that time. For instance, if you were born in February, you were probably conceived in May; if born in December, you were conceived in March. In astrology, this is a square aspect, and the square represents the material world.

8

GIFTS OF THE SPIRIT

L ast year I gave a lecture at an all-day seminar in the basement of a church. The minister, Reverend Paul Higgins, asked if I could tie the lecture in with the theme of the day, "Gifts of the Spirit," from I Corinthians 12:7–10.

To my surprise, but perhaps not really, I discovered there are nine gifts of the spirit, but none of these are meaningful without the greatest gift of all—love. Nine gifts of the spirit, I reasoned, had to tie in with the nine digits, and the greatest gift of them all, love, had to be the 0, the God symbol, the ultimate goal. The Bible says, God is love, and God is represented mystically as the 0. The ancients said: God is a circle whose center is everywhere and circumference is nowhere.

I further reasoned that, since each of us is born under a special number—our Life Lesson Number—then our Life Lesson Number could represent the gift that spirit has given us in each lifetime to use as a tool for growth towards perfection, love, the 0 or God.

Armed with this exciting theory, I began to research the idea. Before going on, I ask that you read the following verses from I Corinthians, Chapter 12 and Chapter 13, so that you will be more familiar with the reasoning behind the following analyses. I have quoted from I Corinthians out of the Lamsa Bible. George Lamsa, an Assyrian, was brought up in the Biblical lands and spoke pure Aramaic, the language of Jesus. Up until World War I, Lamsa's homeland was isolated from the outside world; therefore his people retained the customs, culture and language of their ancestors, those people who lived in the same land and spoke the same language as Jesus. He was brought up speaking this tongue. So I feel, as do many, that his translation of the Bible from the original Aramaic is more accurate than the translations of other scholars of other nationalities who had to learn Aramaic before they could translate the Bible from the original manuscripts. Many nuances and subtleties can be lost to a "foreigner" trying to interpret another language.

I Corinthians, Chapter 12, v. 7–11:

7. But the manifestation of the Spirit is given to every man as help to him.

8. For to one is given by the Spirit the word of wisdom; to another the word of knowledge by the same Spirit.

9. To another faith by the same Spirit; to another gifts of healing by the same Spirit.

10. To another the working of miracles; to another prophecy; to another the means to distinguish the true Spirit; to another different languages; to another the interpretation of languages.

11. But all of these gifts are wrought by that one and the same Spirit, dividing to every one severally as he will.

I Corinthians, Chapter 13:

1. Though I speak with the tongues of men and of angels, and have not love in my heart, I am become as sounding brass or a tinkling cymbal.

2. And though I have the gift of prophecy, and understand all mysteries and all knowledge; and though I have all faith, so that I could remove mountains, and have not love in my heart, I am nothing.

3. And though I bestow all my goods to feed the poor, and though I give my body to be burned, and have not love in my heart, I gain nothing.

4. Love is long-suffering and kind; love does not envy; love does not make a vain display of itself, and does not boast,

5. Does not behave itself unseemly, seeks not its own, is not easily provoked, thinks no evil;

6.Rejoices not over iniquity, but rejoices in the truth;

7.Bears all things; believes all things, hopes all things, endures all things.

8.Love never fails; but whether there be prophecies, they shall fail; whether there be tongues, they shall cease; whether there be knowledge, it shall vanish away.

9.For we know in part and we prophesy in part.

10.But when that which is perfect is come, then that which is imperfect shall come to an end.

11.When I was a child, I spoke as a child, I understood as a child, I thought as a child; but when I became a man, I put away childish things.

12.For now we see through a mirror, darkly; but then face to face. Now I know in part; but then shall I know even as also I am known.

13.And now abide faith, hope, love, these three; but the greatest of these is love.

After reading these passages from I Corinthians, I began pondering them. Finally, through analysis, discussion—and here I especially thank my daughter, Melanie (Bunker) McIlveen, for some very insightful thoughts—, and practical application, I arrived at the following associations. Perhaps the gift associated with your Life Lesson Number is one you should seriously think about. It could be a very valuable tool for your growth in this lifetime.

Number 1 - The means to distinguish the true Spirit
Number 2 - The interpretation of languages
Number 3 - Faith
Number 4 - Healing
Number 5 - Different languages
Number 6 - The working of miracles
Number 7 - Prophecy
Number 8 - Knowledge
Number 9 - Wisdom
The Goal - 0 - Love

The Bible says we are given these gifts; therefore, as gifts, we can choose to use them or not. They are given, however, "as a help."

I will attempt to explain why I feel the above correlations between the gifts and the Numbers are appropriate. I do not maintain they are absolutely infallible. You may have a different idea, and if so, I would appreciate hearing from you. At the moment, however, these seem to work especially well.

1 THE MEANS TO DISTINGUISH the true Spirit: Although 0 is the God symbol, 1 represents a sort of unity as we know it in this material world. 1 is a centered number: ego-centered in the lower sense; Ego-centered in the highest sense, associated with Mars and Aries. An ego-centered individual is not divided by outside interests but is rather totally centered on self, aware only of self, much like a child who, in innocence, demands its personal needs above all else. A child is closer to its original source than an adult; therefore it often speaks or lives out the true essence or spirit of life, totally immersed in enjoying each moment to the exclusion of all else. "Out of the mouths of babes" come words of wisdom. A child sees the oneness in life, and becomes one with it. The child can distinguish the true Spirit of life because of its centeredness.

Those under a Life Lesson Number 1, should be expressing their total individuality in accordance with the wholeness of living. They should be Number 1 in the sense that they can, by example, show how best to enjoy every moment of living with a single mind—if thine eye be single, thy whole body is full of light. They can show best how to experience the world full of wonder, zest, enthusiasm and total absorption in their pursuits.

Zachary Taylor, Sir Isaac Newton, Napoleon Bonaparte and Aristotle Onassis are good examples of a Life Lesson Number 1.

2 THE INTERPRETATION OF LANGUAGES: As we know from analysis, Number 2 is the peacemaker and mediator, the companion who settles disputes because he or she must have harmony. Vulcan, the mediator between the gods and humanity, and Uranus, god of the heavens, ruler of intuition, belong to Number 2.

The interpretation of languages involves translation. When we translate, we "re-word" an idea so that others may understand what was formerly unintelligible. Often the understanding comes in a flash—like lightning, a bolt out of the blue (Uranus and the heavens). The Living Bible says this gift helps "get others to work together." When we aid two people with differing ideas in understanding each other, then we are helping them to work together. Henry Kissinger exemplified Number 2, interpreter of languages, in his role as the intermediary, the peacemaker.

And is it not the misinterpretation of another's words that causes division? Have you ever taken what someone has said in an entirely different way from the way they intended? I know I have. One occasion comes immediately to mind. During a business arrangement with a gentleman, I suggested that his fee was too high. He hesitated, then reluctantly agreed to the price I felt was fair, with the comment, "Well, if you won't spread it around..." I took his comment to mean that I was too close with my money, when, as it turned out, he merely meant that he would agree to my terms if I would not tell anyone that he had adjusted his fee—if I wouldn't spread it around.

Language is often a poor means of communication—words are loaded with all kinds of meanings. It can be a trigger mechanism that sends people off on tangents, depending on their past association with the words you happen to be using. These word associations are deeply embedded in our subconscious as a result of past experiences. Since the subconscious is involved here, again we find a tie-in with the Number 2, or Key 2, the High Priestess in the Tarot, which rules the hidden workings of the subconscious mind.

The subconscious is the translator, the mediator between the superconscious and the conscious, just as the Number 2 individual is the mediator in the experiences of life.

Calvin Coolidge, Noah Webster, Bob Hope and Henry Kissinger are exemplary Number 2 Life Lesson personalities.

3 THE GIFT OF FAITH: 4 is form and manifestation, and 3 is the activity behind that form and manifestation. There is an expression: Things happen in threes. "Things happen," there is activity, activity that brings results, activity that causes manifestation. But 3 is not form—it is the life behind the form, that moving force we cannot see but we know, nevertheless, is there and is real. It is a point of faith, because before it becomes visible we cannot see it, we can only know it. Faith is a knowing without visible proof. Faith is seeing in one's mind the activity behind the form, the reason behind the act.

Jupiter, ruler of Sagittarius and the 9th house of the higher mind and the church, is unanimously associated with the Number 3. Jupiter also rules professional people like doctors, lawyers and the clergy; those persons we like to have faith in. We put our trust in these people, often our very lives, because we have faith in their ability, knowledge and wisdom to help us solve our problems.

One Oriental philosophy teaches that all humanity walks one of three paths each lifetime: the path of work, the path of knowledge, or the path of faith. Anyone with a Life Lesson Number 3 surely walks the path of faith.

My dear sweet mother-in-law, Ginny, is a perfect example. Her Life Lesson Number is a 39/3. She has an abiding faith that is a joy to see. She believes in love, life, goodness, friendship and above all, that she is going to heaven. If all else fails, that is one belief that will never be shaken from her—she knows she is going to heaven—and I plan to stay close on her heels.

Two of my four children have 3 Life Lessons, and I can see the beginnings of that same beautiful attitude—that things will always work out; God will provide. And life has a way of handing them the things they expect. They seem to be "lucky." But remember—luck is a 3 word. We do not get what we *want*—we get what we *expect*. 3 is faith, and its lesson is to expect the very best.

Famous Life Lesson Number 3 personalities are Thomas Jefferson (O.S.), Louis Armstrong, Eli Whitney and John Wayne.

4 THE GIFT OF HEALING: With Number 4, we are in the 4 square world of form—everything we can see and touch. 3, as the 3-sided triangle, represents the energy behind the form, the spirit of things, the mind within the body. 4 is the body, the square with four sides, which contains the 3, or the triangle: e.g., two triangles within the square.

It is the world of form that suffers the illusion of division, of separateness, of disease or dis-ease (out of ease or harmony). It is the body, number 4, that must be healed. But since the body, Number 4 or the square, contains the mind, Number 3 or the triangle, it is through the mind that the body is healed. Some day the medical profession will publicly state that all disease is psychosomatic, or from the mind. This does not mean that disease is not real—it is very real, but it stems from a misalignment of the mind, the thinking. Remember the times you have not felt too well and were moping around the house—until someone called and said, "Let's go to a movie," and suddenly you felt fine. A small example but an example nonetheless. Much more serious diseases have been cured by miracles, by the use of the mind's will over the body. And this truth will become more widely recognized in the coming years.

The gift of healing belongs to the Number 4, the window with four sides through which to see the inner workings of the world of form. The earth and Pluto rule Number 4. The earth rules form in that sense that it is the visible part of form, and Pluto, ruler of Scorpio, is the great healer, the surgeon, the destroyer of outworn or decayed life, and the transformer.

Number 4 is life; God is life. Number 4 is the square of 360 degrees and God is the circle of 360 degrees: 360=360, ☐ = ◯, form = God. We are God in the flesh. We are

183

the breath of God; we are the "word" of God. When God spoke (when life spoke) we were created (we were born).

Those born under Number 4 have the gift of healing because they are true disciples of life. They worship life as the living temple of God; they know the life force within the world of form; they can feel it and they love it. Through this devotion they pledge themselves to its purity and health and well being, whether through growing vegetables and grains to maintain the body's health, or through the healing touch of the surgeon's hand.

Andrew Johnson, Krishna, Will Rogers, Grandma Moses, Woody Allen and Carl Sandburg are Life Lesson 4 personalities.

5 THE GIFT OF DIFFERENT LANGUAGES: The gift of different languages, or the ability to speak anyone's language, seems a natural for the Number 5, the communicator, speaker, salesperson or public relations executive. Different languages refers not only to the languages spoken in the various countries, but also to the different ways of speaking. You have heard the expression, "You speak my language," That means, you understand me and I understand you, we can communicate. And what better assignment than Number 5, Mercury, the messenger of the gods, the character who carried messages from one place to another, the celestial postman. This gift gives one the ability to influence countless other people because the person with it has the ability to communicate what others feel.

My father-in-law, Reid, has a 50/5 Life Lesson Number. He is an easy going, rambling kind of man who is well liked. He gets along with everyone, and no matter where he is, he strikes up a conversation with whatever age person happens to be around. Regardless of the subject, he can converse on it. People automatically listen to him because they sense something in him that they see in themselves. He speaks different languages in the sense that he speaks the universal language of understanding.

My son-in-law, Richard McIlveen, Jr., has a 32/5 Life Lesson Number. He too has this unique ability to "speak my language." I come home and find him on the living room rug with my eleven-year-old daughter, Sarah. He can get her to do anything because he speaks her language. Sarah was quite crushed when Richard married her sister because she felt there was not another Richard in the entire world. I finally convinced her that someone will come along someday who will make her just as happy as Richard does. She has finally forgiven her sister for marrying him. Richard can just as easily converse with me on metaphysics, with his friends on sports, and with his colleagues on accounting and government affairs. Number 5 is very versatile, and the gift of speaking different languages fits here well.

Famous Life Lesson Number 5 personalities are Abraham Lincoln, Reverend Jim Jones and Patrick Henry.

6 THE WORKING OF MIRACLES: According to *The Randon House Dictionary*, the word miracle means: 1. "an effect or extraordinary event in the physical world which surpasses all known human or natural powers and is ascribed to a supernatural cause. 2. such an effect or event manifesting or considered as a work of God."

In numerology, the Master Number 33, which reduces to a 6, is called the Christ vibration. Jesus is said to have been a worker of miracles. Venus and Neptune, Libra and Pisces, which relate to the 6, represent love, perfect balance, mysticism, suffering and eternal life, all qualities and experiences Jesus the Christ knew, and which he used to work his miracles. If a miracle is "ascribed to a supernatural cause" and is considered as a work of God, then what better assignment for this gift of working miracles than the Number 33, Neptune and Pisces, great compassion and feeling, the Christ vibration, and the Number 6, Venus and Libra, love and balance. Love can be returned to those who have lost faith through the miracle of compassion or through unknown mystical experiences. A miracle can be a healing like Number 4, but it can also be an anonymous gift of money in time to save a home from repossession, or an unpredicted heavy rainfall during a terrible drought that could have caused thousands of deaths from thirst and hunger, or a child kidnapped for seven years suddenly returned home safe after all hope had been abandoned, or a baby falling from a third story window and landing unhurt on bushes lining a paved sidewalk. These are miracles and we say, "It's a miracle," because we can find no "earthly" reason why it should have happened that way. We attribute it to an "act of God," and we feel blessed and humbled that we were chosen for that special gift.

And miracles happen every day in quiet ways—a man and a woman producing a child, the miracle of life; the miracle a child sees when a father fixes a broken toy and it works again or a mother kisses a cut and it does not hurt any more; the miracle of pride when a teenager makes a mature decision against all peer pressure; the miracle of a seed dropped into the soil re-emerging as a tiny green shoot; the miracle of a thought transformed into Swan Lake, the Mona Lisa or the *Brothers Karamazov*, the miracle of a gnarled pair of hands sculpting

185

the Pieta, the miracle of the human heart pumping unceasingly for seventy years. Miracles are not always showy. They happen every moment of the day, and those who know the miracle of life and living stand as an example for us all.

Famous Life Lesson 6 personalities are Dwight D. Eisenhower, Galileo, Thomas Edison, Eleanor Roosevelt, Charles Schultz and Reverend Jesse Jackson.

7 THE GIFT OF PROPHECY: In ancient days, a child born under the Number 7 was placed in the temple to become a priest or priestess because it was recognized that 7 bestowed heightened mental capabilities. 7 rules retreat, contemplation and isolation. Scientists, priests, philosophers, mystics, metaphysicians and all deep thinkers come under this number. Ruled by the Moon, 7 reflects the rhythms of life (the seven day quarters of the moon) and all fluids (the ocean and the body fluids). The Moon has always been associated with mystical processes—the witches' coven meeting under a full Moon, and the magical effect of the full Moon on the human emotion. In mythology Diana was the Moon goddess as well as the Great Hecate of Greek occult philosophy. The Sun is the "chief male elder," the primary active aspect of the life force; the Moon is the "chief feminine elder," or the "primary receptive aspect" of the life power.

As the primary receptive aspect, 7 and the Moon contain all knowledge of life's experiences at deeply hidden levels of mind. The Holy Mother, the Goddess Isis, the Oracle at Delphi and Gibran's Prophet are all manifestations of the Number 7, the holders of truth, the oracles to whom the masses look for answers and guidance. They have the gift of prophecy.

One of my daughters has a 43/7 Life Lesson Number. She is extremely intelligent and restless with a curious and very active mind. She, along with a few family members, took a fine course called Silva Mind Control, which reveals the latent powers of the mind within each individual to him or herself. The 40-hour intensive course guarantees that you will perform psychic readings at the end of the sessions—even if you do not believe you have a psychic bone in your body. The claim was true. To our amazement, we all did psychic readings. Melanie is especially good. At one of my seminars, Melanie and a few other Silva Mind Control graduates demonstrated their abilities before the audience. Given only a name and an address, Melanie gave an incredible reading on this particular person. Her mind is her strength, and although she is young enough now so that she does not know what to do with it, I know that one day she will develop this gift of prophecy in her own way. To prophecy does not necessarily mean one will climb the White House steps and between streaks of lightning and rolls of thunder, shout proclamations to the world, or at least to those who will listen, but prophecy can be the insight that comes through in the great works of a philosopher or a scientist or a holy person, insight that is left behind them for the ages.

Shakespeare, P.D. Ouspensky, Voltaire, Feodor Dostoevski and Maharishi Mahesh Yogi are a few famous Life Lesson Number 7 personalities.

8 THE GIFT OF KNOWLEDGE: With the 8, we are back to a type of analysis similar to that of the Number 4, with differences, however. 4 is the material world, as is 8; 4 is practical application, as is 8. However, in the 8, the 4 square has solidified to become a cube. Results are evidenced. As ye sow, so shall ye reap; as it is above, so it is below; you are going to get exactly what you deserve. 8 is karma or cause and effect. What we send out now comes back. The 8 shows this in the way it is drawn: as it is above, so it is below.

In the 8, emphasis is on the practical business world and financial dealings, the sports field, and deep personal relationships which must be expressed on the physical plane. The person with this number learns not from books necessarily but from direct experience. A physical act is carried out, a physical result occurs. After repeated physical acts and results, or causes and effects, the person learns and profits.

What better assignment here than the gift of knowledge. Knowledge is something acquired, learned from observing cause and effect. *The Random House Dictionary* says knowledge is: "acquaintance with facts, truths or principles, as from study or investigation" (or from observing cause and effect).

Saturn, ruler of Number 8, is lord of the earth and all form. Saturn is the teacher, the one who shows us where we have to concentrate right now, right here, in this material world. When Saturn speaks, we listen, because it touches us in very visible places and in very tangible ways. Saturn rules land, bankruptcy, employment, age, arthritis, the teeth and bones and "well-established things."

My husband has a 35/8 Life Lesson Number. He is a banker. The world of business and finance has been his life and he has always learned from practical experience. He hates to read. His claim to literary fame is the reading of one book, *The Late George Apley*, forced upon him by a (so he claims) sadistic high school teacher. Regardless of this gap (?) in his character, he is intelligent, practical and highly respected in his profession. People respect his opinion. He reminds me of the brokerage advertisement, "When E.F. Hutton speaks, everyone listens." His material strength is a result of the experiences he has been through in the business world, just as his physical strength is the result of his canoeing and hiking and not from medicines or mind control. He experiences everything through his senses—sight, smell, touch, sound, taste. If it is "real," he learns from it.

The gift of knowledge and Number 8 seem fitting partners.

Gerald Ford, Oliver Cromwell, Andrew Carnegie, George Orwell, Timothy Leary and Justice Brandeis are Life Lesson Number 8 personalities.

9 THE GIFT OF WISDOM: *The Random House Dictionary* defines wisdom as "the quality or state of being wise; knowledge of what is true or right coupled with just judgment as to action; sagacity, discernment or insight."

As opposed to 8 which is knowledge or the act of learning from cause and effect, wisdom is the state of *being* wise. The knowledge is already acquired, there is no action involved; it is there, it exists, it is in a state of being.

The Sun, ruler of Number 9, is in a state of being; it is there, it exists, there is no action (in the sense that all planets revolve around it; it does not revolve around the planets). The Sun has always been a symbol of "The Father," the all-wise, the all-knowing, the all-powerful, the Life-giving force, the crucible of the celestial blacksmith. It is the outward manifestation, the representative, of the force we call God. It is therefore omniscient; it knows all.

The gift of wisdom seems appropriate only in this place because wisdom is the ultimate attainment before Love, which is the 0 and God power. With wisdom, we are just, loving and forgiving. With wisdom we cannot hold grudges, hate, be envious, or immoral, because we know the truth. We understand the emptiness of such emotion, we see the oneness, we throw off the little ego and put on the Higher Ego, we aspire to that level of unemotional and impersonal caring. We can only achieve this state through experience, through discovering, through understanding and knowledge. We must climb the numbered steps that begin with the first step, until we reach the 9th, the Sun, the gift of wisdom.

The 9th gift, that of wisdom, allows us to be an example for others. Here it is not mere words that make the difference, though they may be quite eloquent with this number, but it is how we live. Our life is the example. Others will hear our words and see that we live by them as well, and that the fruits of our efforts are full and ripe. In 9, we are the supreme teachers by our example.

John Adams, Albert Schweitzer, Confucius, Charles Lindberg and Paul Revere are Life Lesson Number 9 personalities.

9

THOUGHTS FROM

MY NOTEBOOK

I KEEP A NOTEBOOK beside my bed in which, each night, I record the ideas, thoughts, questions, experiences and significant passages I read during the day. In the morning, I make note of any unusual dream. This notebook is invaluable in my work. It seems that I can think better holding a pen, writing my thoughts, trying to give form to the ideas that are floating somewhere in my brain cells. As a practice that is now a habit, this process has in the past and continues now to reveal information that, for me, is startling, exciting, meaningful and worthwhile. My notebook is a world of free-floating concepts, from Pythagoras and the musical scale to sketches of cubes, from triangles and multipointed stars to various arrangements of the letters of the alphabet and their numerical values, from quotes out of a fascinating book to a dream of flight and crystal chandeliers.

I sometimes wonder what and where is the hand that will

unite these separate pieces into a cohesive picture. And then, a moment occurs, a precious moment which brings tears to my eyes because it reveals a truth for me. A few pieces come together and I begin to see and to understand the beauty and delicate intricacy of the cosmic puzzle that God presents to us in such an array of infinite pieces. So many pieces, in fact, that we often fail to see the unity of it all. As David Spangler says in *Revelation: The Birth of a New Age,* through experimentation in the laboratory, science has come to realize that "the observer and the observed are one," an idea long taught by the mystics of all ages. In quantum physics, Heisenberg's Uncertainty Principle "destroys the myth" of the detached objective observer. Every scientist approaches experimentation with some bias, expecting certain results, and "the act of observing on a subnuclear level alters that which is being observed." We and our reality are one and inseparable. Physicists say that for every action there is an equal and opposite reaction. The mystics say it another way: *as ye think, so are ye; as it is above, so it is below.* Or, as it is in your mind (above), so it is in your body (below) and your material world. We control our health and our lives through our thought forms. Mind and body (the physical body and the physical world) are inseparable. There is unity in spite of seeming separateness and, for me, my notebook is testimony to this "fact"; therefore I would like to share some of my reality with you. Take note if you wish; store it somewhere in the recesses of your mental notebook, and you may find that some of this information will click for you—perhaps not now, but at some moment a few pieces will fall into place, and then you too will smile in amazement at the simplicity of it all.

A New Language

The strokes of a pen on a piece of paper, or the typesetting in this book, convey a message that you understand, because you were taught at an early age what these particular strokes mean when used singly and in combination. You first learned the letters of the alphabet, made up of particular lines in various combinations. These letters probably conveyed no message at that time but you knew that eventually they would. You then put these letters into groups forming words which did convey an idea. The words were grouped together and suddenly a sentence was born. I remember the thrill I felt when, in the first grade, I realized I had read my first sentences: Spot. See Spot run. I can still recall the colored picture above the large lettering, a picture of Dick and Jane running, followed by their faithful dog, Spot. That sentence conveyed an idea to me.

These various combinations of strokes form words and sentences which make up our language and serve as a means of communication. Numbers and geometry, too, are composed of different combinations of lines which compose a language and convey a message to those who have learned the meaning of the individual lines, the lines as shapes, and finally the shapes in combination.

The following are the basics of the language of geometry:

The line represents matter, the body, and the material world because it has a beginning and an end, a birth and a death. It represents time. Various combinations of the line present this definition in different ways.

Spirit entering the material world creates and angle.

The angle where the two lines intersect is a point of consciousness.

The triangle is the first perfect form created with straight lines. It contains three angles, or three points of consciousness, and represents the trinity of mind, soul, and spirit. It is symbolic of the energy behind manifestation. Note that we say, things happen in threes.

The square is the second perfect shape formed with straight lines. The square adds the fourth line, the body and the world of form, to the triangle.

The circle is Spirit, God, the alpha and omega. It has no beginning and no end but is infinite. The ancients said that God is a circle whose center is everywhere and circumference is nowhere.

The square, circle, and triangle are the basic forms of geometry. The square is also represented thusly: ⌐ Note that a carpenter uses a tool shaped in this manner and calls it a square.

An amazing revelation occurs when we look at the basic geometric shapes and the Greek letters corresponding to the letters of the word God.

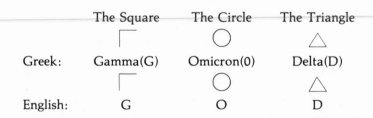

	The Square	The Circle	The Triangle
	⌐	◯	△
Greek:	Gamma(G)	Omicron(0)	Delta(D)
	⌐	◯	△
English:	G	O	D

The basic shapes in geometry spell the word God! God is the square, the circle, and the triangle. In other words, God is the relationship of matter (the square), spirit (the circle), and the connecting energy between the two (the triangle).

The Hebrew of the Old Testament and the Greek of the New Testament used letters in their alphabets to represent numbers; therefore each letter in the Hebrew and Greek alphabets has its own numerical value. Note how Roman numerals are designated by letters: I=1, V=5, X=10, L=50, C=100, D=500, and M=1,000.

The numerical value of God, using the Greek values, is:

$$G \quad O \quad D$$

$$3 + 70 + 4 = 77$$

7 is the perfect number. God finished the creation in six "days" and rested on the 7th. We in the body must now use the creation given us by God and become God's hands as it were. God or Spirit needs form in order to continue creating in the world of form. God can only work through form, or through us, in the material world.

In God, or the square, circle, and triangle, we have:

○   God, the Father-Mother/Unity/Spirit

□   The Son-Daughter/Apparent Separateness/Form

△   The Holy Ghost/Connection/Life Energy

In this analysis, we begin to understand what is meant by "God Geometrizes." The letter "O" in the Greek alphabet is sometimes designated by the Hebrew letter *Vau* with the value of 6. This substitution yields the following total for the name God:

$$G \quad O \quad D$$
$$3 + 6 + 4 = 13$$

13! the number that so many people consider unlucky. The New York Stock Exchange building has no 13th floor, nor do many other buildings. Ski lifts have no 13th chair. Friday the 13th is considered unlucky. The United States Navy will not launch a ship on the 13th or on a Friday. And yet 13 is the number of an aspect of God—that of initiation. Initiation requires discipline, sacrifice, and hard work—the path is indeed narrow and dangerous; and very powerful. For this reason the ancients cast more fear and superstition around the number 13 and the process of initiation to protect themselves from death, that is, annihilation at the hands of a public who at that time were fearful, superstitious, and controlled by outside ignorant forces. They knew that the ones who truly sought the path would find them and come to understand the truth and transforming powers of the number 13.

S/he, The Wo/man

A numerologist knows that each word has its own particular vibration that sets it apart from every other word. This awareness causes one to be extremely careful in the use of words—the way one writes and speaks. Words are truly energies, energies that impress themselves upon every cell of the body through repetition; which brings me to the feminist movement arising in this century as a result of the birth of the Aquarian Age.

Since it is not obvious from my name, Dusty, I tell you here that I am a woman. I am not a "feminist" or a "masculinist," but I am an "equalist." And as an equalist, I object to God referred to as He and the Christian Trinity excluding the female principle. Most trinities in the world contain Mother-Father-Child, but, as is well known from even a cursory look at history, the early Hebrews and the early Christian sect that became dominant were extremely patriarchal or male-centered. Women were chattel, or possessions, and considered inferior. The use of the male pronoun did not at one time include women. When it was said, "all men are created equal," that is exactly what was meant—all men. Less than seventy years ago in this country, the United States of America, supposedly the most enlightened and advanced nation in the world, voting was denied to lunatics, criminals, and women. What do you think that does to the consciousness of a people? Certainly this world has been male dominated. List the names of famous women painters in history—the only one I can think of is Grandma Moses. It is a fact that women artists have resorted to signing male names on their works in order to have them accepted. Think of the names of famous female composers, sculptors, scientists, and writers before this century. And then, the most horrendous condition of all: How many holy avatars or saviors have been women?

Our language reflects our consciousness and our level of awareness. And when we use "he" and "mankind" and "brotherhood" supposedly to include women we are grossly misled. The male pronoun and nouns do *not* include "she," "womenkind," and "sisterhood." The vibrations of the words are entirely different; and the longer we continue to use these male terms the longer we will all, both male and female alike, be in bondage to an outdated and archaic system of thought. It is horrifying to think of the talent that has been and is still denied, destroyed, or allowed to lay fallow because it happens to belong to a woman. It is time to change our vocabulary so that we can all benefit by becoming equalists.

H   E
8 + 5 = 13 The Death Card in Tarot

S   H   E
1 + 8 + 5 = 14 The Temperance Card in Tarot

13 = The number of initiation, death of the body, and the rebirth of the consciousness at another level: or the death of the body as the creative, fertilizing, energizing fluid, the male semen, leaves the body to be reborn in another body.

14 = The value of the diameter of the circle in many oriental philosophies. Pi, or 3.1415, adds up to 14. Pi expresses the relationship between the circle and its diameter. Pi, or 14, is the creative, receptive expression of the circle, or God. The diameter or the horizontal line symbolizes matter (the linear world of space and time). The female principle is the creative, receptive, formative aspect of the Trinity. The male semen, through the death process, leaves its creator and is received in the female body for the process of transformation and creation. The female is the transforming power after the death process.

M   A   N
4 + 1 + 5 = 10/1 The Wheel of Fortune Card in Tarot

W   O   M   A   N
5 + 6 + 4 + 1 + 5 = 21/3

The World Card in Tarot

It is interesting to meditate upon the corresponding Tarot keys for a fuller realization of the meanings of these words.

195

When we continually speak of all people as "he," we emphasize the male, aggressive, dominating, forceful side of human consciousness and deny the female, receptive, nurturing, and compassionate side of that same consciousness. We, as human beings, contain both male and female expressions; however, in most cases, one side far outweighs the other, and imbalance results. The imbalance has propelled the human race into war, death, and destruction, while ignoring the "she" side of themselves—the caring, gentle, nurturing aspect which is as much a part of all of us as is the male side. We need to use the positive aspects of both parts of ourselves—the yin and the yang, the female and the male, the receptive and the aggressive—and bring them into balance in our lives. A dominance of either spells pain, turmoil, and disaster, not only within the human psyche but also throughout the world as we all try to live in peace and harmony.

Pi Proportion, The Living Logos

π, or pi, the mathematical value, popularly attributed to the Greek mathematician and engineer Archimedes (280 BC), represents the relationship between the circumference of a circle and its diameter. Now, if geometry is a language, then the pi value contains a message. Frank C. Higgins, in *Hermetic Masonry*, a book I highly recommend to number addicts, says, "the pi proportion is something that is never absent, in one form or other, from every one of the world's primitive religions..." and is incorporated into present-day philosophies. Mathematicians have discovered in this computer age that they are unable to complete the pi value because, at a certain point, pi begins to repeat itself. The pi value is infinite.

The curious fact is that the first sentence of the Bible contains pi. The Bible says: "in the beginning God created the heaven and earth." The Hebrew word for God is ALHIM or Elohim. If ALHIM is placed in a circle, which is the God symbol, and the values of the Hebrew letters are placed appropriately, see what happens!

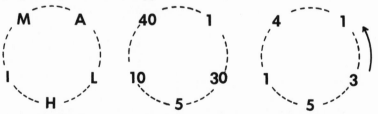

ALHIM has a numerical value of 31415, the value of pi.

God is infinite. Pi is infinite. Pi represents the relationship between the circle and its diameter. We know the circle
represents Spirit and the diameter or horizontal line represents
matter; therefore pi represents the infinite relationship between God and Man and Woman (and all life forms).

Archimedes may have used pi in 280 BC but Moses,
author of Genesis, trained in Egypt by the Masters and himself
a Master, also knew the value of pi and incorporated it in the
first sentence of the Bible in the name of God. The builders of
the Great Pyramid (constructed, some claim, 6,000 years ago)
also knew of pi and used its value in the measurements of this,
the most magnificent structure on earth.

Frank Higgins also mentions in *Hermetic Masonry* that
"Almost all the ancient names of Deity, when their letters are
resolved into numbers, are found to consist of what are
sometimes called "cosmic numbers" in that they express some
great planetary or terrestrial cycles.

The Number 26 and Karma

Continuing on with the theory of cosmic numbers as expressed
through the various names of the ancients for God, we now
look at the number 26.

Another Hebrew name for God is Jehovah or Jod Heh
Vau Heh. The value of the Hebrew letters in this name are
10-5-6-5, for a total of 26. By taking the English word, God,
and adding the placement of the letters in the alphabet, or
$7+15+4$, we also arrive at 26.

Now, if God is the 0, how can God also be the 26?
Geometry again provides the answer. A circle has 360 degrees,
a triangle 180 degrees, and a square 360 degrees (or two
t r i a n g l e s) :

$$\bigcirc = 360°$$

$$\triangle = 180°$$

$$\square = 360°$$

Therefore, the circle equals the square, since they are
both 360 degrees. The circle, God, equals the square, matter.
God and matter are one and the same in that matter contains
God and is a perfect and equal expression of God. St. Paul
said, "*In* God I live and move and have my being." He said, *In*
God, or in matter, in the human body, in this physical world.

Rather than try to escape the physical world, we are meant to live in it, expressing our spirituality every day.

The square solidified becomes a cube.

The cube symbolically represents the three-dimensional world of height, width, and depth. The square is the two-dimensional representative of matter, and the cube is the three-dimensional indicator of the physical world. The ancients used the cube as the symbol of the physical body, the stone that must be worked, shaped, and perfected. The number of the cube is 26: 8 points, 12 lines, and 6 planes = 26. The cube is the fullest expression of God in the three-dimensional world; therefore the ancients used a name for God other than ALHIM and the Unspeakable Name, which was Jod Heh Vau Heh, or Jehovah, which symbolized God working through matter.

$$7 + 15 + 4 = 26$$
$$G \quad 0 \quad D$$

$$10 + 5 + 6 + 5 = 26$$
$$\text{Jod} \quad \text{Heh} \quad \text{Vau} \quad \text{Heh}$$

God = ◯ = Spirit

God = ▢ = Matter

Therefore Spirit = Matter

Cube (solidified square representing the three-dimensional world) = 26

God = 26

Therefore Cube = God (in action in the three-dimensional world)

Cube = Human body
Therefore God = Human body

The Bible says: Ye are the salt of the earth. Salt crystallizes in cubes, the symbol of the body. Solid deposits of salt exist all over the earth, some many thousands of feet thick. The oceans which cover the major portion of the earth's surface contain salt. Salt is an essential part of the human diet. When we perspire excessively, salt tablets are required. The word salary comes from the Latin word salarium, or money paid to soldiers for the purchase of salt. Wherever salt is scarce, its value is very high. In ancient times, much of the salt was probably impure because it contained insoluble earthy material. On the other hand, the *Encyclopedia Americana* states: "salt can be grown by very slow cooling into large and perfectly transparent cubes. . . ." The metaphysical implications here are tremendous. (Remember, the Bible says *Ye are the salt of the earth.*) Salt is an essential part of the earth and the human body: We are an essential part of the earth. Salt crystallizes in cubes: The cube is symbolic of the human body. Salt that contains insoluble earthy material is impure, fit only "to be trod underfoot," according to the Bible (Matthew 5:13): The human body that cannot purify its earthy needs is trapped in a useless existence. On the other hand, "salt can be grown by very slow cooling into large and perfectly transparent cubes. . . ." The human body can grow by a very slow process (hard work and understanding) into a greater and purified being. A transparent cube is the body purified! God is a 26 vibration. A cube is 26. The human body and the physical world is 26. The numerical value of salt is 52, or 26+26.

$$S \quad A \quad L \quad T$$
$$19 + 1 + 12 + 20 = 52$$

In other words, the 26 is the fullest expression on any level in the physical world that we can attain to because it is the God energy in matter. Let's see how this 26 applies in the world around us.

We have 26 letters in our alphabet. I suspect the ancient Hebrews did also. Only twenty-two are known, but it is also known that they considered their vowel sounds sacred, and it is not impossible to believe they might have concealed four of those vowel sounds. At any rate, we have 26 letters in our alphabet which is the most widely used in the world—English, French, Spanish, Portuguese, Italian, Dutch, German and Polish. Even the Turks and the Chinese are starting to use it. These letters form words that form sentences that create books and speeches and poetry and communication on all levels. The 26-letter alphabet is the total expression our minds are capable of. It represents our ability to think, to comprehend, to conceive, to express, to create, and to communicate.

Consider the Boston Marathon. Why is the Marathon 26+ miles? When people speak of the Marathon, they mean the 26-mile run. But why 26? One would logically expect 25 or 30 miles. It is 26 because we innately know the truth and we express it on every level. Although there are other marathons, some shorter distances and some longer, the 26-mile Marathon is still considered the ultimate achievement. The Marathon is run physically of course, but as every runner knows, there is a "wall" at about the 18-to-20-mile point beyond which physical endurance no longer matters. Those last miles are run on sheer will. The 26-mile Marathon is a test of the will. It is the total expression of the manifestation of the human will.

So we have a trinity of expression in the 26: The physical body expressed through the cube is 26, the 26-mile Marathon expresses the human will, and the 26-letter alphabet expresses the human ability to comprehend and communicate.

This does not mean that we have to run a marathon or write a book to express ourselves. These are just examples of the areas of our lives in which we strive for perfection, and how the 26 is the number of that perfection. We place the proper number on such pursuits to tell the world that we know this pursuit is meaningful and worthwhile.

The Great Pyramid in Egypt is believed by many to be a mathematical measurement in stone of time and space. Many also believe it was used as an initiation temple for the highly evolved souls in history. The Ascending Passage, called the Hall of Truth, has a slope of 26 degrees, 18 minutes, and 9.7 seconds. The upward slope, according to Peter Lesmerurier in *The Great Pyramid Decoded*, represents "evolutionary progress," and the 26-degree angle of ascent indicates "human evolution." Again, the pyramid is expressing the number that indicates our ability to fully reach our potential.

The angle itself is important here because the juncture of two lines is a point of consciousness or awareness. Look at a graph which is constructed by numerous parallel lines at 90-degree angles to each other. The crossing lines on a graph mark junctures through which a readable line moves, giving information on the event for which the graph was originally constructed. For example:

The line running through the graph reveals points at which information is available. The graph line runs through angles formed by the background of parallel intersecting lines. These angles are points of information or points of conscious awareness at which certain truths can be understood. In cosmic geometry, an angle represents a point of awareness. Therefore, the 26-degree angle in the Great Pyramid is stating that the number 26 is a point at which we are consciously able to understand and reach our fullest expression.

26 is also incorporated in the deck of playing cards. The cards, so ancient their origin is unknown, contain symbology which is extremely esoteric. There are 26 red cards and 26 black cards, representing perhaps the positive and the negative, life and death. These two sets of 26 could indicate the positive and negative use of the God energies we are born into when we take on the physical body, the cube, the 26. The 26 black and 26 red cards add up to 52 which, as you recall, is the number of the word salt, and also happens to be the number of the outer angle of the Great Pyramid (51 degrees and 51 minutes rounded off is 52). The 52 represents, again, the positive and negative uses of our will while in this 26 physical world. There are 52 weeks in the year—a year being one complete cycle of our lives in which we can see the results of our efforts; e.g., the personal year cycles in numerology. Our birthday is always a new beginning.

The cards contain symbology far beyond what is given here, up to incorporating the value for pi and the Great Year related to the precession of the equinoxes. For further study on this subject, I recommend *Nuggets From King Solomon's Mine* by John Barnes Schmalz (see bibliography). Note that the full precession of the equinoxes, or the Great Year, rounded off, is 26,000 years and the Geat Year, metaphysically, represents one full spiritual cycle for the human race.

Wherever you find the 26 operating, you will find the total expression the human is capable of. 26 is the number of human evolution. 26 is an expression of God that takes place in the world of form.

In numerology, 26 is the number of karma. Karma, which means "the result of doing," refers to cause and effect. A certain action causes an equal and inevitable reaction. We build good karma through positive action and bad karma through evil action, and we carry this karma from one lifetime to the next. Karma comes back to us on the positive side under the guise of good luck, and on the negative side under the guise of bad luck. So, examine your 26's carefully.

The Number of the Beast, 666, and the Computer

Perhaps you have had the experience of being with a special person who activates your creative energy. It seems that when you are with this person ideas flow back and forth in a continuum which draws from each of you just the right response—the lines of communication to your deep inner well of knowing, Jung's collective unconscious, are opened, and you see things and say things and hear things you might not have experienced with someone else. There are a handful of people who trigger this experience for me. These people are some of the ones mentioned in the acknowledgements. I had this privilege of exchange again on the afternoon near the close of this writing when Norris Viviers and I shared our ideas on the number 666. I would like to thank him here for that special day.

According to Christian teaching, Revelation, the last book in the Bible, is the prophecy of the Lord through St. John. In Revelation, Chapter 13 speaks of the beast that shall gain sovereignty over the world for forty-two months. Verses 16–18 read (parentheses mine): "And He (the beast) causes all, both small and great, rich and poor, free and bond, to receive a mark in their right hand, or in their foreheads: and that no man might buy or sell, save he that had the mark, or the name of the beast, or the number of his name. Here is wisdom. Let him that hath understanding count the number of the beast: for it is the number of man: and his number is Six hundred threescore and six (666)."

The 666 has puzzled theologians and lay persons alike for centuries. That it has an evil connotation no one doubts. Note how the 666 was placed on the head of the devil's child, Dameon, in the film *The Omen*. Nevertheless I had never heard a satisfactory explanation of why the 666 was used in Revelation rather than 333 or 999 or even 5 or 13. And as a numerologist, I know that numbers are not chosen arbitrarily.

Through a series of recent events, I found an answer that satisfies me. At a convention a few months ago, I happened to overhear a man mention the number 666. I turned to ask what he was discussing and he said—the carbon atom which, he explained, contains 6 electrons, 6 neutrons, and 6 protons. A flash went off in my head. Here was the 666. He went on to say that carbon is found in all living matter. He was, however, unaware of the passage in Revelation and the number of the beast. I was tremendously excited about this information and when I arived home, I did some research. The atomic number of carbon is 6. Carbon is a component of all living matter and carbon 12 contains 6 electrons, 6 neutrons, and 6 protons.

And would you believe the word *carbon*, assigning digits to the letters, reduces to a 26—the number of the cube and the physical body! Our bodies and the living material world are a product of carbon. The body contains the 666, the beast, but *only* when we are trapped by and in that body because of our physical needs and desires. We can enjoy these physical experiences—we are meant to—but we must own them; they cannot own us so that we are driven to commit evil deeds in order to satiate the body's needs, then the temple becomes a den of the beast, controlled by the needs of the carbon atom, the 666.

Beyond the metaphysical interpretation, there is a very real beast in the world that lurks in many places under the guise of the 666. With the invention of the computer, it would be an easy matter to mark every person in the world with a number, and then record that number in a computer. Note that Revelation states that "no man might buy or sell save he had the *mark* of the beast or the *number* of his name." A cashless system of exchange is seriously being considered and is actually being tested in certain areas of the world. People go into a store and make a purchase which is transacted by running their number into a computer terminal connected to a central computer where the person's paycheck is automatically deposited each week. The computer then deducts the amount of the purchase from the customer's account. No money is exchanged. And to further protect this customer from the loss or theft of a card, it may be suggested and eventually insisted upon that each person be marked with their number on their flesh. It may be invisible, seen only under a certain light, but nevertheless, the person is marked as Revelation stated. On the surface this might seem simpler and easier; however, the implications are horrendous. If society does away with cash as a medium of exchange, and you refuse to be branded or marked, you could not purchase the necessities of life—you could not buy food, clothing, or medicine. And the forces that control the computer could eventually control your actions—how you vote, how you live, what you will submit to because they have a weapon. They can deny you food and shelter and medicine. The carbon body, the 666, is then under the control of a greater 666, the computer. And to add weight to this argument, although the pronoun referring to the beast in Revelation is usually translated, "he." the Greek passage could, be interpreted as "it." The translators merely assumed that the pronoun was "he." The computer is an "it!" The world ruler, the beast, could very well be a computer run by a powerful group of individuals who see to it that everyone in the world has the mark their flesh. The people are then controlled and controllable. We seem close to George Orwell's *1984* with Big Brother close in pursuit, watching our every move and monitoring our lives. If you read nothing else from this point on, read pages 184–185 in Jerry Lucas and Del Washburn's book, *Theomatics* (see bibliography). They wrote a chapter on the number 666 which specifically makes note of the computer and the system that could control us.

So the beast may well show up in the guise of a computer, the 666 in form, that controls the supply of our physical necessities. We would then see the 666 manifesting biological-ly in the carbon atom of the body, metaphysically in the inter-pretation of such, and in the "real" world of computers.

Wherever you find a number, as I said before, the energies are operating in that realm. Look at the following symbol:

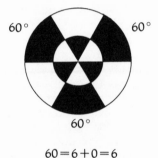

60°   60°

60°

$$60 = 6 + 0 = 6$$

The circle has 360 degrees. These six pie-shaped segments are therefore 60 degrees each. There are three black and three yellow, or two groups of 60-degree segments. If we add the zero to the 6 in 60, which is allowable in numerology, we have two groups of 666! This drawing is the universal symbol for the presence of radioactivity.

One last note on the 666. My daughter, April (Bunker) Worley pointed out the following information to me. As many years as I have looked at it, I never saw it in this light which is a good example of how we can find the number operating everywhere around us—and that we all see the numbers in dif-ferent ways. What I might overlook, you could find very ob-vious, and vice-versa. Therefore, it is worthwhile to exchange ideas with other people.

Look at the number-letter code:

1-AJS
2-BKT
3-CLU
4-DMV
5-ENW
6-FOX
7-GPY
8-HQZ
9-IR

Under the number 6, we have the letters F-O-X which spell *fox*. The value of the letters in this word is 666. E.G.:

6 6 6
F O X

There is no other word I can think of that can be formed out of the letters f-o-x. The fox represents the 666. Note how we use the animal, the fox, and its qualities in our language and culture. Remember the story of the Little Gingerbread Man who tried to cross the river without getting wet? It was the fox who offered its services in the form of a ride on its tail across the river. The Gingerbread Man was deceived, and ended up in the fox's mouth as dinner.

Our everyday language expresses the qualities we assign to this furry little creature. We might call someone "sly as a fox" or "clever as a fox," Or simply "foxy." In caricatures and cartoons we depict sly, crafty people with the features of a fox—narrow eyes, long, pointed nose and wide pencil-line grin.

Our consciousness views the fox, with the value of 666, as a deciever—one who fools others into believing his or her actions are kindly when in reality the actions are evil and destructive. Therefore, when we view the 666 as a negative force (remembering that every number is just an energy and is neutral), we should apply these attributes—deception and trickery under the guise of helpful actions—to the situation in question.

Think on these things whenever you are faced with the 666 whether it be in the form of excessive amounts of radioactivity or a computer.

Geometrical Thoughts

0. ( ) God, love, eternity, fulfillment, wholeness, oneness, cyclicity

1. · The point, the point of awareness.

2. ·——· or ‖ or + , duality, yin and yang, female and male.

3. △ The triangle, trinity, activity behind form.

4. □ The square, form.

5. ☆ The 5 lines of the star, the 5 senses, the 5 races, humanity, the Star of Bethlehem whereunder the saviour of humanity was born.

6. ✡ The interlaced triangles, the Philosopher's Stone, perfect harmony, love on the physical plane reflecting love on the spiritual plane.

7. ___ Matter (horizontal line)

 meeting point, point of consciousness, where spirit meets matter

 spirit (upright line, spinal column).

8. The cube, form solidified into matter, karma.

 as above—so below

 sow—reap

 cause—effect

 action—reaction

9. Fully conscious, point of consciousness rounded out, fully developed, wisdom attained.

 spirit (upright line, spinal column).

7 and 9 seem to defy geometrical definition, except in figures that are difficult to construct; e.g., the 7- or 9-pointed stars. They both represent cycles; 7, the physical and 9, the metaphysical. Perhaps, as transitional points in a state of flux, they cannot be readily defined.

One last numerological note. I wrote this chapter today, June 19, 1980, between 9:00 AM and 10:00 PM, completing the book. Today is a 43/7 day. My name, Dusty Bunker, is a 43/7. How about that.

10

PERSONAL

NUMBER DELINEATIONS

THE FOLLOWING PERSONAL Number Delineations are brief. This book is geared to the future and so it does not stress character analysis; however, a number retains its meaning regardless of when it is operating or how long it is in effect. Keeping this in mind, you can add to your understanding of your Personal Number Delineations as you work with future cycles and observe how they affect your life.

These delineations are written as if they are your Life Lesson Numbers, or what you are here to learn. However, they also describe your Soul, Outer Personality, and Path of Destiny Numbers as well. Use them in the proper context. For instance, if 9 is your Soul Number, then the number delineation describes what you already are, and you should read it in that context. If 9 is your Outer Personality Number, then the 9 shows how others see you but not necessarily how you really are. You should read the number with this idea in mind.

If you wish to explore character analysis in depth, my
first book, co-authored with Faith Javane and entitled
Numerology and the Divine Triangle, will interest you.

1 AS THE LIFE LESSON NUMBER: You are an individual:
unique, first, and best at what you do. You are the pioneer setting out on a perilous journey unconcerned with warnings of danger. Others cannot tell you what to do or how to do
it, because you need to learn and do and experience for
yourself. For this reason you have a forceful personality that
cannot be subdued by others. On the other hand, you must be
careful that you do not ride over others.

In many ways you are a loner. You have learned to stand
on your own two feet without the support of others. Others
may look to you for leadership because they sense your ability
to take control and make decisions. They may think you
strange and aloof, or they may admire your powerful personality; but at any rate, they will recognize your individuality. You are definitely not one of the crowd. You are here to
learn independence, leadership, and decisiveness.

Famous Life Lesson Number 1 Personalities:
Aristotle Onassis—January 20, 1906—Life Lesson Number
37/1.
Susan B. Anthony—February 15, 1820—Life Lesson Number
28/1
Karl Marx—May 5, 1818—Life Lesson Number 28/1.
Napoleon Bonaparte—August 15, 1769—Life Lesson Number
46/1
Daniel Webster—January 18, 1782—Life Lesson Number 37/1

2/11 AS THE LIFE LESSON NUMBER: With the
Master Number 11 or even with the Number
2, you will find that you fluctuate between the two energies.
Master numbers have such a high intensity that a respite is oc-
casionally needed in its base digit, and often the base digit side
of the Master Number will tune in to its Master Number vibration.

As the 2, you are the peacemaker, the mediator, the go-
between who sees communication as an essential cog in the
wheel of life. Peace and harmony are necessary for your
health and well being. You can see both sides of the situation
so clearly that it is often hard for you to make decisions. For
that reason, you are often called upon to settle disputes, solve
problems, enter into partnerships, and express truths that you
are able to discern when others cannot. You will work hard
when called upon and will not let others down who depend on
you. There is a bit of the perfectionist in you that drives you
towards service, devotion, and peace.

With the Master Number 11, you are tuned in to the Cosmic Mind and are therefore subject to laws beyond the earth plane. You must be careful that this attitude does not develop into rebellion for rebellion's sake. Truths come to you like bolts out of the blue. Because you have such a finely tuned mind, you will be called upon to make important decisions in your lifetime that could have far-reaching effects. This number may put you before the public often for recognition. It bestows creative ability because you have an awareness of opposing energies and therefore seek to balance them harmoniously. Your work has a touch of divine inspiration and cosmic insight.

Famous Life Lesson Number 2 Personalities:
Jane Wyman—January 4, 1914—Life Lesson Number 20/2.
Hans Christian Andersen—April 2, 1805—Life Lesson Number 20/2.
Samuel Butler—February 8, 1612—Life Lesson Number 20/2.

Famous Life Lesson Number 11 Personalities:
Noah Webster—October 16, 1758—Life Lesson Number 47/11.
Wolfgang Mozart—January 27, 1756—Life Lesson Number 47/11.
Henry Kissinger—May 27, 1923—Life Lesson Number 47/11.
Bob Hope—May 29, 1903—Life Lesson Number 47/11.
Cecil B. DeMille—August 12, 1881—Life Lesson Number 38/11.
Robert Louis Stevenson—November 13, 1850—Life Lesson Number 38/11.
Jules Verne—February 8, 1828—29/11.

3 AS THE LIFE LESSON NUMBER: As a combination of the 1, individual drive, and the 2 (11), creative cooperation (divine inspiration), 3 may be the most versatile of all the numbers. You are multitalented, expressive, full of zest and joy. You are center stage—acting, expressing, communicating—for your presence brings joy into the lives of others. This is a very social number, one that needs others as an audience with whom to enjoy and expand all life's experiences.

You should always maintain your faith in the goodness of life, for this will be an inspiration to others. They see you coming and they smile because you actually light up their lives.

Expression is your key to life. You should develop this ability in any way you can—elocution, acting, public speaking, politics, the arts. Be careful, however, that you do not spread yourself too thin and scatter your energies—a very real danger with this number.

Famous Life Lesson Number 3 Personalities:
Louis Armstrong—July 4, 1900—Life Lesson Number 21/3.
Eli Whitney—December 8, 1765—Life Lesson Number 39/3.
Charlton Heston—October 4, 1924—Life Lesson Number 30/3.
Benjamin Franklin—January 6, 1706—Life Lesson Number 21/3.
John Wayne—May 26, 1907—Life Lesson Number 48/3.
Alfred Hitchcock—August 13, 1899—Life Lesson Number 48/3.

4/22 AS THE LIFE LESSON NUMBER: You will fluctuate between the Number 4 and the Master Number 22. Master Numbers are intense and require occasional periods of rest in their lower digit; the base digit often tunes in to the Master Number side.

As a 4, you are concerned with earthly matters. The world of form and the senses appeal to you. When you work, you like a visible product at the end of your endeavors. You are organized, efficient, creative, and down to earth. There is an extremely spiritual side of some Number 4s who are able to see the God energy at work in all life forms.

Your work appeals to the basic earthly qualities of those who experience it. You are a builder in the world of form—a tradesperson, an accountant, an artist who explores tangibles, a humorist with an earthy touch—and you are here to experience the world as a structured place.

As a Master Number 22, you function in a powerful physical world where you are in supreme control. Military leaders come under this number's influence. You have an uncanny touch that discovers the people's pulse, and tunes in to their needs. You may find you have control of the reins of power in very wealthy circles. You can build an empire in this physical world, an empire that reflects the world around it—something built on tangible needs and desires.

Famous Life Lesson Number 4 Personalities:
Max Planck—April 23, 1858—Life Lesson Number 49/4.
Krishna—July 19, 3227 BC—Life Lesson Number 40/4.
Grandma Moses—September 7, 1860—Life Lesson Number 31/4.
Will Rogers—November 4, 1879—Life Lesson Number 40/4.
Woody Allen—December 1, 1935—Life Lesson Number 31/4.
Carl Sandburg—January 6, 1878—Life Lesson Number 31/4.

Famous Life Lesson Number 22 Personalities:
P.T. Barnum—July 5, 1810—Life Lesson Number 22/4.

James Otis—February 5, 1725—Life Lesson Number 22/4.
P.H. Sheridan—March 6, 1831—Life Lesson Number 22/4.
Julius Caesar—July 12, 102 BC—Life Lesson Number 22/4.
David Farragut—July 5, 1801—Life Lesson Number 22/4.

5 AS THE LIFE LESSON NUMBER: There is no doubt about it—with Number 5 you are a communicator. In some sense and in some way, you will find the masses and speak to them. You are extremely versatile, clever, witty, and charming. Language is your strength, for you speak most everyone's language. There is a restlessness here, a curiosity, a need to discover and experience. Your mind is ever active, always wondering, always moving—almost afraid that something will escape your attention. You will probably physically need to move often during your lifetime; if not physically, then certainly mentally, for you are here to experience life on all levels. Therefore, you need freedom—room to move. You cannot feel that you are bound in any way.

Famous Life Lesson Number 5 Personalities:
Abraham Lincoln—February 12, 1809—Life Lesson Number 32/5.
Charles Darwin—February 12, 1809—Life Lesson Number 32/5.
Reverend Jim Jones—May 13, 1931—Life Lesson Number 32/5.
Mme. Blavatsky—July 30, 1831—Life Lesson Number 50/5.
Adolph Hitler—April 20, 1889—Life Lesson Number 50/5.
Johnny Carson—October 23, 1925—Life Lesson Number 50/5.

6/33 AS THE LIFE LESSON NUMBER: You may move between the Number 6 and the Master Number 33 side. Master Number 33 needs relief from its intense energies and finds it in the base digit, whereas the 6 often taps the resources of its Master Number side, 33.

As a 6, love, beauty, and balance are your keywords. One side of the 6 is very concerned with domestic issues—the home, the family, and all loved ones. Domestic occupations come under this vibration—perhaps builders, plumbers, electricians, and so on—all trades that require a certain artistry. Other types of professions that seek to beautify apply here as well—interior decorating, hairdressing, landscaping. Many artists are born under this number: those who need to bring balance into the world through their ideas. This can express itself as invention, music, or writing, but always with the

211

same theme—the need for love and balance. This balance may come through the courts—through judges and lawyers, those who seek balance through justice.

33 is known as the Christ vibration. You are a deep, compassionate individual, feeling the hurts of the world. Your love reaches out in waves of emotion. You are willing to martyr yourself for a cause, and must be careful that the cause is worthy of the sacrifice you make. Emotions can overwhelm you, causing you to remain dedicated to a belief, an idea, a cause against all opposition. If the cause is just, the sacrifice is well made.

Famous Life Lesson Number 6 Personalities:
Johann Strauss—October 25, 1825—Life Lesson Number 51/6.
Ralph Waldo Emerson—May 25, 1803—Life Lesson Number 42/6.
Pearl Bailey—March 29, 1918—Life Lesson Number 51/6.
Eleanor Roosevelt—October 11, 1884—Life Lesson Number 42/6.
Charles Schulz—November 26, 1922—Life Lesson Number 51/6.
Joan of Arc—January 6, 1412—Life Lesson Number 15/6.

Famous Life Lesson Number 33 Personalities:
Thomas Edison—February 11, 1847—Life Lesson Number 33/6.
Galileo—February 15, 1564—Life Lesson Number 33/6.
Reverend Jesse Jackson—October 8, 1941—Life Lesson Number 33/6.
Danny Kaye—January 18, 1913—Life Lesson Number 33/6.
Jimmy Durante—February 10, 1893—Life Lesson Number 33/6.

7 AS THE LIFE LESSON NUMBER: Your strength is your mind. Had you been born in another time, you would have been placed in the temple to become a priest or priestess, because the ancients recognized the 7's mystical powers. You may need time by yourself in which to think, meditate, and ponder upon the ideas that flow freely through your mind. Periods of isolation are necessary for you—periods in which a renewal of your energies occurs and you have time to think. Time spent in the woods or by the ocean and away from the crowds are especially healing. Some may think you spend too much time alone, but it is vital that you have these seclusive periods. You should train your mind in some discipline—philosophy, science, religion, metaphysics—so that your fine mental capabilities may be put to their proper use.

Famous Life Lesson Number 7 Personalities:
Horace Greely—February 3, 1811—Life Lesson Number 16/7.
Maharishi Mahesh Yogi—January 12, 1911—Life Lesson Number 25/7.
Oliver Wendell Holmes—March 8, 1841—Life Lesson Number 25/7.
P.D. Ouspensky—August 19, 1897—Life Lesson Number 52/7.
Feodor Dostoevski—October 30, 1821—Life Lesson Number 52/7.
Voltaire—November 21, 1694—Life Lesson Number 52/7.
Emily Dickinson—December 10, 1830—Life Lesson Number 34/7.
Shakespeare—April 23, 1564—Life Lesson Number 43/7.

8/44 AS THE LIFE LESSON NUMBER: You will fluctuate between the 8 base digit and the Master Number 44. Master Numbers are intense but respite is found in the base digit; and the base digit often taps the potentials of its Master Number side.

As an 8, you are especially tuned into the physical world. You need to experience life directly. This is a number of strength and responsibility which requires a keen sense of balance because it is especially karmic. What you send out has great repercussions. You may be involved in business and finance as an executive, because 8 bestows power and control. Many important and well-paid executives operate under this number. Because of 8's organizational abilities on a large scale, coupled with strength, leadership, and karma, many military men come under this number and the Master Number 44/8. 8 bestows unusual strength, endurance, and balance: many famous athletes are born with an 8 Life Lesson Number. At any rate, close personal physical relationships are vital. You need intense sexual relationships which must be fulfilling. You give much and need an equal return, whether in work or play or love.

With the Master Number 44 side, you are so tuned in to the basic needs of humanity that you may very well become a sort of "guru," a spokesperson for the needs and feelings of others. You understand the hurts, the loves and hates, the hunger and sickness, and you seek to relieve that suffering on the physical plane. Your influence is so wide that you may very well be able to help alleviate humanity's pain and restore some semblance of order to everyday basic existence. The emphasis here is on material needs.

213

Famous Life Lesson Number 8 Personalities:
Alexander Graham Bell—March 3, 1847—Life Lesson Number 26/8.
Gerald Ford—July 14, 1913—Life Lesson Number 35/8.
Andrew Carnegie—November 25, 1835—Life Lesson Number 53/8.
Jesse Owens—September 12, 1913—Life Lesson Number 35/8.
Oliver Cromwell—April 25, 1599—Life Lesson Number 53/8.

Famous Life Lesson Number 44 Personalities:
George Orwell—June 25, 1903—Life Lesson Number 44/8.
Timothy Leary—October 22, 1920—Life Lesson Number 44/8.
Justice Louis Brandeis—November 13, 1856—Life Lesson Number 44/8.
Douglas MacArthur—January 26, 1880—Life Lesson Number 44/8.
Ulysses S. Grant—April 27, 1822—Life Lesson Number 44/8.
George Patton—November 11, 1885—Life Lesson Number 44/8.
General William Westmoreland—March 26, 1914—Life Lesson Number 44/8.

9 AS THE LIFE LESSON NUMBER: With 9, you are one who cares for all of humanity, with a heart as big as an ocean and a love just as boundless and impersonal. You are the universal teacher and example, the one others look to for guidance, because they sense a depth of understanding beyond the ordinary ken. You will meet many people in your lifetime—famous ones at that—and all will be impressed by your breadth of understanding and your tolerance. You must learn not to hold on to people once your work is done, once the need has been fulfilled, for you belong to the world. Give others the benefit of your knowledge and wisdom; go beyond your own needs and see what you can do for others. With a 9, you are charitable, forgiving, and loving—you must personify the best qualities in all people because you are the messenger of light. When you leave this earth, be sure that your lamp has been well filled and is burning brightly so that others will not stumble in the darkness.

Famous Life Lesson Number 9 Personalities:
Albert Schweitzer—January 14, 1875—Life Lesson Number 36/9.
Charles Lindbergh—February 4, 1902—Life Lesson Number 18/9
Cole Porter—June 6, 1893—Life Lesson Number 36/9.

Confucius—June 19, 551 BC—Life Lesson Number 36/9.
Henry David Thoreau—July 12, 1817—Life Lesson Number 36/9.
Paul Revere—January 1, 1735—Life Lesson Number 18/9.
Mahatma Gandhi—October 2, 1869—Life Lesson Number 36/9.

11

TEMPORARY NUMBER

DELINEATIONS

T HE FOLLOWING DESCRIPTIONS of the numbers are for those cycles you experience only temporarily, and they will be in effect only for as long as the number influences your life. If you are in a 3 cycle for a day, it will influence you for the day; if the 3 cycle is in effect for a year, then you will feel its energies for the year. The longer the duration of the cycle, the greater its effect on your life.

There is an infinite variety of ways in which each of the numbers will manifest in your life, depending of course upon your present circumstances and your previous actions to that point. However, a 1 is always a 1, a 2 is always a 2, and so on. Whatever the experience you are currently involved in, it will have the basic flavor and characteristics of the number under which it manifests, and no other.

At this point, I suggest a loose-leaf notebook with, for the moment, a single page for each of the numbers 1 through 9, and the Master Numbers, on which you can record the events that occur in your life under the appropriate numbers. On each page you might want to mark the date and then label each event as a PD (Personal Day), PM (Personal Month), PN (Period Number), or PY (Personal Year) so that you will know how long a period was in effect when the event occurred. The page might look something like the accompanying sample.

Number 3
Keywords: expansion, travel, attention to appearance,
pleasure, growth

date	cycle	event
May	PM	fun weekend in the mountains
7/77-3/78	PY	took acting lessons
10/11-10/18	PN	went to England
January 27...	PM	bought new wardrobe
March 13...	PM	month of parties

In this example, we can see that the Number 3 energies of expansion, travel, pleasure, recognition, and a new image are manifesting.

This is an easy method of recording your memorable events, as well as a quick way of coming to understand how specific numbers will operate in your life. Keywords can easily be gleaned from this method and you might want to list these keywords at the top of the page or on a separate sheet of paper as your record grows. Eventually, you may decide to refine this method or develop your own process for a more specific analysis.

1 NEW BEGINNINGS, INITIATIVE, decisions, individuality. Here you are—alone in the world; born anew as it were. This is the beginning of a brand new cycle in your life, and you may wonder what in the world you are going to do, how you are going to make it on your own. Because that is probably how you feel—quite alone. Though you may be surrounded by family and people, you still feel a sense of isolation and aloneness. This is a necessary attitude on your part because it is time to center your energies, concentrate your will, and think very hard about yourself and your place in the world and what you are going to do in the coming cycles.

Decisions must be made, decisions that will determine your course for some time to come. That is why you are feeling alone now. You must be free from outside distractions, cares, requirements, and demands so that you can make those decisions wisely. Therefore, the Higher Forces see to it that you feel removed from the activity around you, however or whatever it takes to accomplish that state of affairs.

This is the beginning for you, and you feel a strange surge

of energy and determination. You know you have to do things yourself because no one will do them for you. And right now you probably do not want anyone to do things for you. You would rather do them yourself. Defeat is not a word you will accept now. You shut yourself off from outside advice feeling that your own instincts are more accurate. You become very centered, concentrating on your own needs and desires and self-expression. You come first now; it is time for Number 1. You recognize that you are an individual with special needs and, although at other times you put your own needs last, now they must come first. This is your time.

You are unafraid; at least you will attempt now to do things that you might have shuddered at a while ago. You become focused, your "eye is single," and you reach out for life in new ways. You try things, pioneer new methods, examine fresh courses. You begin to exercise your initiative. You find you can draw upon a higher source of power to energize your activities and bring about your desires. There is a sense of unity here as the evolutionary process begins again.

One important person may come into your life now who acts as a guide, an example, a teacher. You may develop meaningful friendships during this period but you must select your friends carefully because they will be with you for some time to come.

This is an aggressive time in your life when you must assert your will in order to accomplish your goals, make yourself heard, speak out, be decisive and unafraid to take a stand, even though it may seem unpopular with those around you. If you feel you are right, then "stand up and be counted." The stand you make now determines the course and perhaps the outcome of your future.

You should avoid partnerships now and go it alone. It is a time for independence. Be careful that you do not become overly aggressive and trample those around you. And be aware of impulsive moves that you might regret later. You are teeming with energy. Use it wisely.

This is an extremely creative period. The Number 1 represents the spinal column, the shaft of life through which the creative spinal fluid, the kundalini, flows. Geometrically, 1 is the point. Both meanings imply and require concentration of will as a necessary beginning in order to move the creative life force, and to move it in the direction desired. In the Number 1 period, tremendously creative forces are awakened, the sleeping serpent stirs, and you must direct its future course carefully.

2 COOPERATION, PARTNERSHIPS, passivity, creativity. As opposed to the 1's direct, ego-centered action, 2
requires a passive, calm, waiting attitude. In the 2, and aware
of the needs and desires of others, you now become concerned
with working in unison to bring about harmonious conditions. Situations arise in which you see the duality, the yin and
the yang, the negative and the positive. This attitude
necessitates discrimination on your part, the need to define
and balance. Often, being able to see both sides so clearly, you
find it hard to make decisions. You may vacillate, preferring
to remain in the background, the silent shadow, while others
take the lead. However, because you have the ability to
discern now, you are the peacemaker, the mediator, who can
settle disputes and bring about peaceful settlements. This is a
good time for partnerships because you are concerned about
the other person's welfare as much as your own.

If 1 is the will to create, then 2 is the power to create, and
it is here that artists find great moments of inspiration. The
hidden works of the subconscious are very active, and the
energies flow through creative works as well as through
telepathic experiences. You are tuned in to the polarities, the
delicate sense of balance, the equilibrium of the cosmos. The
seeds dropped by number 1 are now sprouting beneath the
surface and, although hidden at the moment, they will soon
burst forth.

You should not make decisions now because this is a
waiting period, while the seeds of Number 1 establish
themselves firmly in the ground. If affairs seem unstable, fluc-
tuating, uncertain, it is only because you are meant to wait
and remain passive while nature takes its course. There is a
time for action and a time for reaction. This is the period of
reaction. You have already sown, now await the results. Take
action only upon those affairs that are absolutely necessary.

Love affairs under a 2 may be unstable with hidden
elements involved. Or the relationships could be deeply satis-
fying if each is attuned to the other's needs. Certainly the 2 implies a coming together of two entities seeking harmony and
balance; therefore a perfect relationship could result.

There may be secret energies at work that you are
unaware of. Be alert to those who would deceive you. Approach life confidently and with faith but expect the unexpected. For goodness, return goodness, for evil, return justice.

2 is the law of polarity. Whenever one force begins,
another opposite force manifests itself simultaneously.
Geometrically, 2 is a division of unity represented by the
following symbols: ⟶ , ‖ , + , ⊕ , ∟ , all of which
imply points of conscious awareness. Conscious awareness is

219

only possible when one is aware of self as separate from unity. That separateness can be expressed harmoniously, ‖ , or in-harmoniously, + . At any rate, polarity and duality bestow potentially reproductive periods in which creativity is revealed.

Read Number 11 also, as Number 2 often tunes in to its Master Number side.

11 SUDDEN EVENTS, LEGALITIES, inspiration.

Under the Number 11, sudden unexpected events occur which require decisive action on your part. You may have to make important decisions, overnight or on the spot. This is a testing period during which you must balance any inharmonious situations that arise or are already existent. You must relinquish wrong ideas and the negative circumstances in your life and set about to bring the correct combination of attitudes within yourself that will ensure desirable results in the future. The need for a balanced mind may urge you towards education during this time.

Since justice is required to bring about balance, you may become involved in some kind of legal dealings involving court situations and legal counsel. Financial settlements, legacies, wills, accident claims, and sales agreements that occur now are bringing to an end inharmonious circumstances.

Because the energy of the 11 is tuned into the higher mind and the cosmos, you may very likely have flashes of intuition, insight, and understanding that will aid you in solving difficult situations. These illuminating flashes may also bring moments of inspiration in which exquisitely beautiful works of art are produced.

Lightning, an illuminating flash from the heavens, casts light on the darkened world beneath. Just so, the lightning flashes of your 11 period can cast light upon you, make you shine, so that you become very noticeable to the people around you. Sudden recognition is therefore possible, perhaps for some act or work long forgotten, and then again, perhaps for something you are presently doing but never expected recognition for.

The events of this period are quick, exciting, and totally unexpected. And your entire system will be highly electrified.

The two upright columns found traditionally before every mystery temple symbolize the 11, the male and female principles in perfect equality. They represent the perfect equilibrium you should strive for within yourself, balancing the male and female parts of yourself. 11 is again the two points, the two parallel lines, the cross and the angle—imperfection seeking perfection. Under the 11, we are presented with imbalance so that through testing we may reach perfection.

Please read Number 2 as well. Master Numbers are highly charged; therefore they often find respite in the base digit.

3 ACTIVITY, EXPANSION, TRAVEL, LUCK. You need room to move and express yourself freely now. You need to experience life, freedom, and the joy of living. All the experiences you encounter during a 3 have one purpose—to help you grow and expand your horizons. If a long trip to another part of this land or another country will do the job, then the opportunity for such a trip will present itself. You will meet people who will enlarge your idea of the world and your role in it. Positive feedback will encourage you to speak out and express yourself as never before. Since this cycle is very social, you will be invited to parties, engagements, and various public functions where you suddenly become the center of attention. People notice you. Because of this new exposure, you become more aware of your appearance, and may possibly indulge yourself with a new wardrobe and other new beauty aids, even though this may not be your usual habit. It is important that you look well because your appearance will make a difference with those you contact now. You have a new image and those around you will take notice.

You may feel the need to take elocution or acting lessons, or to become involved in other activities that will help you express yourself more eloquently.

This could be a very lucky period in your life. If you discover that it is, now is the time to buy that sweepstakes ticket or try for the big bingo pot. Enter every free contest and buy those one-dollar tickets from your local organizations. Money as well as material winnings can start coming in now. Because you feel "lucky," you transmit positive energies, which draw positive results back to you—the law of cause and effect.

As an expansive period, 3 can bring growth and fertility in all areas of your life. If you are in the child-bearing years, the birth of a child is certainly possible. Or the baby could be a creation of the mind through an artistic pursuit. Everything is growing now, the life force is active.

Enthusiasm and optimism are attitudes you express freely now and they can help you mix business with pleasure. Some of the people you meet socially may turn out to be important business contacts in the future.

Be careful that the optimism and expansion of this period do not lead you towards extravagance, overindulgence, and wastefulness. Loss of money and material possessions could result. Trouble could upset the home front. A danger under the 3 is the scattering of one's energies in too many directions, thus depleting their effectiveness. Indulgence can also cause an overweight condition, so be careful that you body does not expand along with your bank account.

3, as the activity behind all manifestation, is a fundamental in nature—"Things happen in threes." E.g., length, breadth, and width; the three-dimensional world; the primary colors—red, yellow, blue; the head, trunk, and limbs of the human body; the past, present, and future; and so on. The Father (Spirit), Mother (Soul), and Son (Body) concept is reflected throughout every major religion in the world, now and in the past. This concept is expressed geometrically through the equilateral triangle, the first perfect figure that can be drawn with straight lines, thus exemplifying the perfect equilibrium of the three parts of self—Spirit, Soul, and Body—the perfect condition.

4 WORK, LAW AND ORDER, budgeting, foundations, sex. This is a period of work on the material plane. You have such an urge to organize your life that you may begin by cleaning the attic, the cellar, the closets, desks, and drawers, the garage, and the shed. No corner is safe from your organizing energy. It is an overriding need to build strong secure foundations in your life that drives you to clean up your environment and put it in order. Your subconscious takes its suggestions from what it sees every day; so if you live in a mess, your subconscious thinks that is the way you want things and sets about to create a "mess" in other areas of your life as well. Under a 4, you sense this truth and are driven to clean up your living area. Now your subconscious sees order, and once convinced that this is what you really want, sets about to bring order to all levels of your life.

Emphasis under the 4 is on material things. You desire money and possessions now because they add to your sense of security and satisfy your heightened physical desires and needs. You may purchase goods or services that require setting up a budget and making payments. Land and property, building and remodeling come under this vibration, and you may seek to purchase or beautify in this area. But you should be economic and practical now, organizing your funds carefully and wisely. Take care of your money and it will take care of you.

Your body is your home as well, and, after that disastrous expansive 3 cycle, you may find that your body expanded as well as your mind and income. So out come the jogging pants, the diet book, and the bathroom scales. Or you may choose to go to Weight Watchers or a physical fitness center to tone up, flatten, and lose.

Since all physical senses are heightened, your sexual relationships can be very rewarding and physically stimulating. You are aware of sensations now that are often muted under the other cycles. For males, 4 can bring fatherhood.

This can be a money cycle for you—money that comes in direct proportion to the effort you have expended. 3 is called "lucky" money, or so it would seem. There is no such thing as luck. It is just that the effect cannot be consciously connected to the cause. Somewhere along the line, you earned it. However, 4 is earned money, directly visible. You work—you get paid.

4 is also law and order. I know of one case where a woman was called to jury duty in a 4 cycle. 4 is also a doorway to worldly success and acquisition of material possessions, or a window to heaven where insight, perception, and finely tuned senses reveal the essence of life—the God energy at work in all form. And 4 is, perhaps, a little of both.

Negatively, under a 4 you may put yourself in too much debt to satisfy your desire for material possessions. You can be stubborn, tenacious, and overly sensitive. Be careful you do not become a prisoner in bondage to your earthly desires. Enjoy them, own them, but do not let them own you.

In a 4, we find the divine life principle working in substance or matter. The earth was formed on the 4th day of the Biblical story of creation. 4 relates to all earthly matters: the four seasons, the four points of the compass, the four elements (fire, earth, air, and water), the four rivers in the Garden of Eden, the four letters in the sacred Hebrew name for God, IHVH, and on the Christian cross, INRI. Geometrically, 4 is the square, the second perfect figure formed with straight lines. 4 is the foundation stone upon which the temple (the body) is built. In the 40, a high-powered 4 working with the God energy 0, debts are paid. Christ overcame temptation during his 40 days in the desert—overcame and cleansed himself on 4 levels—physically, mentally, emotionally, and spiritually.

Please read Master Number 22 as well, for sometimes the Number 4 will tune in to its Master Number side.

22 POWER, POSITION, STRENGTH, travel, completion. You are now in a position of great strength. The advancement you have been waiting for could be yours. The power may be placed in your hands to control a large enterprise, business, or organization. This is vast power on a material plane. The cycles have come full circle, and your energies have manifested in supreme accomplishments. You have already put in the necessary work and gleaned the required experience to handle whatever rewards you will now receive. The training and testing is over, the real exercise begins. You are the leader now.

Travel may be part of this cycle, but not for pure enjoyment as much as for business reasons. Of course, business for some is pure enjoyment.

You may find yourself removed from friends and the people you usually associate with because of your newly acquired position. Often a period of isolation, silence, and solitude accompanies this vibration, as if you need the quiet to discover how well you can handle the vast power that has been handed to you.

This is the time to think big, plan big, and dare great deeds, always with both feet planted firmly on the ground and one eye on the bank account. Be practical, but dare to dream and use your dreams efficiently.

It is as if you are now finely tuned, with your finger on the material pulse of the people. You have a sort of X-ray vision, a depth of insight that would frighten others if they knew, as it is almost a supernatural phenomenon. Use your reason and intuition hand-in-hand as you build an empire. Rely on your past experiences as guides because you are ready for the job. Listen to the advice of those you respect and who are "in the know," then carefully screen the results.

An uncanny supply of physical endurance and strength will be supplied you when the going gets tough, and, as a great coach once said, that's when the tough get going. And right now, that is you. You will not allow obstacles to defeat you. You have a goal in mind and you pursue it intensely, without a sideways glance. You now have a one-track mind and a full-powered locomotive to pull it to your destination.

22 holds a unique position in metaphysical literature. The ancients used it as the symbol for the circle, and the Hebrew alphabet had 22 letters. In these respects, it represents a full cycle, a completion. Tau, or the cross, as the 22nd letter in the Hebrew alphabet, represents victory over limitation and the material world. The individual has come "full circle" and is now victorious. In the Tarot, there is no Key 22. The Major Arcana contains Keys 1–21, and the Minor Arcana embraces cards numbered 23–78. Key 0, the Fool, stands alone, as the Life Force about to step into manifestation, about to take on the physical body. However, once the Fool has stepped into the flesh and walked the 21 Keys of the Major Arcana, the Fool then steps out of the flesh fully initiated, complete, balanced, and whole. Therefore, 22, as the ancient's circle, is

also the Fool after incarnation, when experience on the earthly plane has been completed and wisdom earned.

Please read Number 4 as well, because Master Numbers are highly charged, requiring brief periods of rest in their base digits.

5 COMMUNICATION, DECISIONS, CHANGE, experience, sexual magnetism. You are so busy now that you do not know which end is up. Activity, experience, and change are key issues here. You are totally involved in the activity of life—meetings, errands, answering mail and the telephone, making arrangements, attending parties and public functions. All of a sudden, everyone needs you, and you feel as if you are on a merry-go-round.

This is a period of communication. You meet many people and become involved in various activities because you are in a changing cycle. You need these experiences so that you will have enough information available to make the decisions that eventually must be made. Experience is your most important activity now, and change will be the end result. You are in the midst of a turning point in your life when the sanctuary must be cleansed, when you can look at your life and decide whether you like the direction in which you are heading. If you are dissatisfied with the status quo, then this is the time to do something about it. Paths will open through the many encounters you experience now, and you will find solutions.

You feel a restless energy which keeps you on the move. You want to get into the mainstream of life and be doing and living. You do not want to miss anything. Your curiosity is heightened.

Some people decide to take courses under a 5 in order to satisfy their need for experience and learning. New interests continually pop up, enticingly.

Under a 5 vibration, you are sexually magnetic. The opposite sex suddenly "discovers" you and your date book is filled. You are the life of the party, surrounded by admirers.

All this activity requires traveling. Your wheels will be rolling continually in an endless stream of places to go and things to do. Be careful that you do not deplete, not only your gas tank, but your own fuel reserves. Your nervous system is highly activated now so you should avoid alcohol and drugs; and be careful of accidents because you are in high gear. Do not deplete your energies through superficial activities and in meaningless relationships. And resist temptations that may plague you during this period.

The pentagram, or 5-pointed star, is the symbol for the Number 5. The pentagram represents the human body, stand-

225

ing erect with arms stretched to either side and feet set apart. 5 also represents the five senses and the five human races. We have five vowels in the English alphabet (our means of communication), and the ancient Hebrews claimed that the vowels were the centers of good or evil depending upon how they were used. Doctors are coming to realize that diseases reach a crisis on the 5th day or the 5th hour after midnight. In longer illnesses, it is the 5th week that is critical, the turning point as it were. All these associations indicate that 5 is a point of instability and oscillation where choices must be made.

5 is the central digit in the 1 through 9 series, i.e., 1-2-3-4-(5)-6-7-8-9, having four numbers on either side. As such, it has been called "the keystone in the arch of the structure of life."

6 LOVE, HOME AND FAMILY, justice, beauty. In a 6 period, the emphasis is usually on the home and family members. There will be changes here in the domestic scene. Family members may enter or leave the home. Children go off to school or get married. Babies are born or relatives need financial assistance or may move in with you temporarily. Responsibility on the home front increases: a family member may become ill, or may need your emotional support.

6 is the number of advantageous partnerships with the opposite sex and therefore rules marriage. After the Number 5 cycle of sexual magnetism, in which you had an opportunity to experience relationships with different types, you may have selected a mate and decided to settle down and establish your own home. 6 is a seeking for balance at the very roots of your being, manifesting in your home, your relationships, and yourself.

Beauty becomes important. You may remodel or redecorate your home because of a need to bring harmony into your environment. Like your home, your own body begins to get your attention—you decide to begin a program in beauty care with facials, makeup, and hair styling.

Your sense of artistic proportion is sensitized; therefore, any works of art portray a lovely symmetry and beauty. This sense of proportion may manifest in a need to involve yourself in community projects that beautify your town or city, or in legalities that bring unity to the political scene.

You are so tuned in to the requirements for balance that others sense your present awareness and come to you for help in settling their differences. People seek your advice. Everyone cries on your shoulder, telling you their problems. You become the Father/Mother Confessor in this cycle. Some court decisions may be forthcoming which will restore balance and harmony.

If balance is not restored, then separations occur. The home and close relationships may suffer because differences are irreconcilable. Many wars have been fought under the 6 influence. A gentleman engaged in war games as a hobby told me that during the middle ages, most wars occurred under 6s.

Metaphysically, 6 is the force of generation, the seeking for perfect balance in the uniting of the human and divine, substance and spirit. It is the urge to reunite with the higher self and therefore is associated with the sexual act. The early Christians taught that 6 was synonymous with sex and, since chastity was an issue with them, this number took on negative meanings. In Revelations, the number of the beast is 666, or degeneration (immersion in negative physical satisfactions) on all three levels: physically, mentally, and spiritually. Geometrically, the 6 is associated with the interlaced triangles, ✡ , called the Philosopher's Stone, the Star of David, and the Sign of Vishnus. It represents Spirit and Matter intermingled in perfect harmony.

Please read Master Number 33 along with this delineation. Often the Number 6 picks up its Master Number side.

33 SACRIFICE, COMPASSION, martyrdom. Since Master Number 33 is the higher side of the digit 6, you should read number 6 in conjunction with this number. Master Numbers frequently fluctuate to the base digit for a moment of respite.

Master Number 33 is called the Christ Vibration, and is believed to be very difficult to live up to. Great sacrifices are required here involving understanding, love, compassion, forgiveness, tolerance, and service. Home and family members may need services beyond what you believe you are physically and emotionally capable of giving. Or that demand could come from a larger humanitarian group or organization which needs your time, effort, and total dedication.

You need deep faith in your higher self and a willingness to give freely if the request is truly for the overall good and not a wasteful act on your part. Only the most urgent causes should be attended to because you need to be selective if your energies are not to fall on fallow earth and wither.

Look for courage to help you accept the responsibilities that may be heaped upon you, and energy from your wellspring of faith to keep you going. Once you have selected the proper cause, be steadfast in the face of all opposition, because surely under this number, the law of karma, as ever, will reward you in great measure.

The Master Number 33 may also be associated with the two interlaced triangles, ✡ , which draw energy (3 and the triangle are the activating principles) from above (heaven, God) through the upper triangle, and from below (earth) through the lower triangle, uniting these energies in a oneness that knows no fuel shortage. Here the pumps are always full.

7 REST, PHYSICAL COMPLETION, perfection, health, analysis. This is a period of retreat. You may feel more tired than usual and not want to socialize. You need to be alone, to think, meditate, reflect, and retreat within yourself. It is a good time for vacations, weekends at the mountains or by the sea, or just being left alone in your home. You would rather be alone, or at least with people of a more contemplative nature who complement your own mood. 7 is a time to rest. God rested on the 7th day.

Outer activity and interests will cease, or be maintained at minimal levels, while the activity is transferred to the inner realms of the mind. You will do a lot of necessary thinking now as gathered experiences are synthesized. This is a pause in the life cycle during which you need to think and become partially conscious of your spiritual side, your inner workings. You have done enough work. Now let nature take her course.

Set material worries aside. The things you have been worrying about will mysteriously take care of themselves. You are not to push your affairs or aggressively assert your energies in order to accomplish worldly goals. If you persist in these attempts, you may become ill. The higher forces say stop, look and listen; if you do not heed them they will place you where you have to listen—in a sick bed. Slow your pace and take care of your health.

This introspective period is a perfect time to perfect skills you already have. Take a course to polish your talents. Or enroll in a philosophical or metaphysical course, such as yoga, TM, Silva Mind Control, religion, astrology, or numerology.

Your intuitions are working well now. Dreams, visions, and telepathic experiences are all possible as you delve into the mystical side of life.

7 brings attainment and completion on the physical level. The efforts you have expended in past cycles can bring rewards now that may not necessarily be material, although they can be. 7 is the number of perfection, and it is here that you need to feel you have done well. You analyze your past cycles, think about your present conditions, and look towards perfecting the future. Here your mind is your strength. Use it to overcome any negative conditions in your life by concentrating on the power of positive thinking. External laws are not important here, but rather the discovery of the true "I" within, one's individuality in its purest form.

Do not become so reclusive that you shut yourself off from everyone. Watch your health. Rest, pace yourself, eat well, and sleep wisely. If signing any legal documents, check the fine print: cross the t's and dot the i's with care. 7 demands perfection.

Metaphysically, 7 represents emergence from the outer world of chaos into a more perfect realm of mental and physical perfection. Hepta, the Greek word for 7, means holy, divine, motherless. 7 is perfection, a combination of 3 (spirit) and 4 (form): $3+4=7$, or perfection. Perfection is holy, divine. It has no parent; it is not born; therefore, it is motherless. Perfection is; God is; it exists; the original state of being. 7 is perfection on the earth plane, reflected through the seven original planets or spirits governing our solar system; the seven colors of the rainbow, God's convenant or promise to humanity; the seven white keys of the musical scale, the music of the spheres; and the seven year stages in human development; e.g., at 7 we go to school, at 14 we reach puberty, at 21 we become legal adults (metaphysically at any rate), at 28 we gain our souls according to Plato and the Saturn return in astrology, and so on. 7 is reflected in minerology. Salt solidifies first in triangular shapes or pyramids, and secondly in squares, or cubes. Again, 3 (the triangle) plus 4 (the square) equals 7 (perfection). We are told that we are the salt of the earth. Our bodies (the square) containing spirit (the triangle) equal perfection (the 7).

The average life span today is 70–72 years. The procession of the Equinoxes, where the sun moves through all 12 zodiacal signs in periods called ages, takes 25,920 years. Plato called this the "great world year." If you divide the great world year by a single year of 365 days plus, you will have 70–71 years, the "alloted life span" of a human being. $70=10\times7$, or the perfect 7 comes full cycle (10). 7 is the physical cycle, 9 the metaphysical cycle, and 10 solidifies the cycle by beginning again.

8 KARMA, RESPONSIBILITY, BUSINESS, finances, sex, balance, strength. If you have ever been in doubt about how effective you are as a moving force in this material world, now under the 8 you need doubt no longer. Under the 8 truth is clearly defined, and karma reigns. The law of cause and effect is completed, and you will receive exactly what you deserve. For some, great rewards are bestowed; job advancement, raises, public recognition, honor, awards, legacies; for others, there will be only material loss, financial hardships, unemployment, and sometimes bankruptcy. The difficult side of this number does not mean you are a "bad" person necesarily, but it does indicate that you have not handled your energies wisely, you have not pursued the proper goals, or you have not taken the appropriate steps or perhaps put in the required effort to achieve those goals.

8 is the number of material domination. The world of business and finance is governed by the 8. (Note that the WATS line, the free telephone service for consumers calling business concerns, is an 800 number.) You may first feel the effects of this cycle at your job when pressures and responsibilities begin to mount. You may strain at the extra work load others heap upon you. Responsibilities increase perhaps through promotion as you are placed in positions of command because you are a person with a force of character that is recognized in the material world. Additional monies are then available, and your finances improve. Since 8 is karmic, you might receive an inheritance or win a lottery—all ultimately the result of positive efforts previously spent.

The negative reaction might be the loss of a job and the ensuing financial burdens. At any rate, pressure and responsibility become key issues.

Intense sexual relationships are needed now. 8, related to the 8th sign of the zodiac, Scorpio, and 8, as the glyph itself representing a need for balance and equal pay for equal work, both indicate an intense need to fulfill oneself through a balancing, a coming together, a union of equality. Sex is one outlet for this need. Because 8 is physical, the pure physical enjoyment of the relationships must be experienced. And since 8 is spiritual (containing 2 God zeros), the relationships must be spiritually fulfilling as well—the meeting of mind and body, heaven and earth. And under an 8, your physical sexual relationships can be heaven on earth because you and your partner both feel a responsibility to it and each other.

Negatively, as said above, the loss of material possessions and resources is possible. Base materialism can overcome an individual, who then launches a power drive that crushes all who get in the way. There can be deliberate blindness to the suffering of others, and displays of cruelty because the person is so driven by a fear of poverty, loss, and helplessness.

8 is "either personal limitation or spiritual freedom." It requires a keen sense of balance between the material and spiritual worlds. The figure 8 drawn horizontally, ∞ , is the lemniscate, a mathematical symbol for infinity, God, the "signature of the universe," the current of life that sweeps through the universe, over the earth, and through our bodies. 8 is the dragon, or the serpent, the serpentine flow, whose misuse caused expulsion from the Garden of Eden. It is the sexual, creative current that flows through our bodies and up our

spines. As serpents it is wrapped about the caduceus, the medical staff, carried by Mercury (Hermes), the messenger god.

Drawn to reflect *as it is above, so it is below*, it is the law of cause and effect, or *as ye sow, so shall ye reap*. It is the spiral of evolution and the promise of reincarnation, whose crossover point →8 represents the "eye of the needle" through which materialistic individuals find it hard to pass. 8 is immortality, the only number other than 0 that can be drawn over and over endlessly without lifting the pen from the paper.

The densest of all minerals, salt, crystallizes in cubes, the geometrical symbol for the 8. 8 is the material world in harmony with the spiritual world. 8 is reflected truth.

Please read Master Number 44 as well, since it is the higher side of this digit 8, and one under the 8 often responds to its vibrations as well.

44 EARTHLY SERVICE, KARMA, productivity, material progress, opportunity. Under this Master Number 44 period, you are given an opportunity to re-evaluate your present conditions and the events that brought you to this point. You begin to think about the processes that bring you the rewards and material goods you may now be receiving. Friends can help you now. Opportunities come from out of nowhere, and your stores increase. You may be tempted to sit back and relax. This attitude would be a mistake because you now have the opportunity to accomplish much.

By examining your methods of operation, your attitude, and your philosophy about getting ahead in the world, you may find the missing link in your makeup, the one thing that seems to hinder your progress in all that you do. You question values and goals, and look for answers that can put your world together more effectively. Your intuitions are especially keen as you search for the link between the material and the spiritual worlds.

44 requires that you give service to others in ways that ease their physical burdens. Through practical, down-to-earth types of work, you reveal the goodness of the physical world to others. You might volunteer to work with the sick or the mentally impaired, or grow a garden whose vegetables will feed a hungry family, or help build an animal shelter, or raise funds to eradicate hunger, or become involved in beautifying your town—cleaning the park and planting flowers and thus providing a scene of beauty that lifts the spirits of those who walk there.

There are many works you can become involved in under

this number; however, the key thought is—work to produce material results that have healing effects. Your reward comes from sharing your talents in very visible ways.

Advice and counsel are other ways to heal; however, the counsel should be on issues that are basic necessities of life—health, finance, occupation.

Approach all affairs with a calm, patient, quiet determination, and above all keep your mind keyed to practicality. As a Master Number, 44 can bring great spiritual growth for you through the works you perform in God's physical world.

9 ENDINGS, TRANSITION, CHARITY, friendships, wisdom. It is time to let go. This is a cleansing period in which those things that are no longer necessary in your life must be relinquished. They are used up, worn out, useless in relation to you, and they have to be discarded to make room for the new. We cannot always know what we need and what we do not need, so if we cannot or do not want to let go of our unnecessary "things," the higher forces step in and remove them for us. People may leave your life. You may have to change jobs or relocate, and things you are attached to may have to be given up. The status quo is upset.

This can be an emotionally trying experience if change and transition are difficult for you. You may feel like crying frequently, and you will need some time alone to sort out the pieces. You need to come into full contact with your inner self. Do some serious house-cleaning or body-cleaning—mentally, physically, emotionally, and spiritually. However, if endings occur under a 9, it is because there is something new just around the bend. When one door closes, another opens.

Use some of your energies in charitable deeds. You have gathered much from the past cycles, and in this final phase, you should give back to the universe some part of what you have gained. This is tithing time. Your giving is a demonstration of your faith in the unending flow from the conucopia of life. When you give, you physically demonstrate that you do not fear not having, because you are willing to give, knowing that life will supply you abundantly. You should not work alone now but rather with others for a common good.

Be sympathetic, compassionate, understanding, and loving to all those you encounter in this cycle. Old friendships become especially meaningful, and heartwarming and beautiful new relationships can develop. Gifts and favors may be bestowed upon you. You should observe this cycle closely. Many of your goals will have been accomplished by now, and you should finish any that are still hanging. Much wisdom can be gathered here through observation.

Negatively, some people become overly emotional, refusing to listen, to reason, or try to understand. They cling to those things that they can no longer have and thereby prolong a transitional period that could have passed quickly and painlessly.

9 is boundless, unlimited, ever changing, yet retains its identity. It governs cyclicity and humanity's evolution. It eternally reproduces itself, resisting destruction. Pythagoras said it was the symbol of matter constantly changing its form but never destroyed. "The Greeks compared 9 to the ocean," constantly flowing around all the other digits. 9 is the final digit in the series 1 through 9 and all numbers are bound by it. Multiplied by any number, 9 returns to itself; e.g., $1 \times 9 = 9$, $2 \times 9 = 18/9$, $3 \times 9 = 27/9$, etc. The 9 multiplied by another number returns to itself. Or the 9 goes out to multiply (in the next 1 cycle) but always returns to itself (back to 9). A mathematical truth and a metaphysical truth—evidence of cyclicity, eternity, and reincarnation on some level. The ending is the beginning. 9 is wisdom, spiritual knowledge, because one can see the cyclicity before it manifests in the 10/1, or the solidification of the 1–9 cycle.

The circle of 360 degrees and the square of 360 degrees reduce to a 9. ($360 = 3 + 6 + 0 = 18/9$). The circle (God) and the square (matter) unite in 9 in a point of transition, energy indestructible in a state of change. The Bible expresses humanity's cycle as 9 through Revelations and the number of the Beast ($666 = 18/9$) and the Redeemed ($144,000 = 9$). 9 is duality and flux in the life of humanity, which can go either way, the way of the Beast (the unregenerated who fight their higher side) or the way of the Redeemed.

9 is 6 (sex) reversed, the creative, sexual energy, the serpent power, which in the 9 is elevated to head level (the 0 at the top of the upright column, the spine). The serpent power in the 9 is now transmuted in service to fulfill the needs of others rather than the needs of self. The 9th letter of the Hebrew alphabet is TETH, or "serpent", meaning wisdom. The Bible says, "Be ye wise as serpents..." The cat, a universal symbol of wisdom and mystery, is said to have "9 lives." 7 is a physical cycle—animals are said to live 7 years to our one; and 9 is a metaphysical cycle, designated to humanity as an extra two years in which to absorb the esoteric meaning of life.

Postscript

Each individual language expresses the truth of any "word" through its numerical vibrations for the people who speak that language. The Hebrews and Greeks used their language and number code to express truths just as we use the English language, and Italians use Italian, Germans, German, and Spaniards, Spanish. The given number vibration in each language will express how that culture views any word they use. The word "table" in English has a different vibration from the word *tavola* (table) in Italian because the two cultures see the "table" in different ways. In America, the table is something you pound on at a meeting, or drop your school books on as you rush to change for an early date. In Italy, the table traditionally is the focus of the family meal where accounts of the day's activities are exchanged and a few leisurely hours are spent. Each culture expresses its own traditions through its language, and the numerical vibrations of that language reveal the truth that each culture has learned. We speak, in our own tongues, as much truth as we know.

"In the beginning was the Word, and the Word was with God, and the Word was God." (St. John 1:1) Words are truths that can set us free and keep us free if we but look beneath the surface for the hidden nuggets of wisdom.

Revelation states in Chapter 13 in the passage about the beast, the 666: here is wisdom, here is truth. Let all that understand count the number and be aware. And if you have ears, it is time to hear.

Look around you. Observe the messages written in nature, in your personal life, in the business world, in your religions, in symbols, and in words. We are unconsciously urged to express the truth in all that we think, say, and do. Study God's language, the language of geometry and numbers, and you will hear *May your life be blessed with Love and Light*.

I hope that our combined efforts in this book—the writing and the reading of it—have provided insight and some food for thought. I have had my moments of awareness in its writing and if you have had your moments of awareness in its reading, then our experience is doubly fruitful. And now, until the next book...

Answers to Exercises

Page 12:

Soul Number: 24/6
Outer Personality Number: 43/7
Path of Destiny Number: 67/4
Life Lesson Number: 48/3

Page 19:

$9 + 10 + 1981 = 9 + 10 + 19 = 38/11$

Page 28:

April 20-Aug. 20	Aug. 20-Dec. 20	Dec. 20-April 20
1982	1982	1982
23	48	24
2005 = 7	2030 = 5	2006 = 8

Age: 23
Life Lesson: 48/3
Soul Number: 24/6

Page 36:

April 20 - May 20 48/3
May 20 - June 20 49/4
June 20 - July 20 50/5
July 20 - August 20 51/6
August 20-September 20 52/7
September 20 - October 20 53/8
October 20 - November 20 54/9
November 20 - December 20 55/1
December 20 - January 20 56/11
January 20 - February 20 45/9
February 20 - March 20 46/1
March 20 - April 20 47/11

Page 43:

May 7 53/8	May 15 61/7	May 23 69/6	May 31 77/5
May 8 54/9	May 16 62/8	May 24 70/7	June 1 48/3
May 9 55/1	May 17 63/9	May 25 71/8	June 2 49/4
May 10 56/11	May 18 64/1	May 26 72/9	June 3 50/5
May 11 57/3	May 19 65/11	May 27 73/1	June 4 51/6
May 12 58/4	May 20 66/3	May 28 74/11	June 5 52/7
May 13 59/5	May 21 67/4	May 29 75/3	June 6 53/8
May 14 60/6	May 22 68/5	May 30 76/4	June 7 54/9

Bibliography

American Heritage Book of the Presidents. New York: Dell Publishing, 1967.

Case, Paul Foster. *The Tarot A Key to the Wisdom of the Ages*. Richmond, Virginia: Macoy Publishing, 1947.

Crockett, James. *Crockett's Victory Garden*. Toronto: Little, Brown, 1977.

Encyclopedia Americana. New York: Americana Corporation, 1966.

Field, Paul. *50,000 Birthdays*. Richmond, Virginia: Macoy Publishing, 1964.

Golden Home and High School Encyclopedia. New York: Golden Press, 1961.

Gray, Eden. *A Complete Guide to the Tarot*. New York: Bantam Books, 1972.

Gribbin, John, R., and Plagemann, Stephen H. *The Jupiter Effect*. New York: Random House, 1976.

1980 Hammond Almanac.Maplewood, New Jersey: Hammond, 1979.

Heline, Corrine. *Sacred Science of Numbers*. La Canada, California: New Age Press, 1971.

———. *Star Gates*. La Canada, California: New Age Press, 1965.

Higgins, Frank C. *Hermetic Masonry*. Ferndale, Michigan: Trismegistus Press, 1980.

Javane, Faith, and Bunker, Dusty. *Numerology and the Divine Triangle*. Rockport, Massachusetts: Para Research, 1979.

King James Bible. New York: World Publishing Company.

Lamsa Bible, I Cor. 12:7-11; 13. Philadelphia, Pennsylvania: A.J. Holman, 1968.

Lesmerurier, Peter. *The Great Pyramid Decoded*. New York: St. Martin's Press, 1977.

Lucas, Jerry, and Washburn, Del. *Theomatics*. New York: Stein and Day Publishers.

Luxton, Leonora. *Astrology, Key to Self Understanding*. St. Paul, Minnesota: Llewellyn Publications, 1978.

Ogg, Oscar. *The 26 Letters*. New York: Thomas Y. Cromwell Company, 1948.

Random House Dictionary of the English Language. New York: Random House, 1969.

Schmalz, John Barnes. *Nuggetts From King Solomon's Mine*. Ferndale, Michigan: Trismegistus Press, 1980.

Spangler, David. *Revelation: The Birth of a New Age*. Scotland: Findhorn Publications.

Books from Para Research

THE AMERICAN ATLAS
by Neil F. Michelsen

Provides all American time changes and time zones from 1883 to 2000 for over 100,000 birthplaces, virtually every incorporated or unincorporated city, village, neighborhood, airport and military base in the United States. "Whether or not you already have an atlas, buy Neil Michelsen's American Atlas if you're serious about computing horoscopes."—Richard F. Nolle. Cloth, $19.50.

THE AMERICAN EPHEMERIS
by Neil F. Michelsen

Has everything you need to cast horoscopes. Perfect for beginners, with its chart casting instructions and Placidus house tables, it is the required tool for practicing astrologers. Daily midnight positions: Sun and Moon longitudes to the nearest second of arc, true *and* mean node of Moon, planetary longitudes, latitudes and declinations. Also includes a complete aspectarian, Moon phenomena and much more. The combined volumes of the American Ephemeris cover the 20th century.
1901 to 1930 paper, $14.95   1931 to 1940 paper, $5.00   1941 to 1950 paper, $5.00
1951 to 1960 paper, $5.00   1961 to 1970 paper, $5.00   1971 to 1980 paper, $5.00
1981 to 1990 paper, 5.00   1991 to 2000 paper, $5.00   1931 to 1980 & Book of
Tables, cloth, $25.00

THE AMERICAN EPHEMERIS FOR THE TWENTIETH CENTURY
by Neil F. Michelsen

For the first time, an inexpensive paperback ephemeris which covers the entire 20th century with the accuracy and detail you expect from *The American Ephemeris*. Sun and Moon longitudes to 1 second; planet longitudes to .1 minute; calculated for GMT time; Solar and Lunar eclipses; aspectarian of Jupiter thru Pluto and much more. Noon or Midnight, each volume: Paper, $15.95.

ASTROLOGICAL INSIGHTS INTO PERSONALITY
by Betty Lundsted

This book combines principle and practice. The first section introduces the author's basic concepts in a clear and readable way. The second and largest section discusses each of the major planetary aspects as a context for personality development. The third section presents the author's approach to chart analysis and synthesis and uses two case histories to illustrate how you can use the material in this book. Paper, $9.95.

ASTROLOGY INSIDE OUT
by Bruce Nevin

This is an excellent introduction to astrology and much more. Its theoretical framework, integrating esoteric tradition with modern harmonic research in astrology and recent developments in physics and psychology, will interest every astrological reader. Through its many ingenious visualization and meditation exercises, even seasoned astrologers will learn new ways to recognize and interpret astrological patterning from the 'inside out.' Paper, $12.95

ASTROLOGY, NUTRITION & HEALTH
by Robert Carl Jansky

Explains how to use the natal horoscope to foresee and prevent health problems. This concern is as old as Hippocrates and Ptolemy, but there are few books on the subject written for the layman. The author, a professional astrologer trained in biochemistry, demonstrates, in readable nontechnical language, how a knowledge of astrology can help the reader understand the components of metabolism and health. Paper, $6.95.

COMPLETE RELAXATION
by Steve Kravette

Complete Relaxation is unique in its field because, unlike most relaxation books, it takes a completely relaxed approach to its subject. Interspersed with text and beautifully drawn illustrations you will find a series of poetic explorations designed to put you in closer touch with yourself and the people around you. *Complete Relaxation* is written for all of you: your body, your mind, your emotions, your spirituality, your sexuality—the whole person you are and are meant to be. As you read this book, you will begin to feel yourself entering a way of life more completely relaxed than you ever thought possible, because *Complete Relaxation* speaks directly to the inner you. Paper, $8.95.

DEVELOP YOUR PSYCHIC SKILLS
by Enid Hoffman

The author's long experience with psychic phenomena is integrated with the practical implications of recent brain research showing how we all have psychic abilities waiting to be developed. The book includes excercises for training both perceptive and projective skills, for clearing obstructing beliefs, for past life recall and many more experiences now available to all who would develop their potential psychic powers. The author says, "I have always felt it important for my students to understand how natural and human a process it is to develop one's psychic skills." She also makes it a lot of fun. Paper, $7.95.

DREAM CYCLES
by Dusty Bunker

Dream Cycles offers a new and exciting approach to dream interpretation. It draws on the author's extensive experience as a numerologist, as a teacher of metaphysical subjects, and as the author of a newspaper column on dreams, as well as her knowledge of scientific dream and sleep research. Writing in the lively, engaging style familiar to readers of *Numerology & Your Future* and *Numerology & The Divine Triangle*. Dusty Bunker spreads before the reader as tasty a banquet of knowledge and skills as anyone could desire. Paper, $9.95.

GRAPHOLOGY HANDBOOK
by Curtis Casewit

This authoritative text spells out the fundamentals of graphology and illustrates them with over one hundred handwriting samples ranging from presidential proclamations to notes jotted down by ordinary people. The author, who currently teaches graphology at the University of Colorado, has studied with the leading graphologists of Europe and the United States. He presents the science of handwriting as a means to discover undeveloped talents, diagnose health conditions, screen prospective employees, understand friends and family, and reveal your own personality. Paper, $6.95.

HOROSCOPE SYMBOLS
by Robert Hand

This book, representing four years of writing and twenty years of research, presents an in-depth reexamination of astrology's basic symbols. Core meanings are analyzed in detail so that the astrologer can see for himself why traditional meaning and significance have been attributed to each astrological symbol. In many cases, these core meanings also establish new interpretations as the author develops the substance and symbolism of images which astrologers have employed for centuries. Paper, $14.95

HUNA: A BEGINNER'S GUIDE
Revised Edition
by Enid Hoffman

Centuries ago, the Kahuna, the ancient Hawaiian miracle workers, discovered the fundamental pattern of energy-flow in the universe. Their secrets of psychic and intra-psychic communication, refined and enriched by modern scientific research, are now revealed in this practical, readable book. Paper, $6.95.

NUMEROLOGY AND THE DIVINE TRIANGLE
by Faith Javane & Dusty Bunker

At last a truly comprehensive and authoritative text on numerology! *Numerology and the Divine Triangle* embodies the life work of Faith Javane, one of America's most respected writers and teachers of numerology, and her student and co-author, Dusty Bunker, a teacher and columnist on metaphysical topics.

Part I is a complete introduction to esoteric numerology and includes a section on the life of Edgar Cayce as a case study of numerology in action.

Part II includes extensive delineations of each of the numbers 1 to 78 and, for the first time in book form, a synthesis of numerology, astrology and the Tarot. Each of the Tarot cards is illustrated. *Numerology and the Divine Triangle* is number one in its field, the book to which all books on the subject will be compared from now on. Paper, $9.95.

THE ONLY WAY TO LEARN ASTROLOGY
by Marion March & Joan McEvers.

A success in its earlier typewritten version, *The Only Way to Learn Astrology* is now available in a completely revised, redesigned and re-typeset edition. This new edition is more compact, clearer and easier to read. If you are looking for a comprehensive basic astrology book, *The Only Way...* is the ideal text for beginning self-study. It is also an excellent basic reference book because each planet is completely delineated in each sign and house position, and in each of the major aspects.

The book, developed over many years of successful teaching, is based on Marion March and Joan McEver's tested course outline. Now, with the republication of *The Only Way to Learn Astrology,* this proven method of learning astrology is available to everyone. Paper, $9.95.

PLANETS IN ASPECT: Understanding Your Inner Dynamics
by Robert Pelletier

Explores aspects, the planetary relationships that describe our individual energy patterns, and how we can integrate them into our lives. Undoubtedly the most thorough in-depth study of planetary aspects ever published. Every major aspect—conjunction, sextile, square, trine, opposition and inconjunct—is covered: 314 aspects in all. Paper, $10.95.

PLANETS IN COMPOSITE: Analyzing Human Relationships
by Robert Hand

The definitive work on the astrology of human relationships. Explains the technique of the composite chart, combining two individuals' charts to create a third chart of the relationship itself, and how to interpret it. Case studies plus twelve chapters of delineations of composite Sun, Moon and planets in all houses and major aspects. Paper, $13.95.

PLANETS IN HOUSES: Experiencing Your Environment
by Robert Pelletier

Brings the ancient art of natal horoscope interpretation into a new era of accuracy, concreteness and richness of detail. Pelletier delineates the meaning of each planet as derived by counting from each of the twelve houses and in relation to the other houses with which it forms trines, sextiles, squares and oppositions, inconjuncts and semisextiles. Seventeen different house relationships delineated for each planet in each house, 2184 delineations in all! Paper, $12.95.

PLANETS IN LOVE: Exploring Your Emotional and Sexual Needs
by John Townley

The first astrology book to take an unabashed look at human sexuality and the different kinds of relationships that people form to meet their various emotional and sexual needs. An intimate astrological analysis of sex and love, with 550 interpretations of each planet in every possible sign, house and aspect. Discusses sexual behavior according to mental, emotional and spiritual areas of development. Cloth, $12.95.

PLANETS IN TRANSIT: Life Cycles for Living
by Robert Hand

A psychological approach to astrological prediction. Delineations of the Sun, Moon and each planet transiting each natal house and forming each aspect to the natal Sun, Moon, planets, Ascendant and Midheaven. The definitive book on transits. Includes introductory chapters on the theory and applications of transits. Paper, $18.95.

PLANETS IN YOUTH: Patterns of Early Development
by Robert Hand

A major astrological thinker looks at children and childhood. Parents can use it to help their children cope with the complexities of growing up, and readers of all ages can use it to understand themselves and their own patterns of early development. Introductory chapters discuss parent-child relationships and planetary energies in children's charts. All important horoscope factors delineated stressing possibilities rather than certainties. Paper, $13.95.

To Order Books: Send purchase price plus fifty cents for each book to cover shipping and handling to Para Research, Dept. PC, Rockport, MA 01966. Massachusetts residents add 5% sales tax. Prices subject to change without notice.

How well do you know yourself?

This horoscope gives you answers to these questions based on your exact time and place of birth...

How do others see you?
What is your greatest strength?
What are your life purposes?
What drives motivate you?
How do you think?
Are you a loving person?
How competitive are you?
What are your ideals?
How religious are you?
Can you take responsibility?
How creative are you?
How do you handle money?
How do you express yourself?
What career is best for you?
How will you be remembered?
Who are your real friends?
What are you hiding?

Many people are out of touch with their real selves. Some can't get ahead professionaly because they are doing the wrong kind of work. Others lack self-confidence because they're trying to be someone they're not. Others are unsuccessful in love because they use the wrong approach with the wrong people. Astrology has helped hundreds of people with problems like these by showing them their real strengths, their real opportunities, their real selves.

You are a unique individual. Since the world began, there has never been anyone exactly like you. Sun-sign astrology, the kind you see in newspapers and magazines, is all right as far as it goes. But it treats you as if you were just the same as millions of others who have the same Sun sign because their birthdays are close to yours. A true astrological reading of your character and personality has to be one of a kind, unlike any other. It has to be based on exact date, time, longitude and latitude of your birth. Only a big IBM computer like the one that Para Research uses can handle the trillions of possibilities.

A Unique Document Your Astral Portrait includes your complete chart with planetary positions and house cusps calculated to the nearest minute of arc, all planetary aspects with orbs and intensities, plus text explaining the meaning of:

★ Your particular combination of Sun and Moon signs.
★ Your Ascendant sign and the house position of its ruling planet. (Many computer horoscopes omit this because it requires exact birth data.)
★ The planets influencing all twelve houses in your chart.
★ Your planetary aspects.

Others Tell Us "I found the Astral Portrait to be the best horoscope I've ever read."—E.D., Los Angeles, CA "I could not put it down until I'd read every word...It is like you've been looking over my should since I arrived in this world!"—B.N.L., Redding, CA "I recommend the Astral Portrait. It even surpasses many of the readings done by professional astrologers." —J.B., Bristol, CT

Low Price There is no substitute for a personal conference with an astrologer, but a good astrologer charges $50 and up for a complete chart reading. Some who have rich clients get $200 and more. Your Astral Portrait is an analysis of your character written by some of the world's foremost astrologers, and you can have it not for $200 or $50 but for only $20. This is possible because the text of your Astral Portrait is already written. You pay only for the cost of putting your birth information into the computer, compiling one copy, checking it and sending it to you within two weeks.

Permanance Ordinarily, you leave an astrologer's office with only a memory. Your Astral Portrait is a thirty-five page, fifteen-thousand-word, permanently bound book that you can read again and again for years.

Money-Back Guarantee Our guarantee is unconditional. That means you can return your Astral Portrait at any time for any reason and get a full refund. That means we take all the risk, not you!

You Hold the Key The secrets of your inner character and personality, your real self, are locked in the memory of the computer. You alone hold the key: your time and place of birth. Fill in the coupon below and send it to the address shown with $20. Don't put it off. Do it now while you're thinking of it. Your Astral Portrait is waiting for you.

© 1977 Para Research, Inc.

Para Research, Dept. NF, Rockport, Massachusetts 01966 I want to read about my real self. Please send me my Astral Portrait. I understand that if I am not completely satisfied, I can return it for a full refund. □ I enclose $20 plus 1.50 for shipping and handling. □ Charge $21.50 to my Master Charge account. □ Charge $21.50 to my VISA account.

Card number _____ Good through Mo. _____ Day _____ Yr. _____

Mr/Ms _____ Birthdate Mo. _____ Day _____ Yr. _____

Address _____ Birthtime (within an hour) _____ AM/PM

City _____ Birthplace City _____

State _____ Zip _____ State _____ Country _____

Para Research Horoscopes

Own your own computer generated text-horoscope with portions written by Robert Hand, Robert Pelletier and John Townley. We are the world's leading astrology publisher of books and horoscopes. More than two million people own one of our horoscopes and more than 100,000 people use our books. How many of our publications do you own?

ASTRAL PORTRAIT. Our most popular horoscope. All planetary positions and house cusps calculated to the nearest minute of arc, all planetary aspects with orbs and intensities. Text explaining the meaning of: Sun/Moon polarity, Ascendant sign and the house position of its ruler, house position of each planet, all planetary aspects including the inconjunct. Approximately 15,000 words, 35 pages. Professional version*, $14; deluxe version, $20.

ASTRAL COMPOSITE. The horoscope for the two of you. All planetary positions and house cusps of two natal charts plus the composite chart (midpoints of like planets). All composite aspects with orbs and intensities. Delineations of house position of each composite planet and of each composite aspect. Approximately 10,000 words, 25 pages. Professional version*, $14; deluxe version, $20.

ASTRAL GUIDE. Your personal transit calendar. Each Beautiful 16- by 22-inch poster-sized page gives one month's transits to your natal chart with explanatory text. Compiled using your exact time and place of birth. Specify starting month if not the current one. Twelve months, $24.

YOUTH PORTRAIT. The horoscope for children that grownups love. All planetary positions, house cusps and aspects with orbs and intensities calculated. Delineations of sign position, house position and aspects for each planet. Text stresses the developing personality. Use it to understand your children or your childhood. 10,000 words, 25 pages. Professional version*, $14; deluxe version, $20.

LOVE PORTRAIT. An intimate analysis of your emotional and sexual needs. For the adult native only. All planetary positions, house cusps and aspects calculated. Delineations of sign position, house positions. Professional version*, $14; deluxe version, $20.

BIORHYTHM CHART. Graphs your 28-day emotional cycle, your 33-day mental cycle and your 23-day physical cycle. Shows critical days. No text. $5.

NATAL CALCULATIONS. Sign and house positions of all planets and all house cusps to the nearest minute of arc. All aspects with orbs and intensities. $3.

COMPOSITE CALCULATIONS. Sign and house positions of all planets and all house cusps to the nearest minute of arc given for two natal charts plus the composite chart. All composite aspects with orbs and intensities. $5.

*Professional and deluxe versions of a horoscope contain exactly the same calculations and text. Deluxe version comes printed on bond paper and bound in permanent gold-embossed vinyl. Professional version is unbound on plain white paper.

TO ORDER, send birth information (name, date, local clock time, place) your name and address plus $1.50 for shipping and handling. For composite, send two persons' birth data. No time needed for biorhythms. Sixty-four-page horoscope catalog sent free with all horoscopes. Book catalog sent free on request.

PARA RESEARCH DEPT. NF, ROCKPORT, MA 01966